REPARATIONS AND ANTI-BLACK RACISM

A Criminological Exploration of the Harms of Slavery and Racialized Injustice

Angus Nurse

BRISTOL
UNIVERSITY
PRESS

First published in Great Britain in 2022 by

Bristol University Press
University of Bristol
1–9 Old Park Hill
Bristol
BS2 8BB
UK
t: +44 (0)117 954 5940
e: bup-info@bristol.ac.uk

Details of international sales and distribution partners are available at bristoluniversitypress.co.uk

© Bristol University Press 2022

British Library Cataloguing in Publication Data
A catalogue record for this book is available from the British Library

ISBN 978-1-5292-1682-0 hardcover
ISBN 978-1-5292-1683-7 paperback
ISBN 978-1-5292-1685-1 ePdf
ISBN 978-1-5292-1684-4 ePub

The right of Angus Nurse to be identified as author of this work has been asserted by him in accordance with the Copyright, Designs and Patents Act 1988.

All rights reserved: no part of this publication may be reproduced, stored in a retrieval system, or transmitted in any form or by any means, electronic, mechanical, photocopying, recording, or otherwise without the prior permission of Bristol University Press.

Every reasonable effort has been made to obtain permission to reproduce copyrighted material. If, however, anyone knows of an oversight, please contact the publisher.

The statements and opinions contained within this publication are solely those of the author and not of the University of Bristol or Bristol University Press. The University of Bristol and Bristol University Press disclaim responsibility for any injury to persons or property resulting from any material published in this publication.

Bristol University Press works to counter discrimination on grounds of gender, race, disability, age and sexuality.

Cover design: Namkwan Cho
Front cover image: Shutterstock/Alessandro Biascioli

Contents

List of Abbreviations		iv
Acknowledgements		v
Preface		vii
1	Black Lives Matter: The Legacy of Slavery	1
2	Slavery and Reparations: A Criminological View	16
3	Reparations Litigation: An Overview	30
4	Victims of Slavery and Reparations: Who Suffers?	48
5	A Comparative Analysis of Reparations	61
6	Unjust Enrichment and the Socio-Legal Case for Reparations	73
7	The 'Value' of Reparations	85
8	The Nature of Reparations	97
9	Reparations in the 21st Century: Contemporary Debates and Issues on Reparations	111
Appendix: Reparations Litigation and Settlements		130
Notes		132
References		135
Index		157

List of Abbreviations

ANC	African National Congress
BAME	Black Asian and Minority Ethnic (term used to refer to members of non-White communities)
CAH	Crimes against humanity
CARICOM	The Caribbean Community
CRC	CARICOM Reparations Commission
CSR	corporate social responsibility
ECHR	European Convention on Human Rights
ECtHR	European Court of Human Rights
EJI	Equal Justice Initiative
IACHR	Inter-American Commission on Human Rights
ICC	International Criminal Court
ICCPR	International Covenant on Civil and Political Rights
ICESCR	International Covenant on Economic, Social and Cultural Rights
ICJ	International Court of Justice
ICTJ	International Centre for Transitional Justice
TRC	Truth and Reconciliation Commission (South Africa)
UN	United Nations
UNCAT	United Nations Committee Against Torture
UNHRC	United Nations Human Rights Council
VPS	Victim Personal Statement

Acknowledgements

This book has been several years in the making and would not have been possible without the help, support and influence of several people to whom I owe a debt of thanks.

Firstly, the colleagues with whom I have been able to discuss some of the ideas and policy issues that are explored in this book, Katerina Gachevska, Emma Milne, Erin Sanders-McDonagh, Tony Goodman and Tine Munk. These colleagues, coming from different academic perspectives and experiences have been invaluable in both supporting and questioning some of the assertations made about reparations and the contemporary experience of racism, sometimes forcing me to explore basic ideas in more depth in order to better explain the conceptions on anti-Black racism that have found their way into this book.

Thanks are also due to the human rights and criminology students I have worked with at Birmingham City University, the University of Lincoln and at Middlesex University over the past ten years. Many of the questions raised in our classroom discussions and in their excellent work have inspired the examination that has found its way into this book. In particular, the Human Rights and Contemporary Justice postgraduate students who I worked with at Middlesex showed a willingness to engage in debates around critical race theory and to critique the merits of human rights law as a tool to address contemporary racism and race-based discrimination. Their questions and critical analysis have at times been invaluable in bringing to light some of the gaps that exist in mechanisms that in principle exist to remedy human rights violations and in identifying where such tools may be ineffective in practice.

I am also grateful to the anonymous reviewers who commented on the initial outline for this book and the draft manuscript. Their comments prompted some areas of reflection as well as identifying some areas of clarification and expansion in the original text. Last but by no means least, thanks are due to Rebecca Tomlinson for her enthusiasm for this project and for encouraging me to extend the book from my original intention of a short policy book into the more expansive book it has turned into. This is a challenging subject, and my original idea of a short book would doubtless not have done it justice. Even within the longer format that this book developed into I found that several ideas could not be accommodated and there are some topics I will examine further in other projects and that probably require more depth than has been possible within the confines of this book. I am grateful to Bristol University Press for supporting this project.

Preface

This book examines the case for reparations in the context of slavery's enduring harms including persistent social attitudes of Black people as second-class citizens. Its starting point is that despite the undoubted successes of the civil rights struggle and legal recognition of the equality afforded to or due to Black citizens, systemic anti-Black racism is still a fact of life for many in contemporary Western society. Numerous studies and the lived experience of Black citizens provide testimony to the reality that anti-Black racism remains embedded in society. Regrettably, it is also a factor in how policy is implemented and has effect in a number of areas. This is most notable in criminal justice practices, but also exists in areas of social policy, education, housing and in negative perceptions of Black citizens that feed into media representations and perpetuate stereotypes of Black citizens as criminal.

By this point I may already have turned off some potential readers, particularly those unwilling or unable to accept the notion of systemic racism within society. Defensiveness towards the idea of systemic racism is prevalent in the attitudes of many politicians and media commentators on both sides of the Atlantic. Resistance to policy change and unwillingness to carry out detailed examination of society's problems also seems to be common to both the US and UK experience notwithstanding social and political differences between the two countries. The scramble to argue that racial problems are largely a thing of the past or a minor problem in Western societies, and notably the US and UK, borders on the indecent and suggests large-scale denial that the injustices identified in the racial struggles of the 1960s and 1970s have somehow been 'fixed'. Underlying policy responses to claims that policing has an element of racism or that Black citizens are treated differently is an almost constant refrain of 'this is not about race'.

Really?

In October 2019 as election campaigns kicked off on both sides of the Atlantic, attitudes towards and the treatment of Black citizens became a topic of debate. Around that time, I explored the topic of slavery reparations in a blog post that set out some of the research being conducted for this book. That post argued that evidence from both the US and UK consistently indicates that Black citizens are disadvantaged in their treatment at the hands of the state and state agencies, particularly criminal justice ones.

In the US, the Black Lives Matter movement shed light on the killing of unarmed Black citizens (mostly men) and alleged disproportionate use of force by policing agencies against the Black community. In 2020 this turned into global protests following the killing of George Floyd by police in the US.

In the UK, research continues to suggest disproportionate use of police stop-and-search powers against Black and Minority Ethnic people. In both the US and UK, Black people are disproportionately represented in prison populations, and evidence suggests they receive harsher prison sentences compared to their White counterparts.

Underlying these issues are social attitudes towards Black people arguably situated in cultural perceptions of inferiority and of Black communities as being predisposed towards crime. However, social inequalities between Black and White communities are visible in a range of areas including income disparity, access to professions and discrimination in the workplace and provision of services.

The racial disparity in US society is arguably more pronounced and visible than that in the UK to the extent that there has been public race-based dialogue such as recent debates about whether calls to send elected (non-White) politicians 'home' is racist and about the perceived racism of senior mainstream politicians. UK politicians and public policy professionals seemingly argue that this is a US problem, apparently believing that the UK has been spared such problems. However, the UK's Windrush scandal which in 2018 saw the wrongful detention and threat of deportation of Black citizens who were incorrectly classified as immigration offenders also draws into sharp focus the extent to which UK authorities have discriminated against Black citizens and shown at best poor judgement in the creation of a hostile environment towards Black people. The Windrush scandal was the consequence of a deliberate policy to create a 'hostile environment' for immigrants, but which adversely and disproportionately affected Black citizens.[1] At worst, Windrush gives the impression that racist attitudes towards Black people permeate aspects of government thinking and policy.

Against the backdrop of poor attitudes towards Black people and concerns about differential treatment for Black citizens and communities, a renewed campaign for slavery reparations has gathered momentum. At the heart of this campaign is a growing call for recognition of the impact of slavery on current communities. There are also calls for UK and US governments to acknowledge a debt is owed to those who suffered and lost their lives as a result of slavery, while governments and other institutions benefitted.

For those who believe that a long history of forced, unpaid labour, ownership and servitude and persistent social attitudes of Black people as second-class citizens has caused difficulties for current communities, reparations for the harm caused by slavery make sense. However, assigning responsibility at the level of the state and identifying who should make reparations and what form any reparations should take can be difficult.

The focus of this book is a critical, criminological examination of the case for reparations and consideration of how best to implement reparations. In the US, the slavery reparations movement is fairly advanced. In July 2019, Chuck Shumer, leader of the Democrats in the US Senate backed a campaign for reparation. US Presidential hopeful Cory Booker and Congresswoman Sheila Jackson Lee also called for a commission to study and develop reparation proposals for African Americans. A bill known as H.R.40 has been introduced in the US Congress to provide a legislative basis for this commission.

A range of court action has also taken place in the US in recent decades with the aim of having the courts rule that reparations should be paid and drawing some conclusions on who should pay them. Legal cases have included action against major financial institutions that benefitted from slavery as well as claims against the government itself. So far, none of these cases has fully succeeded, with the reasons for failure varying.

In rejecting these claims, reasons given by courts include arguments that present-day institutions cannot be held responsible for the actions of their long-dead predecessors. It has also been argued that whether the state should compensate for something that was 'legal' at the time is a political question rather than one that should be decided by the courts.

Reparations claims have also been rejected because there is nobody alive today who has *directly* suffered from slavery and so in one sense there is no surviving victim who should be compensated. This argument distinguishes the 'legacy' of transatlantic slavery as an institution against Black people who are still feeling its effects, from more recent harms like the persecution of the Jews in the Holocaust. Reparations have been paid for the Holocaust in part because not only is the Holocaust a more recent memory, but a number of its survivors and their children are still alive. As a result, there were living victims whose harm could be addressed when Holocaust reparations were initially agreed in the 1950s with additional payments agreed decades later.

Arguably the same cannot be said of the victims of Black slavery which technically ended in 1863 in the US with the emancipation proclamation, and officially with the 13th amendment after the end of the civil war in 1865, and in 1834 in the UK following the passing of the Slavery Abolition Act 1833. That said, an argument can be made that reparations could be given for the *descendants* of slaves, many of whom continued to suffer the effects of slavery through segregation in the US until the civil rights reforms of the 1960s and 1970s. US civil rights and Black Lives Matter activists might well argue that they are still suffering today, and that anti-Black racism is a structural issue that requires some form of action or redress.

This book critically analyzes various court actions on reparations that have taken place in recent decades as well as examining aspects of the contemporary reparations debate. The objective in writing this book is to examine the case for reparations through a critical criminology and human rights lens. This means that the book is not solely about *direct* slavery reparations but also considers reparations for indirect and ongoing injustice; a wider idea of anti-Black racism. But slavery is invoked as the cause or originator of a system that upholds White supremacy and continually denigrates Black citizens, and this is made clear in some of the litigation analyzed within the text even though some cases are framed explicitly in the context of a legal argument for reparations about slavery. This is in part because civil rights litigators are pursuing legal arguments concerning historical wrongs that have present-day consequences and are using specific legal tools to get the matter in court and bypass political arguments that reparations are not required at state level.

This is a complex and contentious issue, and the topic of reparations has been the subject of scholarly attention in several areas including Black studies, history, law and political science. For some scholars, slavery should be preserved as the central focus of reparations and with particular focus on the issue of unpaid labour. For others it is a political issue concerning recognition of the debt owed to those who suffered the horrors of slavery including its loss of life and human rights abuses. Other debates concern whether states and institutions that benefitted from slavery should make reparations in recognition of the loss of life and unpaid labour costs that arguably they profited from. But as a criminologist and human rights academic I make clear that in this text I examine a broader context of reparations noting that the contemporary reparations movement is wider than just seeking payment for unpaid labour and also considers redress for contemporary injustice and disadvantage. In this context I make clear that the discussion in this book is about reparations for the enduring harms of slavery *and* ongoing anti-Black racism.

The criminological approach adopted in this book differs from a purely legal approach concerned with the legality of slavery, its internal regulation and the slave laws in operation at the time or the legal merits of any reparations' judgements. Instead, the criminological perspective proposed by this text goes further and considers, for example, issues of state crime, the abuse of power in setting up and perpetuating systems of discrimination, and how the criminalization of Black people represents an abuse of state power in *how* police use their powers (and who against) even though they may legally be entitled to use force.

The selection of topics in this book will doubtless not satisfy everybody and inevitably I could not include everything I wanted to and made some choices along the way in deciding the precise focus of this text. There are some excellent slavery and reparations books that examine the machinery of slavery and its legal structures in detail, as well as some excellent overviews of the history of slavery and the campaign for abolition. I use many of these other texts in my own research and teaching and there are several that make for excellent reading. But I am clear in stating that this is not a book about the institution of slavery or its injustices while in operation, although these issues are inevitably touched upon in places. Instead, my aim with this book was to produce a reasonably accessible book with a criminological focus on anti-Black racism as a consequence of slavery and as an ongoing social justice issue. Even as I have edited the book from its initial draft there have been further killings of Black citizens by law enforcement as well as continued denials of a problem of systemic racism by politicians and public institutions initially keen to show their support for the Black Lives Matter movement but at time of writing seeming to be in something of a backpedal when asked to actually engage with meaningful change. But there has also been recognition by some institutions that they have profited from slavery and so should somehow provide some form of redress whether by way of a simple apology or by providing scholarships for Black citizens or contributions to address social inequality. Such action illustrates the complexity of the reparations issue and the debate concerning the scale and form that any reparations should take. The measures needed to achieve social justice and address structural racism extends far beyond the criminological discussion contained in this book.

I have no doubt I will be returning to this topic again.

1

Black Lives Matter: The Legacy of Slavery

This book is about the contemporary reparations movement and the case for redress for ongoing anti-Black racism; considered to be systemic in modern society (Feagin and Elias, 2013; Tourse et al, 2018). Despite the undoubted progress made by the civil rights movements in both the US and UK, and the integration of Black citizens within Commonwealth countries, contemporary Black and African-American citizens arguably continue to suffer disadvantage. Evidence consistently suggests that Black citizens are disproportionately represented in the negative aspects of criminal justice; being more likely to be stopped and searched by policing agencies (Bowling and Phillips, 2007; Torres, 2015) to be disproportionately represented in prison populations (Pettit, 2012; Lammy, 2017) and are believed to receive stiffer sentences for offending compared to their White counterparts (Burch, 2015). In addition, Black citizens are more likely to be in the lower socio-economic bracket in society and suffer disadvantage in areas of housing, education, access to certain professions and representation in the higher areas of social life. As Oliver and Shapiro explained when assessing the position in the US, 'African Americans are vastly overrepresented among those Americans whose lives are the most economically and socially distressed' (2007: 91). The same is true in the UK, where Black citizens are overrepresented in respect of inner-city, low-income housing, educational attainment, an area where we speak openly of an attainment 'gap' (Richardson, 2015) and where Black citizens are rarely represented at the higher levels in criminal justice agencies such as the police, the judiciary and higher political office. In addition, Black citizens regularly raise concerns about disadvantage, unequal or unfair treatment and contend that even when they do play by the rules of society their ability to achieve some types of success may be adversely affected by structural barriers.

The reasons for this apparent disadvantage are varied, but a central issue raised in race and inequality discourse is the existence of systematic and endemic racism; the perception of Black lives as somehow being less important and the concerns of Black citizens as somehow secondary. In the area of criminal justice, the Black Lives Matter movement has drawn attention to the perception of Black lives as being worth less and of Black bodies as being disposable; echoing concerns raised by the civil rights movement, and during the era of the Black Panthers and other activists decades ago (Williams, 2008). Issues such as the killing of unarmed Black citizens by state policing agencies and evidence of seemingly racist attitudes among politicians and in policy raise the uncomfortable idea that despite all of the rhetoric of equality and the existence of equal rights legislation, underlying racist attitudes still exist. This being the case, the disadvantage perceived by some citizens may well become a daily fact of life.

This book examines these issues via a criminological exploration and critical analysis of the case for reparations as both legal and societal remedy for the legacy of slavery and continuing racial injustice. It sets out a core argument of slavery as being 'legally coded White supremacy' that created structural inequality and a system of structural racism that has continued into contemporary society. It also explores aspects of contemporary anti-Black racism and the legacy of inequality still experienced by Black citizens. A core part of the book's analysis is the contemporary reparations movements and debates about how reparations for slavery, Jim Crow and their legacies might be achieved (Martin and Yaquinto, 2007b). While much of the reparation litigation brought to the courts is based on slavery as a cause of harm, one aspect of the contemporary reparations movement is that of engagement with both historic injustices and the ongoing inequality of structural racism. From the outset this book's focus is also clarified as being also concerned with more recent injustices, thus its consideration of reparations is one concerned with slavery *and* its legacy in the form of contemporary anti-Black racism, rather than just on slavery alone. These are challenging issues to consider and go beyond a simple calculation of unpaid labour costs within the transatlantic slave trade. They can also include consideration of reduced economic opportunity and social costs of African-American and Black citizens as well as redress for African and Caribbean nations who may claim they have been impoverished as a consequence of slavery and colonial rule. They may also consider aspects of contemporary disadvantage and inequality caused by institutional racism.

The criminological perspective employed by this book examines structural racism as a crime of the powerful and considers its basis within historical injustice. While the book is deliberately brief on the history of slavery and its moral wrong, it acknowledges that within contemporary reparations discourse an argument can be made that reparations could be given for the descendants of slaves, many of whom continued to suffer the effects of slavery through segregation in the US until the civil rights reforms of the 1960s and 1970s. Black British citizens would join with US civil rights and Black Lives Matter activists to argue that they are still suffering today and to identify that the UK and other Global North countries have problems with systematic, societal racism. While this is not a book about slavery as much as it is a book about the contemporary legacy of slavery and other injustices, this introductory chapter links the social impacts of slavery to contemporary issues that have created the need for movements like the Black Lives Matter movement. This introductory chapter also sets out the structure for the remainder of the book.

Slavery and anti-Black racism

While it is beyond the scope and focus of this book to provide a comprehensive analysis of the institution of slavery and its operation, some discussion is necessary to contextualize the book's remaining discussion. The *Cambridge Dictionary* defines modern slavery as 'the condition of being forced by threats or violence to work for little or no pay and of having no power to control what work you do or where you do it' (*Cambridge Dictionary*, 2020: np). This definition arguably reflects modern slavery as defined within the context of labour exploitation. Indeed, the preamble to the UK's Modern Slavery Act, 2015 denotes this as 'an Act to make provision about slavery, servitude and forced or compulsory labour and about human trafficking, including provision for the protection of victims; to make provision for an Independent Anti-slavery Commissioner; and for connected purposes'. Thus, within the opening sections of the legislation, offences are created as follows:

(1) A person commits an offence if:
   (a) the person holds another person in slavery or servitude and the circumstances are such that the person knows or ought to know that the other person is held in slavery or servitude, or
   (b) the person requires another person to perform forced or compulsory labour and the circumstances are such that the person knows or ought to know that the other person is being required to perform forced or compulsory labour;
(2) In subsection (1) the references to holding a person in slavery or servitude or requiring a person to perform forced or compulsory labour are to be construed in accordance with Article 4 of the Human Rights Convention. (Modern Slavery Act, 2015)

These contemporary legal definitions highlight both the moral and legal wrong of holding another person in servitude and forcing them to work against their will or to perform forced, compulsory or unpaid labour.

Crucially, the definition contained in the UK legislation also makes explicit reference to Article 4 of the European Convention on Human Rights (ECHR). This contains a prohibition on holding a person in slavery or servitude and states that 'no one shall be required to perform forced or compulsory labour' (European Court of Human Rights, 2020: 5). The definition of slavery contained within the ECHR and deployed by the European Court of Human Rights (ECtHR) is drawn from the 1926 Slavery Convention which defines slavery as 'the status or condition of a person over whom any or all of the powers attaching to the right of ownership are exercised' (European Court of Human Rights, 2020: 7).

While the modern slavery conception is returned to at times during this book, when referring to slavery, this book's discussion primarily refers to the Atlantic slave trade. This involved the large-scale capture and acquisition, transportation, sale and indentured servitude of millions of Black Africans. Thomas (1999: 291) indicates the period of the Atlantic slave trade as being 1440–1870 and notes that for the majority of its operation, the Atlantic slave trade was a governmental enterprise. Thus, it was lawful and carried out with the full knowledge and support of governments and underpinned by legislative mechanisms and rules designed to facilitate the buying, selling and ownership of slaves. Accurately calculating the number of persons involved in slavery is problematic as is identifying its precise end as while Britain and the US arguably banned their Atlantic trade in African slaves in 1807 and 1808 respectively 'in fact the trade survived (mainly to Brazil and Cuba) until it dies away in the 1860s' (Walvin, 2007: 1). Prior to abolition and the ending of the trade 'some twelve million Africans had been loaded onto the Atlantic slave ships. About ten and a half million of them survived to landfall in the Americas' (Walvin, 2007: 1).

Considerable academic discourse and historical record exists to describe the machinery of slavery and its operation. Wacquant described chattel slavery as 'the pivot of the plantation economy and the inceptive matrix from the colonial era to the civil war' (2002: 41). Chattel slavery had the effect of making slaves property and reflected ideological conceptions of White supremacy and Black inferiority that arguably has continued as a dominant paradigm in contemporary society. While slavery technically ended in 1865 in the US following the emancipation proclamation and the end of the civil war, and in 1834 in the UK following the passing of the Slavery Abolition Act in 1833, Black citizens in both the UK and US continue to experience disadvantage linked to their societal status.

The post-slavery period

In principle the end of slavery and the emancipation proclamation put an end to the subjugation of Black citizens in the US and paved the way for equality. Yet various writers note that emancipation was followed by 100 more years of institutionalized subjugation through the enactment of Black Codes and Jim Crow laws, peonage, convict leasing, domestic terrorism and lynching. Lutz (2008: 533–8) provides an overview of American history that argues that even with the end of slavery American citizens were denied equal access to transport, fair terms of employment or voting rights, some of which were not resolved until the 1970s when de facto segregation was considered unlawful. This is acknowledged in various contemporary state and municipal resolutions concerning reparations for slavery. For example, New Jersey's African-American Reconciliation Study Commission Act of 2003 stated:

> Emancipation was followed by over one hundred years of legal segregation and widespread discrimination against African-Americans. Core elements of our Democracy were affected, including voting and other political and constitutional rights and our system of civil and criminal justice. These legacies of slavery impeded African-American efforts to protect themselves and their communities through political action.

The City of San Francisco's (2001) reparations resolution noted:

> Whereas since the end of the period of the Civil War known as Reconstruction, when the Federal Government briefly attempted to compensate the former slave community for hundreds of years of bondage, African Americans have been widely prevented through legal and extralegal measures from obtaining equal education, employment, housing and health care; in short prevented from joining the American middle class in substantial numbers.

The final example to illustrate this point is the City of New York's Resolution 219 (2002) which noted: 'Whereas African-Americans have sought repeatedly to improve their educational status, economic condition, and living situation and have been held back by prejudice, lawless white violence and official indifference thereto.' These, and other reparations acts and declarations are discussed in more detail later in this book. But they are mentioned here as indications of some of the challenges raised in the post-slavery era. While it is beyond the scope and focus of this book to discuss the Reconstruction era in detail, it merits some mention in terms of the underpinning argument that despite the abolition of slavery, structures remained in place which arguably upheld notions of White supremacy. The first Reconstruction period (approximately 1865–77) required measures to address the destruction caused to the defeated Southern states in the US.

It also needed to define the role of emancipated slaves in Southern society. However, while some mechanisms were put in place to address the collapse of the old social and economic structures that were reliant on slavery, as indicated in the earlier quotes, legal segregation continued in the US in the post-slavery era. Kelley (2007: 207) identifies that in 1865 Union General William T. Sherman issued Special Field Order 15 intended to distribute land along the South Carolina coast and on the Sea Islands among freed people. He notes that Sherman was able to settle 40,000 freed people on seized lands and two months later Congress produced the first Freedmen's Bureau Bill which promised to provide male refugees or freedmen with not more than 40 acres of land. However, President Johnson vetoed Congress' proposals and overturned Sherman's order. Ultimately 'under President Johnson, nearly all the land confiscated from the Confederate plantation owners was restored for oaths of loyalty' (Kelley, 2007: 207). Lyons comments that 'new governments in the defeated states established Black Codes, which much resembled the former Slave Codes. Freedmen were coerced into labour contracts. Widespread violence enforced the new system' (2007: 40) including extra-judicial killing by way of lynching.

Lartey and Morris (2018) identify that historians generally consider lynching to be 'a method of social and racial control intended to terrorize Black Americans into submission and into an inferior racial caste position'. Lynching occurred in the US South from roughly 1877 when 'lynching of blacks was widely practiced, reaching a peak in the 1890s, when a lynching occurred every two or three days' (Lyons, 2007: 41). Lynching arguably tailed off from the 1930s but continued into the 1960s. The Equal Justice Initiative (EJI) (EJI, 2017) documented 4,084 racial terror lynchings in 12 Southern states between the end of Reconstruction in 1877 and 1950.[1] EJI also documented more than 300 racial terror lynchings in other states during this time period. The EJI study concluded that racial terror lynching was a tool used to enforce Jim Crow laws and racial segregation. Wacquant describes the Jim Crow era as: '[a] system of legally enforced discrimination and segregation from cradle to grave that anchored the predominantly agrarian society of the South from the close of Reconstruction to the Civil Rights revolution which toppled it a full century after abolition' (2002: 41).

Thus, lynching became 'a tactic for maintaining racial control by victimizing the entire African American community, not merely punishment of an alleged perpetrator for a crime' (EJI, 2017). EJI states that its research confirms that many victims of terror lynchings were murdered without being accused of any crime but instead were killed for minor social transgressions or for demanding basic rights and fair treatment. EJI identified that terror lynchings generally had one or more of the following features:

(1) lynchings that resulted from a wildly distorted fear of interracial sex; (2) lynchings in response to casual social transgressions; (3) lynchings based on allegations of serious violent crime; (4) public spectacle lynchings; (5) lynchings that escalated into large-scale violence targeting the entire African American community; and (6) lynchings of sharecroppers, ministers, and community leaders who resisted mistreatment, which were most common between 1915 and 1940. (EJI, 2017: np)

The reality of lynching set out in the EJI analysis and other reports is one of lynching being normalized and viewed as an effective tool to maintain a social and racial order from which all White people benefitted. It also represented a devaluation of Black life such that lynchings were 'rituals of collective violence that served as highly effective tools to reinforce the institution and philosophy of white racial superiority' (EJI, 2017: np). Lynch mobs were intended to instil fear in all African Americans, to enforce submission and racial subordination, and to emphasize the limits of Black freedom (Banner, 2006). As extra-judicial killings they not infrequently could become public spectacles for White citizens, again reinforcing the notion of White supremacy and serving as a tangible representation of the disposable nature of Black lives (Wood, 2011; Harding, 2017). Arguably it was the lynching of 14-year-old Emmett Till in 1955 (in Mississippi) that served as a pivotal moment in transforming the lynched Black body from a symbol of unmitigated White power to one illustrating the ugliness of racial violence (Harold and DeLuca, 2005) and thus galvanized civil rights power and public opposition to lynching.[2]

The civil rights movement

In theory, the Reconstruction era in the US following the abolition of slavery and the gradual integration of Commonwealth subjects into British life was intended to be a period where Black citizens were accepted into society and were able to access the societal benefits taken for granted by their White counterparts. In practice this proved not to be the case. Instead, a concerted civil rights struggle took place in the US during the 1950s and 1960s that eventually culminated in civil rights legislation that theoretically provided for racial equality if not an actual end to discrimination.

The Civil Rights Act of 1964 outlawed discrimination on the basis of race, colour, religion, sex, or national origin, required equal access to public places and employment, and enforced desegregation of schools and the right to vote. In the UK, the Race Relations Act 1976 contained similar provisions, prohibiting discrimination on the grounds of race, colour, nationality, ethnic and national origin in the fields of employment, the provision of goods and services, education and public functions. Further anti-discrimination provisions are contained in the Human Rights Act 1998 (which implements international human rights law provisions on racial discrimination) and the Equality Act 2010.

Brown et al (2007) identify that the civil rights movement was considered to be successful and suggest this is an important issue in considering how contemporary attitudes towards race are contextualized. They provide the following assessment of why the campaigns of the civil rights era are perceived as being effective and to have largely worked to end discrimination:

- First, they suggest that Americans believe that the existence of civil rights laws ending racial inequality and legal segregation have been successful. Racial extremists are thus a small minority of Americans and exist on the fringes of mainstream White America.
- Second, where racial inequality exists it is because Black citizens have not taken advantage of the opportunities created by the level playing field brought about by the civil rights successes. They identify that 'a substantial majority believe that black Americans do not try hard enough to succeed' but also that they are supported by Government to take what they have not earned.
- Finally, it is suggested that most White Americans think that America is becoming a colour-blind society and thus there is no justification for affirmative action or other colour-blind policies. In short; because the problem has slowly evened itself out. (Brown et al, 2007: 55–6)

While this assessment was published in 2007 and the global anti-racism protests of 2020 drew attention to the reality of life experienced by many Black citizens, many of these ideas arguably still exist. When setting out these perceptions Brown et al identified that 'it was naïve to believe that America could wipe out three hundred years of physical, legal, cultural, spiritual, and political oppression based on race in a mere thirty years' (2007: 57). Fifty years on from the heyday of the civil rights movement arguably this remains the reality.

The arguments highlighted by Brown et al (2007) require a little more discussion. First, the existence of laws should not by itself be taken as evidence that a problem has been resolved. Criminological enquiry frequently identifies that it is in enforcement of laws that problems often exist rather than the content of the laws, and this raises issues around consistency of enforcement, willingness to enforce and the extent to which enforcement regimes resolve identified problems, notwithstanding any issues concerning the adequacy of laws. In both the UK and US, anti-racism laws exist and the notion that discrimination based on race is unlawful is also contained in international human rights law.[3] But in both the US and UK racial tensions continued and following a long history of racial violence in the UK, in 1981 the British government conducted an inquiry into the problem and found that Black people were 50 to 60 times more likely than White people to be the victims of racially motivated attacks (Gordon, 1990). At the time, many racial attacks were not reported to the police. In his review of the statistics on the nature and extent of racial violence in Britain, Gordon (1990) said that the police response to racial violence showed a number of problems: delays in responding, denial of racial motives, an unwillingness to prosecute assailants, mistreatment of victims, and unnecessary special measures. Many of these issues are now being raised again by Black Lives Matter activities who argue that the position has changed relatively little in the last three decades.

Racism in the 21st century: Black Lives Matter

Understanding of contemporary racism is an important aspect of assessing contemporary reparations discourse. Wacquant (2002) argued that in addition to chattel slavery and Jim Crow, the ghetto and the carceral apparatus became mechanisms for containing Black citizens in the US. This argument contended that 'slavery and mass imprisonment are genealogically linked' and that one could not understand the latter 'without returning to the former as historic starting point and functional analogue' (Wacquant, 2002: 41–2). Central to this argument is the contention that Black citizens suffer from continuing stigma affecting the descendants of slaves by virtue of being members of a societal group that is consistently denied of ethnic honour. As the preceding discussion highlights, the ending of slavery did not end the persistence of challenging attitudes towards Black citizens.

An unpleasant reality situated within discussion of systematic and institutionalized racism is that Black citizens continue to suffer at the hands of law enforcement and that violent misconduct perpetrated against Black citizens is not a new phenomenon in criminal justice discourse. After the beating of Rodney King by police officers was caught on camera in 1991, riots took place in Los Angeles after the police officers involved were acquitted. Calls for police reform were also heard following the LA riots and were heard again following the deaths of Eric Garner in 2014, the shooting of Michael Brown and following the Ferguson protests in August 2014. The 2017 UK Angiolini Report into deaths and serious incidents in police custody identified that 'there is evidence of disproportionate deaths of Black Asian and Minority Ethnic (BAME) people in restraint related deaths'. The report recognized that any death involving a BAME victim who died following the use of force can provoke community disquiet leading to a lack of public confidence and trust in the justice system. The report made several recommendations including some concerning police use of restraint techniques and improving the monitoring, safety and scrutiny of police custody environments. It also recommended improvements to the investigation of deaths in police custody in England and Wales. Previously calls for police reform in the UK have followed high-profile incidents such as the 1981 Brixton Riots and the Scarman Report or the finding of institutional racism within the Metropolitan Police by the Stephen Lawrence Inquiry in 1999. Elsewhere in considering incarcerations, Alexander (2019) argues that there has been a rebirth of a caste-like system in the US, one that has resulted in millions of African Americans locked behind bars and then relegated to a permanent second-class status, denied the very rights supposedly won in the civil rights movement. In *The New Jim Crow*, Alexander (2019) contends that racial discrimination was not ended but was merely redesigned, and that by targeting Black men through the War on Drugs and decimating communities of colour, the American criminal justice system functions as a contemporary system of racial control, relegating millions to a permanent second-class status even as it formally adheres to the principle of colour-blindness.

The problems of racism in policing and criminal justice processes identified by anti-racist campaigners and most recently by Black Lives Matter activists have often been dismissed as the problems of 'a few bad apples', rogue officers who do not follow accepted standards of behaviour, rather than there being a systemic problem. What the prevalence of racism incidents in both the UK and US illustrate is that arguably racism is inexorably embedded in the fabric of society, and thus can never be overcome unless by enacting change outside of its core system.

In this respect, social media and public campaigning has at least drawn attention to contemporary racism. Ray et al (2017) analyzed 31.65 million tweets about Ferguson across what they considered to be four *meaningful* time periods (emphasis added). These were: the death of Michael Brown, the non-indictment of police officer Darren Wilson (the police officer who shot and killed Michael Brown), the US Department of Justice report on Ferguson, and the one-year aftermath of Brown's death. Ray et al's (2017) analysis shows that #BlackLivesMatter evolved in concert with protests opposing police brutality occurring on the ground. The significance of this is arguably the increased visibility of the disproportionate use of force against Black citizens and the ease with which evidence relating to this can be circulated through social media (for example, Twitter, Facebook, WhatsApp and so on). Traditional news media are arguably selective in what they report and can also shape the presentation of a story to fit a network's ideological perspectives and support dominant perspectives (Schlesinger and Tumber, 1994; Dixon et al, 2015).

The reality is that some policing and criminal justice reforms have already taken place, but these have not been considered effective. Campaigners in both the UK and the US point to underlying problems in attitudes to Black citizens and in scrutiny and accountability mechanisms when force is used.

If reforms are to be meaningful and effective, they need to target not just the symptoms of problematic justice practices but also their cause and how they might be repaired and addressed.

These issues are the focus of this book discussed through the lens of reparations where litigation and wider reparations discourse seeks to argue that many of the harms and issues outlined here have their origins in slavery but have developed as contemporary society has been reshaped along racial lines.

Reparations in context

The remainder of this book examines the case for reparations and conducts a critical examination of contemporary reparations discourse leading towards a criminological theory of reparations in the final chapter. Chapter 2 situates slavery reparations within criminological discourse, viewing slavery as both a crime of the powerful and as state crime/state-corporate crime which is linked to notions of the state being complicit and involved in harms that may not be strictly defined as crimes but nonetheless can result in mass harms. This chapter also examines some of the legal, political and philosophical aspects of reparations as linked to human rights conceptions and outlines how the reparations litigation movement is arguably situated within state-crime discourse concerning repairing harm and seeking redress for power abuses. The chapter also sets out how contemporary reparations approaches can be pursued through several different tracks: political, legal and social mechanisms. Ruggiero (2015: 3) identifies a schematic distinction 'between law as a set of universal values applying to all and law as a set of techniques for the perpetuation of power'. Slavery arguably fits within the latter notion where the legal mechanisms and state sponsorship of slavery maintained White supremacy and a White hold on economic power. The former conception of universal values is arguably one being deployed in the use of reparations litigation to enforce rights and redress in respect of the harms caused by slavery.

Chapter 3 explores this issue in more detail via a critical overview and analysis of slavery reparations litigation to date.[4] The chapter contains a brief history of the reparations movement's litigation attempts and examines the key themes and issues explored within litigation attempts and court judgments. For example, lawsuits filed against modern American companies in the early 2000s seeking reparations for the companies' alleged complicity in slavery made an explicit attempt to show how present-day private actors had benefitted from a historical wrong. The full extent to which the companies were complicit in or benefitted from slavery was something that had arguably only recently come to light but was advanced as an argument that not only were their profits unfairly obtained, but also that their corporate activity supported slavery and created the subsequent conditions in which racist ideologies remained an integral part of society. Thus, the plaintiffs argued that reparations were owed to all descendants of slaves from corporations for their part in reinforcing race-based second-class citizenship for Black citizens. This is but one of the issues raised in reparations litigation, and Chapter 4 contains four litigation case studies together with some criminological discussion of the themes arising in these cases.

Chapter 4 returns to and examines in more detail the question of harm as one of the issues identified in analysis of reparations litigation and policy debates. A central issue in determining a case for reparations is exploration of the nature of harm and determining whether a plaintiff has directly suffered an injury. In the US, slavery reparations claims have been rejected by the courts because there is nobody alive today who has *directly* suffered from slavery and so in one sense there is no surviving victim who should be compensated. But this argument makes a distinction between transatlantic slavery as a historical mass wrong directed at Black people who are still feeling its effects from more recent harms like the persecution of Jewish citizens at the hands of Nazi Germany. Holocaust reparations have been paid because not only is it a relatively recent mass harm and from which there are survivors with tangible needs, but also because it has been subject to contemporary international law proceedings (that is, the Nuremberg trials) that established guilt according to contemporary ideas of crime and international law. Thus, it fits within contemporary ideas of perpetrator(s) who have caused the harm and victims who are owed reparations. By contrast, the lack of living slaves who directly suffered and for whom no *immediate* descendants are alive has the consequence of making the harm seem more remote. Potentially arguments can also be made that reparations have been provided during the post-civil war reconstruction periods in the US, albeit contemporary litigation might contest the nature of such reparations. Lyons, for example argues that 'reconstruction established the legal basis of some basic rights for 4 million African Americans who had lacked any such rights at all' (2007: 43). In principle at least, Reconstruction also paid compensation in the form of reallocating some land to freed slaves and providing them with ownership rights that had arguably been denied to them primarily on grounds of race. However, the subsequent Jim Crow era of segregation reinforced racial differences and cemented the notion of Black people as second-class citizens in the US. In the UK, racial tensions have continued as a factor in Black citizens relationships with the state. Chapter 4 examines some of the conceptions on victimization that underpin reparations claims. In 2012 Germany revised the original payment scheme agreed in 1952, increasing pensions for those living in Eastern Europe and broadening who is eligible for payments. This chapter also addresses the notion of harm and suffering through its criminological lens, drawing on arguments from race and crime and human rights discourse that contends that harm and suffering exist in both direct (individual) and indirect (wider community, family and descendants) contexts.

Chapter 5 expands on the previous chapter's identification that reparations have been paid in certain cases such as the Holocaust and by the US government where the state acknowledged an obligation to pay reparations for harms attributable to government action; namely the harms caused to native Americans and Japanese Americans. In this case, state acceptance of the case for reparations is arguably linked to direct action that harmed citizens and amounted to direct infringement of rights. Chapter 5 conducts a comparative case study of Holocaust reparations and Black/slavery reparations and identifies how the experience of successful Holocaust reparations cases might inform slavery and anti-Black racism discourse.

Chapter 6 returns to the question of benefit from slavery and anti-Black racism as well as examining the nature of disadvantage and inequality. It examines the arguments raised in reparations litigation concerning the benefit gained by companies and other institutions as being unfairly obtained and thus creating a notion that some of that wealth is illegitimate. This discussion examines how reparations claims and wider reparations discussion challenge the notion that reparations should not be paid by present-day institutions for harm caused by their predecessors due to an activity that was ostensibly legal albeit distinctly harmful to a specific section of society. The chapter examines the unjust enrichment argument from a contemporary criminology/human rights and zemiological perspective, contending that contemporary injustice and social harm arising from the legacy of slavery can be applied to the concept of unjust enrichment. Thus, the concept should be applied not just in the narrow context of whether present-day institutions should be said to have acted legally or illegally at the time of slavery but adopting the Roman Law principle that no one should benefit at another's expense. In part this chapter makes an argument for institutions to recognize that their existing wealth and social prestige amount to unjust enrichment irrespective of any legal arguments that they are not liable for reparations: (a) because their predecessor organization's actions took place within the context of legal activity; and (b) because the institutions themselves have changed since the time of slavery. Yet as Chapter 9 later examines, several universities later acknowledge slavery and segregation as a part of their past with the implicit acknowledgement that this reflects a contribution to segregated education and racial disparity in education that has wider consequences for social mobility and causes injustice.

Chapter 7 considers the 'value' of reparations via the application of a criminological perspective to questions surrounding what is owed by way of reparations, combined with a critical examination of how value is assigned in respect of the harm caused. Litigation and political arguments suggest that one mechanism is to simply assess the value owed to the descendants of slaves and their communities in respect of wages that could/should have been paid in respect of slave labour. However, this chapter also extends the discussion of 'value' to consider the 'cost' of slavery and its relevance to the reparations debate in both narrow and wide sense. Calculating the wages of slave labour is the narrow cost calculation that places financial value on slave labour and the indentured servitude that followed emancipation in the US, and the chapter critically analyzes the literature on financial calculations for reparations and the unpaid labour debates. The wider cost debate employs a zemiological approach that considers cost in the wider sense of economic loss through social harm and the missed opportunities for people of colour. Wider conceptions of cost and value examine how Black people generally remain in the lower socio-economic brackets in both the US and UK and are arguably still denied some of the tools of social mobility. This chapter also considers how inequality in Caribbean and some African states is a consequence of slavery, thus arguments exist that these states should somehow be compensated. Thus, this chapter argues for both narrow and wide conceptions of cost and value to be deployed within reparation discussions.

Chapter 8 examines the case for reparations through a restorative justice and human rights lens. In doing so, it also applies a critical criminological perspective to examining the nature and type of reparations and the purpose of reparations. This chapter draws on contemporary human rights and international criminal law to critically evaluate conceptions on repairing harm. It identifies reparations as a human rights issue and draws on selected case law and judicial principles from the International Criminal Court (ICC) and the ECtHR to discuss issues surrounding remedying international crimes such as war crimes, genocide and crimes against humanity (CAH) and unlawful discrimination and other human rights abuses including modern slavery, with a focus on how these might be remedied within contemporary justice systems. While acknowledging that contemporary law cannot be retrospectively applied, this chapter identifies that reparations can take many forms from apology and state recognition of the harms caused by slavery through to financial compensation, affirmative action or social rebuilding that contributes to social justice.

Chapter 9 concludes the book by examining contemporary debates in reparations and the reparations movement and returns to discussion of political, legal and social conceptions on reparations; comparing the arguments from within the UK and the US where arguably different reparations movements and considerations exist. The chapter's core focus is to construct a criminological theory of reparations, building on discussions in the previous chapters. This chapter sets out the case for reparations as linking to notions of Justice, Forgiveness and Repairing Harm even though in one sense this may not be possible from a criminological perspective where those who died as a direct consequence of slavery clearly cannot now receive a remedy. However, payments to descendants and/or public recognition of the wrong arguably constitute a restorative solution. The chapter critically examines arguments against reparations recently set out by both the US and UK governments using Sykes and Matza's (1957) techniques of neutralization. The chapter also contains analysis of the plan for reparations set out by the CARICOM Reparations Commission (CRC) in the Caribbean as well as proposals for a reparations Commission in the US. The chapter contains case studies on reparations, analyzing some of the reparations mechanisms that have been used to date including: apologies; the setting up of college funds in both the UK and US; and direct payment mechanisms in limited individual cases. This chapter's theory of reparations argues for a menu of reparative tools to be deployed to provide for a holistic approach to reparations.

Before progressing, it is worth once again pointing out that this book explores the issues of reparations and anti-Black racism from a criminological perspective. Thus, it is concerned with issues of inequality, discrimination, state and corporate crime and repairing harm from a criminological perspective rather than a Black studies approach or a broader sociological one. As a result, its discussion is inevitably situated within criminological discourse on victimization and the ability of legal systems (both criminal and civil) to offer some form of justice, restitution or compensation. As a result, while this book may not deal with certain issues of race and Black studies discourse in detail this does not mean that they are considered unimportant, but solely indicates that this book takes a specific approach to its discussion of reparative justice.

2

Slavery and Reparations: A Criminological View

Chapter 1 sets out the starting point for this book's discussion of anti-Black reparations discourse as having its basis in the harms caused by slavery, while acknowledging the contemporary reality of continued racism that is directed at and impacts negatively on Black citizens. This chapter situates the book's discussion of slavery reparations within criminological discourse, viewing slavery as both a crime of the powerful and as state crime (and state-corporate crime) given the (historical) legality of slavery in both the US and UK and its value to Western prosperity (Wilkins, 2020). As Chapter 1 identifies, slavery was underpinned by the state who in both the US and UK received revenues and taxes from slave labour and were thus complicit in the subjugation of African citizens who became property within the confines of the slave system. Whereas today most states have anti-trafficking laws (and international conventions also exist in this area), at the height of the transatlantic slave trade, the movement and trafficking of persons was deemed legal, profitable and supported the fledgling American economy. Thus, it was supported by state institutions, finance and other corporations and provided an economic contribution to states and private wealth (Neuborne, 2003). Thus, states were arguably complicit in slavery's human rights abuses for economic reasons as well as for cultural reasons predicated on beliefs that Black non-Europeans were lesser beings for whom slavery and a status as property was considered acceptable. This ideology rejected any notion of Black people as fellow citizens deserving of respect and equal treatment (Epps, 2006).[1]

Criminological examination of how perpetrators and authorities consider mass atrocities such as genocide identifies some of the barriers to providing redress for such CAH. This chapter examines the political and philosophical aspects of reparations as linked to human rights conceptions and outlines the contemporary reparations movement as situated within state-crime discourse concerning repairing harm and approaching reparations through several different tracks: political, legal and social mechanisms.

Slavery as state crime and state-corporate crime

Mullins (2020: np) identifies the concept of state crime as being concerned with 'the attempt to push the boundaries of both academic and political discourses to provide a recognition of the most harmful actions as states as criminal in nature and to bring social scientific theories of crime and criminality to bear in the identification, analysis, and control of these events'. Thus, violations of law by states are clearly covered by state-crime discourse, but arguably so too are failures by states to comply with international norms. From a criminological perspective, state actions may be drawn within state-crime discourse when social audiences define state acts as criminal (Green and Ward, 2004). Slavery derived its legality in part from governments passing laws that allowed private actors (citizens and corporations) to participate in the slave trade and conduct slave trading across international and domestic borders subject to regulations and in accordance with any legislative constraints (Bravo, 2007). But arguably slavery could always be conceptualized as a crime against humanity (Muhammad, 2003; Tibbles, 2008; Martinez, 2012) and the opposition to slavery that ultimately contributed to its abolition, arguably placed slavery in the category of state crime through its social opposition to the practice. The state's complicity with corporations and financial institutions in unlawful practices in some parts of the slave trade and in contemporary racialized exploitation also invokes discussion of state-corporate crime.

Kramer et al (2002) identify how the state-corporate crime concept developed from Quinney's work on corporate crime (1963, 1964) has been advanced to examine how corporations and governments intersect to produce social harm. State-corporate crime is broadly defined as criminal acts that occur when one or more institutions of political governance pursue a goal in direct cooperation with one or more institutions of economic production and distribution. Michalowski and Kramer (2006) identify how those in positions of political and economic power frequently operate in collaboration; and are often all too willing to sacrifice the well-being of the many for the private profit and political advantage of the few. Thus, in the context of the institution of slavery as well as in contemporary society, states and corporations arguably have vested interests in exploitative practices that result in profits. State-corporate crime discourse also examines such crime as organized crime, which rests on the exploitation of vulnerable groups. For example, criminological discussion of food crime has identified how global trades in food have exploited natural resources and labour. Such exploitation ranges from the use of slaves in the sugar plantations through to 'new slavery' in the form of exploitation in the agriculture, fishing, food processing and packaging industries (Croall, 2013). Michalowski and Kramer (2007) argue that the serious social harms that result from the interaction of political and economic organizations indicate that a class of organizational crimes exist that are the collective product of the joint actions between a state agency and a business corporation. Arguably such state crimes are often 'hidden' or invisible crimes but, as is the case with slavery are often more harmful and costly – socially, politically, economically, culturally, than regular crime (Rothe, 2020). Where they do occur, they may be more problematic to prosecute, particularly in respect of criminal courts where bringing action against states can be problematic, particularly in the context of historical injustices that predate international criminal law mechanisms. Thus, slavery reparations cases, which bring civil claims using tort mechanisms, raise human rights concerns or are aimed at the corporate partner in the state-corporate nexus represent a potential legal strategy to highlight state and institutional complicity in wrongdoing and mass harms (for example, mass human rights harms) in a manner that might otherwise prove difficult to bring before the domestic courts.

Crimes against humanity and reparations discourse

Criminology has long been concerned with large-scale activities that perpetuate criminal acts, victimization and human rights beyond the scale of domestic harm and in the area of international crimes including genocide and CAH; there is considerable scholarship that examines the activities of states in committing mass harms (Green and Ward, 2004; Meron, 2006; Walklate and McGarry, 2015).

Article 7 of the Rome Statute of the ICC provides a contemporary definition of what is meant by CAH (Cassese, 1999: 150). The Article specifies this as follows:

> For the purpose of this Statute, 'crime against humanity' means any of the following acts when committed as part of a widespread or systematic attack directed against any civilian population, with knowledge of the attack:
> - murder;
> - extermination;
> - enslavement;
> - deportation or forcible transfer of population;
> - imprisonment or other severe deprivation of physical liberty in violation of fundamental rules of international law;
> - torture;

- rape, sexual slavery, enforced prostitution, forced pregnancy, enforced sterilization, or any other form of sexual violence of comparable gravity;
- persecution against any identifiable group or collectivity on political, racial, national, ethnic, cultural, religious, gender as defined in paragraph 3,[2] or other grounds that are universally recognized as impermissible under international law, in connection with any act referred to in this paragraph or any crime within the jurisdiction of the Court;
- enforced disappearance of persons;
- the crime of apartheid;
- other inhumane acts of a similar character intentionally causing great suffering, or serious injury to body or to mental or physical health.

Schabas (2012) indicates that the term 'crimes against humanity' (or similar terms) was first used as early as the late 18th and early 19th century, particularly in the context of slavery and the slave trade. The term was also used to describe atrocities associated with European colonialism in Africa. Thus, while transatlantic slavery predates the passing of the Rome Statute (and its provisions cannot be applied retrospectively) the notion of slavery as a crime against humanity is relevant both in a historical context where the practice was institutionally accepted, and in a contemporary context where the legality of slavery might be questioned from a criminological perspective.

There is a contextual element within the Rome Statute which specifies that CAH must involve either large-scale violence in relation to the number of victims or its extension over a broad geographic area (widespread), or a methodical type of violence (systematic). This prohibition would exclude random, accidental or isolated acts of violence but would certainly apply to the systematic operational nature of the slave trade (retrospective considerations notwithstanding). Article 7(2)(a) of the Statute also requires that CAH must be committed in furtherance of a State or organizational policy to commit an attack. The plan or policy does not need to be explicitly stipulated or formally adopted and can, therefore, be inferred from the totality of the circumstances. Arguably the system of slave permits, warrants and organizational mechanism in place provide evidence of its systematic nature and intent (Finkelman, 2001; Campbell, 2010). In addition, the notion of targeting on racial grounds (for example, Black Africans) situates racialized or ethnic-based subjugation within a contemporary notion of a crime against humanity.[3]

The Rome Statute articulates direct contemporary prohibitions on slavery at 7(1)(c) as well as indicating the problematic nature of enforced removal of citizens and reducing them into a state of servitude. Section 7(2) of the Statute further clarifies that enslavement 'means the exercise of any or all of the powers attaching to the right of ownership over a person and includes the exercise of such power in the course of trafficking in persons, in particular women and children'. The specific reference to 'the crime of apartheid' in sub-paragraph (j) is also further clarified in paragraph 7(2) as follows:

> 'The crime of apartheid' means inhumane acts of a character similar to those referred to in paragraph 1, committed in the context of an institutionalized regime of systematic oppression and domination by one racial group over any other racial group or groups and committed with the intention of maintaining that regime.

Thus, contemporary notions of ethnic cleansing or promoting racial superiority in a systematic way meet the contemporary definition of a crime against humanity (Walling, 2000). Arguably this requires considerably more than the existence of racial inequality within society to meet the crime against humanity threshold. But the indicative South African apartheid regime, which codified the nature of White supremacy and created mechanisms to perpetuate and uphold this, clearly meets this threshold. CAH have been prosecuted by the ICC which has power to provide for remedies and reparations on conviction (the nature of remedies is explored further in Chapter 8's discussion of restorative principles). For example, Article 75 of the Rome Statute of the ICC empowers the Court to make a reparations order against a convicted person, specifying reparations to, or in respect of, victims. This requires the ICC to establish principles relating to reparations to, or in respect of, victims, including restitution, compensation and rehabilitation. Since the ICC's jurisdiction relates to international crimes as defined by the Rome Statute its reparative principles are primarily concerned with criminal justice notions of harm inflicted by an identifiable perpetrator who is subject to prosecution and who may be required to make reparations following conviction. However, its principles can consider the wider harm caused in a conflict and the impact on an affected group. Crucial to its existence as a permanent court are the opportunity for victims to participate in its decision-making process as witnesses and the public nature of its hearings.

The principle of reparations: political, legal and social mechanisms

Later chapters of this book examine the contemporary slavery and anti-Black racism reparations movements in detail, examining the causes of contemporary reparations efforts. McCarthy (2009) identifies that modern reparative justice theories seek to put victims at the heart of reparative justice. Thus, reparations litigation cases are concerned with achieving victim redress as an integral part of articulating victim suffering (discussed further in Chapter 3).

De Greiff (2006) identifies that the term 'reparations' can have more than one meaning. Reparations law covers both monetary and non-monetary reparations and incorporates various different elements aimed at addressing harm which includes restitution, compensation, rehabilitation, satisfaction and guarantees of non-repetition (Brophy, 2004). A core underlying principle is that reparation provides for reparative justice by removing or redressing the consequences of the wrongful acts and by preventing and deterring violations. Arguably this is problematic when dealing with historical injustices far removed from present circumstances. But within international criminal law and international criminal justice, reparations as a sentencing tool can achieve multiple objectives, restorative, punitive, deterrent. Accordingly, reparations are an important element in transitional justice which can help to heal relations following a conflict or other mass harm. In international criminal law the use of reparations provides a fair and practical way for the offender to repay the harm caused by their offence, either by personally repairing the damage caused or through assisting within the local community. Thus, different types of reparation may be deployed, as mentioned earlier, a written apology, an oral apology, or financial reparation to the victim.

The International Centre for Transitional Justice (ICTJ) identifies that 'reparations serve to acknowledge the legal obligation of a state, or individual(s) or group, to repair the consequences of violations – either because it directly committed them or it failed to prevent them' (ICTJ, 2021: np). As indicated earlier, the Rome Statute provides a legal mechanism for the ICC to provide for reparations.

In respect of political considerations, Cohen (2006) identifies how both states and perpetrators of atrocities such as genocide and CAH are often engaged in a complex process of denial concerning their complicity in atrocities or facilitation of the conditions in which atrocities can occur. Cohen notes, for example, that the process of turning a blind eye or looking the other way are states of mind that 'may be found in the mass denial so characteristic of repressive, racist and colonial states' (2006: 5). Thus, an elementary form of denial is to dispute the reality of the suffering of repressive forms of treatment like slavery, or to normalize it through discourse that involves 'othering' the victims of slavery. A primary means of doing so is to define slaves as not fully human and to engage in rhetoric that emphasizes their suitability for manual labour and to reinforce their status as property. But in addition, Cohen notes that perpetrators and complicit states also deploy a range of standard neutralization techniques (Sykes and Matza, 1957) that can be used as a form of compartmentalization, justification or rationalization. Criminology routinely engages with such neutralization techniques in examining the behaviour of offenders (including states and corporations). Topalli (2005) explained that Sykes and Matza's theory identified how offenders and delinquents are aware of conventional values, understand that their offending is wrong, and self-talk before offending to mitigate the anticipated shame and guilt associated with violating societal norms. Anderson (2017) identifies how in relation to genocide, individuals may seek to reframe their participation in violence that is later considered to be problematic and in doing so may draw on certain techniques of neutralization such as those articulated by Sykes and Matza (1957). Bryant et al (2018) noted that in the context of genocide, 'classic' neutralization techniques serve as a means of rationalization, impression management and identity negotiation. In respect of this latter point, perpetrators and governments that may have facilitated or actively engaged in atrocities need to reposition themselves from identification as the perpetrator of a mass wrong, to a more positive, or at least neutral position. This may even involve repositioning themselves as the victim. Anderson argues that deployment of such techniques 'may function both as "vocabularies of motive" to ease the violation of moral norms, and as post facto rationalizations for violence' (2017: 39).

Cohen (2006: 76) notes that the forms of denial and rationalization applied to genocide, political massacres, disappearances or torture may not be the same as those applied to 'ordinary crime'. The scale and severity of such crimes arguably requires a distinct language of neutralization appropriate to the scale of the harm, albeit consistent with core ideas of neutralization.

Neutralization techniques, slavery and anti-Black racism

Cohen's discussion of how perpetrators and authorities account for atrocities illuminates arguments used in coming to terms with events once they are brought to light and when perpetrators are caught and are forced to reflect on actions, sometimes in the context of impending prosecution or judicial processes that require construction of a defence. However, neutralization techniques are also relevant to this book's criminological discussion of the reparations landscape, in particular the extent to which responsibility is taken for historical actions and the case for reparations is taken forward. Sykes and Matza's five key neutralizations (1957) are discussed next, in the context of slavery and anti-Black racism:

1. *Denial of responsibility*. Bauman (cited by Cohen, 2006) suggests that evasion of responsibility is not solely a convenient after-the-fact rationalization or excuse for wrongdoing. Instead 'it is the 'unanchored responsibility' which is the condition for ordinary people to participate in atrocities' (Cohen, 2006: 88). Thus, an obedience to authority that denies

individual agency (for example, the 'classic' I was just following orders) can be deployed to deny personal responsibility for actions. However, Cohen also notes conformity, necessity and splitting (2006: 88) as being integral to operationalizing denial such that individuals and indeed sometimes whole societies are able to deny responsibility for committing atrocities or marginalize their involvement in them.

In respect of the practice, operation and acceptance of slavery, individual denial of responsibility for the harms of slavery and the brutality of its institutions is perhaps most obvious at the level of those who benefitted from slavery but were removed from the realities of its wrongdoing. Thus, throughout Southern and colonial society, householders who were provided with free labour in the form of field slaves, nannies, construction labourers and so on during the period of transatlantic slavery could separate themselves from the brutality of the system that provided them with indentured servants. Arguably, the buying and selling of Black people as property was normalized as was their presence in subservient roles. Cohen notes the rationalizations of 'I didn't know' or 'I had nothing against those people but ...' as being deployed by 'good Germans' as 'icons of not-knowing' (2006: 89) in respect of the Holocaust. These rationalizations arguably also apply to many ordinary 'good Southerners' during the Antebellum slavery era who failed to confront the reality of high levels of mortality on the slave ships (Miller, 1981; Klein et al, 2001; Walvin, 2013) or the brutality of disciplinary regimes that upheld the system of slavery. Wider US Southern society as well as colonial British society also benefitted economically from slavery while citizens could arguably remain removed from the realities of the conditions that slaves lived in and deny personal responsibility for slaves' loss of freedom and the brutality visited upon them.

Arguably the denial of *individual* responsibility neutralization continues in respect of present-day racism. For example, in areas where allegedly racist policing and criminal justice practices draws criticism, denial can be employed at an individual level. As Cohen notes 'the lower you are in the hierarchy, the easier it is to deny personal responsibility ... But the higher you are in the authority structure (short of initiating the orders), the further you are from the end results' (2006: 89). Thus, denial operates in different ways, potentially allowing those at the sharp end of actions that directly impact on Black citizens in negative ways to deny their individual responsibility due to being cogs in a machine that arguably dictates that they act or respond in particular ways. Higher up the authority scale, individuals are subject to weaker social controls and restraints because they do not carry out or even see the atrocity, which allows a level of denial of responsibility and the apportioning of blame to those lower in the hierarchy. Sometimes this may be couched in terms of the 'rogue' employee who does not embody the morals and ideals of the organization and who failed to appropriately follow policies. Arguments in this paradigm allow for further denial and neutralization of allegations that an organization (or indeed wider society) is institutionally racist. In respect of contemporary calls for reparations, denial of responsibility neutralizations are raised in the context of arguments that present-day institutions and governments should not be held responsible for historical events that they were not engaged in. This argument is explored in more detail in later chapters in the context of both legal arguments surrounding responsibility and political arguments concerning the extent to which governments should take responsibility for historical injustices.

2. *Denial of injury*. Individuals and organizations employing this neutralization technique arguably acknowledge that an action was wrong but claim that no one was harmed by their actions and thus the allegedly harmful actions should not be considered to be a problem.

As Cohen (2006) notes, perpetrators of mass atrocities, genocide and CAH face challenges in arguing that nobody got hurt. Given the evidence of slave mortality, use of physical punishment, lynchings and killing of disobedient or runaway slaves it becomes highly problematic to deny the reality of injury. Instead, techniques of reframing are used to articulate the nature of injury and violence visited on a group as something other than what we might recognize as 'crime' as part of the denial of injury. This may also be combined with the use of 'othering' (Dervin, 2015) and devaluation to situate the injuries caused to a devalued group as being outside of normative understanding of violence. Thus, 'when victims belong to a devalued ethnic group, though, it is common to claim that they don't feel pain as other people do, their culture is used to violence, it's the only language they understand, look what they do to each other' (Cohen, 2006: 95).

As with the denial of responsibility, denial of injury rhetoric is present in the context of both the Antebellum slavery era and British transatlantic slave period and in contemporary discourse. Evidence exists that Antebellum-era slaves were considered to have a high tolerance for and differential understanding of pain as well as being demonized as savages whose culture of violence was such that they should not be treated the same as civilized society. While it is beyond the scope of this book to explore the topic of scientific racism in depth (Jackson and Weidman, 2005), biological arguments concerning the supremacy of White races and the inferiority of Black ones were deployed as underpinning the conception of slavery as being a 'natural' state for Black citizens. While contemporary discourse has largely moved away from such arguments[4] some discussions of inner-city Black youth and of the 'black crime problem' continue to articulate ideas concerning the propensity towards violence of Black citizens. This is achieved, for example, by contextualizing knife crime and gun crime as a distinctly 'black problem' despite the complexity of assessing the nature of knife crime (Eades et al, 2007) and by highlighting the extent to which Black citizens may be victims of crime and violence at the hands of their fellow Black citizens. Thus, the alleged harms of racist institutions are contextualized in a context in which denial of injury arguments are deployed to suggest that Black citizens do greater harm to each other than is caused by structural racism or racist institutions (see also the following discussion of blaming the victim).

3. *Blaming the victim.* This neutralization technique is employed where there is acknowledgement that people or groups have been hurt, but perpetrators and authorities claim that although the action took place and they may bear some culpability for the harm caused, it was really the victim's fault. Thus, responsibility for any required redress might be denied because the victim brought about or otherwise deserved the behaviour that was visited upon them.

Blaming the victim was routine in respect of the harms inflicted upon slaves and the use of brutal forms of discipline to prevent slaves from running away, harming their masters or killing their masters whether in individual circumstances or via slave uprisings or other forms of revolt. The logic deployed in part blamed the slaves for their failure to accept their position in life (based on notions of White supremacy and Black inferiority) and to show gratitude for being provided with food and clothing and the 'protection' of their masters. Where slaves failed to fully submit to the demands placed on them and were subject to discipline or ran away or otherwise sought freedom and were punished, they were considered deserving of punishment and thus were responsible for forcing slave masters and plantation owners to dole out punishment or death.

Similar blame neutralizations were employed in the post-reconstruction and Jim Crow eras. Chapter 1 identifies the use of lynching as a tool to preserve racial hierarchies and perceived norms in the separation of the races in the post-slavery, Jim Crow-era US. Apel notes that 'racial violence was rooted in both race and gender anxieties that criminalized sexual relations between black men and white women and feared the enfranchisement and education of African Americans that might further such relations and destabilize the white-dominated power structure' (2004: 2). Thus, Black citizens who failed to know their place, particularly Black males engaged in sexual relations with White women, could be characterized as having brought any subsequent violence upon themselves by subverting the perceived natural order. Indeed, when slavery was abolished and the law no longer permitted personal violence against Black people, many White citizens nevertheless considered it their right and duty to uphold the racial order by any means necessary. In particular 'many Southerners regarded lynching and mobs as acceptable instruments in meting out punishment' (Berg, 2011: 28). Black citizens who transcended societal norms and were perceived as threatening decent White society only had themselves to blame.

These conceptions on blaming the victim are problematic to contemporary sensibilities that would reject extra-judicial violence as a legitimate tool to enforce or uphold racial segregation. However, 'in political atrocities, denial of the victim is more ideologically rooted in historically interminable narratives of blaming the other' (Cohen, 2006: 96). Thus, ideological differences between races, religions, political opponents can serve to justify conflicts. Narratives of 'look what they did/are doing to us' provide a powerful justification for ideological conflicts that extend the notion of othering to complete dehumanization that at its most extreme results in genocide and CAH such as ethnic cleansing or the subjugation of the 'other' seen as representing a threat to the normative way of life. Thus, denial of and blaming the victim can engage with narratives that see the oppressor as the victim or that reinforce the notion of deserving punishment.

In the context of neutralizing culpability for contemporary anti-Black racism, victim blaming is often deployed, particularly in respect of the social and economic position of Black citizens in Global North countries. In respect of criminal justice and engagement with major social institutions where there is perceived disadvantage, victim blaming is again deployed to address any negative connotations of Black citizens' disproportionate engagement with criminal justice, lack of achievement within certain professions, or failure to achieve particular social status by Black people (Brown et al, 2007).

Thus, reparations for contemporary racism might be denied on the grounds that the position Black citizens find themselves in is less to do with institutional or structural racism, and more to do with conditions within Black communities that has largely been brought about by the behaviour or attitudes of Black citizens themselves. In the context of criminal justice debates, the propensity of Black citizens (particularly Black male youth) to commit crime and engage in acts of violence is frequently invoked to justify the use of what may be perceived as oppressive policing tactics and even the use of deadly force. Black males are characterized as aggressive, violent and responsible for certain types of crimes (for example, mugging, knife crime, gang violence). Thus, a strong police presence is justified and use of deadly force is a 'legitimate' response to the threat posed. The spectre of Black-on-Black crime is sometimes invoked to argue for the necessity of what may otherwise seem discriminatory policing. Thus, it is acknowledged that people may be hurt by such actions, but it is really the victim's fault – they brought about or otherwise deserved the behaviour visited upon them.

4. *Condemn the condemners.* This neutralization technique is deployed to abdicate responsibility for the problematic behaviour and instead to shift attention onto people raising the condemnation. Those raising the condemnation are perceived as being the problem rather than those perceived as the perpetrators or from whom redress is being sought. Arguably the actions of the condemners either excuses the perpetrator's behaviour or contains some form of flaw or ulterior motive that substantially undermines the arguments being raised and negates any claim for redress.

When deploying this neutralization technique, the core strategy is one of deflection and of 'questioning the critics' right to criticise' (Cohen, 2006: 98). This can be achieved using a variety of techniques that can include, pointing to corruption or partiality on the part of condemners, identifying that condemners have no right to interfere or raise the redress claims they are pursuing, highlighting the hypocrisy of condemnation or simply claiming that there are more serious problems requiring attention or that it is worse elsewhere.

While it is beyond the scope or focus of this book to examine the slavery abolition movement in any great detail, this neutralization technique was deployed by slavery proponents during resistance to the abolition of slavery.[5] Abolitionists risked not just verbal condemnation but also physical violence (Ferrell, 2005). Arguably, the ultimate expression of condemnation was the South's attempts to secede from the Union in the US as arguably 'the key issue in the minds of the advocates of succession was the future of slavery' and ultimately the commencement of the American Civil War sought to portray the South as the real victim of a threat to their way of life (Calomiris and Pritchett, 2016: 2).

5. *Appealing to a higher loyalty.* This neutralization technique may accept that harm has been caused or that there was a violation of some social norms. But in doing so, perpetrators and authorities argue that they are adhering to other norms and loyalties and that the higher principles that they adhere to justify the behaviour.

During the Antebellum slavery era, the appeal to higher loyalties is perhaps most obvious in the context of arguing for the economic necessity of slavery without which US Southern society would arguably collapse. Analysis of the South's economics identifies how slavery became inextricably entwined with Southern life such that one consequence of the emancipation of slaves and the dismantling of the system of slave labour was a collapse of the Southern economy, and the 'need' to compensate former slave owners allied to arguments that a form of 'just compensation' was arguably necessary to redress the change in society (Kleintop, 2018). Similarly, the abolition of slavery in Britain was accompanied by large-scale compensation for former slave owners in respect of the economic losses they suffered. The UK's Slave Compensation Commission distributed compensation estimated at £20 million between 1834 and 1845 (Thorne, 2012). More than 47,000 individuals made compensation claims for the loss of their property and 'the slave owners played an important part in the shaping of modern British society' (Hall, 2020: S174).[6] Thus, one aspect of the higher loyalty being appealed to was the need to ensure and maintain a particular standard of living for White society which relied on slavery as an essential part of the economic fabric of society and as an essential component in the production of certain goods (for example, cotton, sugar) and the generation of revenues for the colonial powers.

In addition, the notion of White superiority mentioned several times already in this chapter operates as a powerful higher loyalty that should be preserved at all costs. Thus, neutralization based on the notion that slavery was necessary to maintain White society and to reinforce White social and religious norms becomes acceptable. Arguably such perspectives are evident in the behaviour of colonial powers that aim to civilize the so-called 'savage' races as well as in the creation and perpetuation of segregated life which continued to treat the races as distinctly separate even after the end of the US civil war and during the Jim Crow era (see Chapter 1's discussion).

In response to contemporary calls for reparations and governmental action to address slavery, neutralization may rest on an appeal to the higher loyalty of maintaining the status quo or identify the potential harm of paying reparations and holding current society responsible for the harms of previous generations. Epstein (2014: np) argues that 'rather than speaking of reparations, we should consider the many constructive steps that could, and should, be taken right now as part of our ongoing social commitments to black Americans'. Such arguments reinforce the notion that contemporary society has already accepted the wrongs of past society and has committed to notions of equality and diversity. Thus, there is no need to threaten society any further with talk of reparations or for innocent members of society to bear the burden of harms they cannot reasonably be held responsible for.

The variations in denial can be deployed in a literal, interpretative or practical sense and are not always deployed as individual neutralizations. Thus, reparations claims may encounter one or several of these neutralizations together.

The victimology of reparations

Within criminological discourse, attention has been paid to a range of ideas around victims and victimization. Criminology's sub-discipline of victimology engages with various debates concerning victims' rights and activism (Tapley and Davies, 2020). Critical consideration of how victimhood has come to be understood and responded to and wider notions of victimhood that go beyond the immediate impacts of an event such as crime are also important considerations in victimology and the study of victimhood.

These notions of victimization and victimhood can be applied to consideration of slavery and anti-Black racism. In consideration of reparations litigation and the political movement for reparations ideas of victimhood extend beyond the binary notion of Black people as slavery victims. Instead reparations discourse seeks to approach the harm experienced by Black citizens as being situated within a broad conception of victimization. What reparations litigation seeks to achieve is the bringing together of individual claims of injury and those of an affected 'class', Black citizens who continue to suffer the societal consequences of an historical mass wrong. However, one potential criticism of reparations litigation is that it perpetuates a cycle of victimhood which is ultimately self-perpetuating and self-destructive (Lu, 2017: 97). Thus, Black citizens remain in a mindset of feeling aggrieved by society and unable to move on from past harms. For critics of reparations, litigation in this area risks perpetuating that mindset. But as the cases in Chapter 3 and the discussion in Chapter 4 illustrate, victimhood and victimization are multifaceted and intergenerational and encompass more than the notion of the passive victim to include considerations of agency and empowerment in highlighting various abuses of power. Thus, the principles of both tort and human rights reparations are arguably required as a response to the identified victimization and as tools to pursue appropriate remedies.

A preliminary criminological view on reparations

As this chapter indicates, the passing of laws that allowed slavery by itself provided for a specific notion of legality in respect of slavery. But this does not exempt slavery from discussions of state crime and in respect of contemporary reparations discourse; the role of the state is an important factor to consider. States were complicit in the perpetuation of a crime against humanity, and arguably corporations and states that profited from this should now face the possibility of reparations as would any other 'offender'. Wenar (2006) argues that reparations should be forward-looking rather than backward-looking and suggests that backward-looking considerations add little weight to claims for reparations. However, the reparations litigation discussed in Chapter 3 (and subsequent chapters) highlight how denial and neutralization are integral responses to such claims for redress.

3

Reparations Litigation: An Overview

This chapter builds on Chapter 2's discussion of reparations as a remedy for slavery and anti-Black racism committed as a crime of the powerful and situated within state crime/state-corporate crime via a critical overview and analysis of reparations litigation to date.[1] The Appendix provides a timeline of reparations cases while this chapter contains a brief history of the reparations movement's litigation attempts and examines the key themes and issues explored within litigation attempts and court judgements.

While it is beyond the scope of this chapter to examine all reparations litigation in depth, an overview of the scope and nature of reparations litigation is provided, supplemented with a discussion of four key cases. These cases illustrate issues arising from claims that have profit or benefit from slavery at their core as well, but some of the selected cases also deal with Jim Crow-era harms as well as ongoing injustice and anti-Black racism. For example, numerous lawsuits were filed against modern American companies in the early 2000s seeking reparations for the companies' alleged complicity in slavery. The full extent to which the companies were complicit in or benefitted from slavery had arguably only recently come to light prompting a series of lawsuits. These cases were consolidated in federal court in Chicago, Illinois into *In re African-American Slave Descendants Litigation*, 375 F. Supp. 2d 721 (N.D. Ill. 2005). A broader case, *Cato v United States* (1995) had earlier sought damages from the US relating to the enslavement of African Americans and subsequent discrimination against them. Another case discussed in this chapter directly considers anti-Black racism by a police department and the subsequent litigation which raised human rights concerns. As this chapter identifies, slavery reparations cases are rarely successful and cases situated within claims of ongoing racism and discrimination arising from slavery and segregation face significant hurdles. But in refusing to pay reparations and in the dismissal of cases, several key issues are raised which this chapter discusses.

Reparations litigation in context

In principle 'a program of reparations is intended to achieve three objectives: acknowledgment of a grievous injustice, redress for the injustice, and closure of the grievances held by the group subjected to the injustice' (Darity, 2008: 656). Thus, reparations claims represent a form of restorative justice, rather than merely being punishment for past wrongs.

Reparations litigation is hardly a new phenomenon. Indeed, as Chapters 1 and 2 indicate, the principle of reparations was established in the US shortly after the end of the civil war and was intended as a core element of reconstruction. Specific attempts to 'adjudicate the legal merits of slave reparations against the United States government date back to 1916' but have largely proceeded without success (Hardaway, 2015: 529). Arguably the notion of reparations was embedded in the civil rights movement, according to Darity's (2008) afore-mentioned articulation of reparations principles, even if the calls and campaigning for equal treatment of the civil rights era did not specifically align with direct reparations litigation. From the criminological perspective adopted by this book, the legal mechanism pursued in reparations claims need not be purely criminal in nature. Indeed, much of the reparations litigation pursued in recent decades has been civil in nature and is worthy of consideration from a critical criminology perspective that has an emphasis on addressing power differentials, hierarchies, and inequalities as explanations for crime and wrongdoing (Lynch, 2010). Such a critical criminological approach also invites consideration not just of crime as defined by the criminal law, but also examination of how harm can be redressed and the potential conflict between notions of justice and human rights (Nurse, 2020a). Reparations lawsuits brought as a class action have the benefit of allowing representatives to constitute the public face of the victim in suits that are about extreme victimization (Dubinsky, 2004). Thus the cases can articulate the stories of individual victims or (as is discussed further on) can emphasize the systemic nature of the wrongs involved, allowing the court to see a pattern that could apply to other, similarly affected citizens. A key issue in contemporary reparations litigation, particularly that linked to the injustices of slavery, is that they have sought to identify particular institutions as having benefitted from the harm caused or profited at the expense of others (see also Chapter 6's discussion of unjust enrichment). Thus, where cases concern reparations for slavery or other historical injustices they share several common characteristics: '(a) they were committed or sanctioned at least a generation ago; (b) they were committed or authorized by one or more collective agents, such as a government or corporation;

(c) they harmed many individuals; and (d) they involved violations of fundamental human rights, often discrimination based on race, religion, or ethnicity' (Buchanan, 2009).

Arguably three broad classifications of reparations litigation have been attempted in contemporary reparations cases in the US:

1. A 'traditional' reparations suit against a defendant or defendants on behalf of a 'plaintiff class' that is usually comprised of defendants of slaves. In these cases, a familial relationship between the ancestor victim who experienced slavery and the contemporary plaintiff is considered sufficient to establish standing to bring a claim.
2. The second classification is based on seeking compensation for Jim Crow discrimination which primarily brings suit on behalf of a group of still-living plaintiffs rather than the descendants of slaves. Thus, standing to bring the case is established not through familial relationship but via a claim of direct harm where the person initiating the claim brings suit directly against the party alleged to have caused the injury. In the context of this chapter's wider discussion of reparations claims, this second category would also include reparations claims for contemporary anti-Black racism where redress might be sought for a particular and specified harm.[2]
3. The third classification might be brought by a private citizen on behalf of a group using a state's 'private attorney general' doctrine where the dictates of justice can be argued to allow this. Thus, a case may be pursued in state rather than federal court where the jurisdiction allows a broader notion of standing to bring a case. (Adapted from Miller, 2004: 93)

The afore-mentioned identified 'traditional' claims arguably dominate the legal landscape and are based in tort or theories of unjust enrichment (Kull, 2004; Dickerson, 2019). Considerable academic legal literature exists on the challenges of bringing contemporary litigation. Analysis identifies that most slavery reparations cases fail but for a variety of procedural and jurisdictional reasons including 'statutes of limitations, the political question doctrine, sovereign immunity, and lack of standing' rather than on the specific merits of the case (Ramchandani, 2007: 541). Several articles examining the traditional reparations cases identify that such lawsuits 'are naturally met with hostility in a legal system that refuses to acknowledge the continuing effects of slavery on the black community' (Lutz, 2008: 539). Legal analysis identifies that, at least as far as the courts are concerned, mere familial relationship may be insufficient both in respect of standing to bring a case and in respect of the claimed injury (Miller, 2004; Lutz, 2008; Dickerson, 2019). Thus, such claims may be dismissed at an early stage, or fail on technical procedural grounds rather than being lost on the specific merits of the claim.

In addition, contemporary reparations suits face the challenge of establishing that present-day plaintiffs have standing to bring a case. Several hurdles need to be overcome to establish this issue, not least the existence of 'an injury personal to the Plaintiffs, not a "derivative harm" uprooted from the soil of another's injury' (Martin and Yaquinto, 2007b: 670). Thus, claims made on behalf of slave descendants may struggle on the grounds that they are removed from the direct injustice caused by slavery (that is, they were not themselves unpaid labourers or subject to the disciplinary mechanisms of the slave system). Societal denial of systemic or institutional racism also provides a hurdle that needs to be overcome where claims are routed in present-day injustice arising from a historical cause. Arguably a failing of reparations litigation is that 'most litigants have advanced only broad descriptions of the communities injured and the harms suffered during slavery' (Miller, 2004: 91). Thus, a specific articulation of the injury suffered and by whom emerges as a prerequisite for pursuing a claim.

A second hurdle for litigation is the statute of limitations which arguably represents an almost 'insurmountable hurdle' (Lutz, 2008: 556). Even where plaintiffs raise a case on the basis of 20th-century harms where the statute of limitations may have only recently expired or the issue of causation can be argued due to the proximity of events, courts may still reject as time-barred cases that have their basis in more recent injuries.

A third hurdle concerns the precise nature of any reparations paid and questions concerning how any such calculation has been made. For example, where the claim being made is based on a conception of lost wages, these are likely to be estimated or speculative and face potential challenges to the accuracy of their accounting. Likewise, where the claims are based on a calculation of corporate profits derived from slavery, such claims may make assumptions about the extent to which such profits can be directly attributed to slavery as well as facing challenges in establishing a causal link to the actions of predecessor companies.

While it is beyond the scope of this chapter to conduct an exhaustive analysis of all reparations' litigation the following discussion examines several of the key recent cases.

Case study: *Cato v United States*

In 1994, two groups of plaintiffs, Jewel Cato, Joyce Cato, Howard Cato and Edward Cato; and Leerma Patterson, Charles Patterson, and Bobbie Trice Johnson (collectively referred to as 'Cato' in respect of the lead female plaintiff) filed complaints against the US for damages due to the enslavement of African Americans and subsequent discrimination against them. The claims sought an acknowledgement of discrimination, and an apology. Cato's complaint also sought compensation of $100 million for forced, ancestral indoctrination into a foreign society; kidnapping of ancestors from Africa; forced labour; break-up of families; removal of traditional values; deprivations of freedom; and imposition of oppression, intimidation, miseducation and lack of information about various aspects of their indigenous character. Cato also requested the court to order an acknowledgement of the injustice of slavery in the US and in the 13 American colonies between 1619 and 1865, as well as acknowledgement of the existence of discrimination against freed slaves and their descendants from the end of the civil war to the present.

The plaintiffs in *Cato v United States* (1995, Nos. 94-17102, 94-17104) alleged injuries based on 'disparities in employment, income, and education' between African Americans and other racial groups. But the *Cato* court found that these allegations were insufficient to establish an injury personal to the plaintiffs so as to establish the plaintiffs' standing; rather, such injuries were 'a generalized, class-based grievance'. Cato's suit was dismissed with the court 'citing the government's failure to consent to suit under the Tucker Act, and the failure of the Thirteenth Amendment to provide a remedy under the Administrative Procedures Act' (Ogletree, 2007: 458). The court, thus concluded that Cato's claims were barred by sovereign immunity, but also identified that the appropriate forum for the policy questions raised by her complaint, that is, concerning the appropriate redress mechanism for the injustice of slavery and the question of whether the state itself should provide a remedy, was a matter for Congress, rather than the courts. Cato appealed on the grounds that the dismissal of her action was premature because she was not given an opportunity to be heard on the adequacy or merits of her complaint, or to amend the complaint. She also argued that the complaint should not have been dismissed merely because the court doubted whether she would prevail. Arguably in dismissing the case the court concluded that Cato had not met her burden of showing a waiver of sovereign immunity but also noted that her claim raised a policy question that fell outside of the judiciary's authority to address. The Court in hearing Cato's appeal held:

> Discrimination and bigotry of any type is intolerable, and the enslavement of Africans by this Country is inexcusable. This Court, however, is unable to identify any legally cognizable basis upon which plaintiff's claims may proceed against the United States. While plaintiff may be justified in seeking redress for past and present injustices, it is not within the jurisdiction of this Court to grant the requested relief. The legislature, rather than the judiciary, is the

appropriate forum for plaintiff's grievances. (*Cato v United States*, 9th Circuit 1995 at 1105)

Following the Cato case, further litigation was attempted when evidence of corporate involvement in slavery emerged.

Case study: in re African-American Slave Descendants Litigation (2005)

In 2002, Deadria Farmer-Paellmann filed suit in New York federal court for reparations seeking 'compensatory damages, punitive damages, restitution, and an accounting of profits from American slavery' (Hylton, 2004: 31). The case was filed against the FleetBoston Financial Corporation, Aetna Insurance, the railroad company CSX Corporation and also up to 1,000 'Corporate [John] Does' that may also have profited from slavery. Any payments from the suit were not intended for individual claimants but instead were aimed at establishing a fund to improve health, education and housing opportunities for Black citizens (Torpey, 2004: 171). Farmer-Paellmann identified slave insurance policies in 1997 and subsequently conducted further research into corporations and private estates that had been involved in slavery (Groark, 2002). The *Farmer-Paellmann v FleetBoston Fin. Corp.* (2002) case was dismissed in 2004 but was amended and resubmitted as further lawsuits.

Subsequently, nine lawsuits were filed in federal district courts around the US seeking monetary relief under both federal and state law for harms stemming from the enslavement of Black people in America. The Multidistrict Litigation Panel consolidated all the suits in the district court in Chicago for pre-trial proceedings. A tenth suit, by the 'Hurdle' group of plaintiffs, made similar claims but was filed in a state court and then removed by the defendants to a federal district court. The plaintiffs filed on behalf of themselves and 'others similarly situated', with the effect of including in the plaintiff class 'all of the descendants of African-ancestored persons who had been enslaved in the United States' (Buckner Inniss, 2010: 652).

The plaintiffs brought suit against 18 companies whose predecessors were alleged to have been unjustly enriched (see further discussion in Chapter 6) and to have facilitated CAH through the transatlantic slave trade and slavery in the US.[3] The core issue alleged was that the various named American corporations had profited from slavery either by insuring slaves, lending to owners, or, in some cases, being slave owners themselves and thus those who were descended from slaves had various civil claims arising from the corporate involvement in slavery. The lawsuits essentially asked the courts to hold various corporate defendants liable for the commercial activities of their (alleged) predecessor companies, before during and after the American Civil War. The corporations were argued to have benefitted from slavery and the plaintiffs as descendants of slaves claimed standing, seeking to 'obtain redress for the harms that slavery caused not only to their ancestors but also to themselves' (Buckner Inniss, 2010: 650). The claim was based in part on the basis that of the 18 defendants, nine were alleged to have 'withheld information or made misleading statements regarding their participation in and profiting from slavery' (Ramchandani, 2007: 541). Thus, the suit invoked issues regarding business practices, for example conspiracy, demand for accounting, piracy, unjust enrichment, and consumer fraud, as well as the international legal framework of CAH and violation of the Alien Tort Claims Act. The harm being claimed from these practices included intentional infliction of emotional distress, negligent infliction of emotional distress and several counts alleging violation of state-based Unfair Deceptive Acts and Practices in the jurisdictions where the cases were initially filed.

Several Counts in the amended and consolidated complaint clarify and specify the manner in which the companies are said to have contributed to or profited from slavery. Count II (demand for accounting) specifies that:

> Defendants knew or should have known of the existence of corporate records that indicate their profiting from slave labour, [and] Plaintiffs and the public have demanded that the defendants reveal their complete corporate records regarding same and that a just and fair accounting be made for profits derived from the slave trade.

The claim argued that a fiduciary relationship existed between the litigants and the companies and that the companies held the proceeds of unpaid labour arising from slavery. They argued that production of corporate records was necessary in order to:

> help Plaintiffs to: 'heal the continuing psychic harm associated with slavery, trace ancestral records, provide a public and historical record of the violent force necessary to maintain a hierarchy to support slavery, provide evidence of past and subsequently established discrimination, provide a historical record of the economic benefits that accrued to the defendant private institutions as a result of slavery to more fully describe and document the connection between the institution of slavery and racist/discriminatory policies that still exist today, and assist in stemming racial discrimination through the knowledge of the role slavery played in its root causes'.

Count III of the claim alleged that slavery has always been a crime against humanity and thus raised the claim of unlawful activity irrespective of the legal underpinning of slavery. This was expanded upon in Count IV which alleged that the corporations activity was 'either directly or indirectly in support for the continuation of the smuggling of Africans'. Count V claimed that:

> Defendants' predecessor companies aided or abetted, or under other theories of third party liability ... participated in, allowed, or implicitly or recklessly, sanctioned, and/or benefitted from an institution that relied in [sic] the sexual exploitation, violent abuse and rape to achieve its goals of a malleable and unpaid work force. Plaintiffs further allege that 'Defendants' predecessor companies aided or abetted, or under other theories of third party liability ... participated in, allowed implicitly or recklessly and/or unjustly benefitted from' the spread of racist ideology concerning the inferiority of the African race.

Count V claimed that:

> Plaintiffs allege that '[a]s a result of defendants' failure and refusal to account for, acknowledge and return to plaintiffs and the plaintiff class, the value of their ancestors' slave labour, defendants have wilfully and wrongfully misappropriated and converted the value of that labour and its derivative profits into defendant's own property'.

This aspect of the claim was expanded upon in Count VI which made a specific claim of unjust enrichment. The relief sought by the plaintiffs included 'an accounting of profits, disgorgement of profits, creation of an "independent historical Commission" to study defendants' actions, a constructive trust, restitution, and compensatory and punitive damages arising out of the named defendants' alleged past and continued wrongful conduct relating to the institution of slavery' (Buckner Inniss, 2010: 653).

Article III, § 2 of the US Constitution provides that federal courts have jurisdiction only if presented with a 'Case' or 'Controversy' which limits the federal courts to considering questions presented in an adversary context and in a form historically viewed as capable of resolution through the judicial process. The court in this case noted that the Article III doctrine requires a litigant to have 'standing' to invoke the power of a federal court and that the Supreme Court in *Raines v Byrd* (1997) had expressed the view that a plaintiff's complaint must establish that he has a 'personal stake' in the alleged dispute, and that the alleged injury suffered is particularized as to him. Thus, the court questioned whether the plaintiffs' claim to the economic wealth of their ancestors' labour was conjectural rather than specific. It stated that 'while most would like to assume that they will be the beneficiaries of their ancestors' wealth upon their demise, this is a mere assumption. Plaintiffs can only speculate that their ancestors' estates would have been passed on to them, and cannot say that they would have inherited their ancestors' lost pay. This is insufficient to show a personal injury to Plaintiffs'. The court also questioned whether the claim sufficiently linked the defendants to the alleged harm. The Court also referred to *Cato v United States* in commenting that 'like the plaintiffs' allegations in *Cato* and the other slavery reparations cases decided after *Cato*, Plaintiffs' allegations of continuing harm in this case do not establish a concrete and particularized injury-in-fact, as these allegations are too speculative and generalized'.

The judgement in this case is succinctly summarized as follows:

> the court (like others) dismissed the lawsuit for lack of standing and found that the plaintiffs failed to prove they suffered injuries sufficient to satisfy Article III's case or-controversy requirement. The court specifically held that the claims were barred by the statute of limitations and argued that the claims were 'generalized' grievances rather than personal disputes. Finally, the court opined that it lacked the authority 'to say that more could have been done in the past' and that such a determination must be made by the Legislative Branch. (Dickerson, 2019: 1259–60)

The case is original in reparations litigation in respect of its approach to the profits of individual corporations. While the case is arguably about the institution of slavery itself and seeks reparations for the harm caused to slaves, it widens the scope of reparations to include descendants, and places its discussion of redress in the context of how present-day corporations are said to have benefitted from slavery. Arguably had the plaintiffs won, 'the case had the potential to reverse hundreds of years of assertions about the responsibility of public and private actors who helped to sustain chattel slavery in the United States' (Buckner Inniss, 2010: 654).

While the previous cases are primarily concerned with slavery as a cause of action, litigation has also been pursued in relation to contemporary police brutality as the following case study illustrates.

Case study: the Burge (Chicago police brutality) reparations cases (2008, 2012 and 2015)

The Chicago police brutality cases are the product of a high-profile US police torture scandal from the 1970s and 1980s and illustrate reparations litigation for wider and more contemporary anti-Black racism. The scandal involved Jon Burge, a police officer and later high-ranking commander, who 'from 1972 to 1991, led a group of white detectives who regularly tortured or otherwise coerced confessions from over 120 African-American criminal suspects on Chicago's majority-black South and West Sides' (Baer, 2018: 770).

A petition for the appointment of a Special Prosecutor filed in 2001 stated:

During the period from 1973 to 1991, at least sixty-six individuals claimed that they were tortured while in the custody of Jon Burge, or police officers under his command at Area 2 Police Headquarters and later Area 3 Police Headquarters in the City of Chicago. The Police Department's Office of Professional Standards (OPS) surveyed the pattern of abuse and concluded in a 1990 report that the abuse of suspects by Burge and those in his command was systematic and methodical. A copy of this report, hereinafter referred to as the Goldston Report, is attached as Exhibit A. Later investigating specific allegations by Andrew Wilson that Burge and others tortured him on February 14, 1982, OPS concluded that such abuse did occur. Sanders Report, Exhibit B. As a result, the Police Board, after lengthy hearings, fired Commander Burge and suspended two officers in his command on February 10, 1993, a sanction which was affirmed by the Appellate Court of Illinois, First Judicial District in an unpublished order dated December 15, 1995. O'Hara v. Police Board, Nos. 1-94-0999, 1-94-2462, 1-94-2475 cons. (1995). (In Re Appointment of Special Prosecutor, No. 2001 Misc. # 4)

In 2005 the issue of Chicago police torture was brought to the attention of the international community 'as a human rights issue by petitioning the Inter-American Commission on Human Rights (IACHR) and the United Nations Committee Against Torture (UNCAT)' (Flint Taylor, 2016: 336). The IACHR granted a request for a hearing and several witnesses testified but no further action was taken. A submission to UNCAT:

> decried the failure of the US government to properly investigate or prosecute Burge and his collaborators, highlighted the systemic nature of the torture, called for financial compensation and full rehabilitation for survivors of torture at the hands of the Chicago police, and also detailed how the US government had failed to comply with the Convention Against Torture. (Flint Taylor, 2016: 336–7)

In July 2006 UNCAT's report noted the limited investigation and lack of prosecution in respect of the allegations of torture perpetrated in areas 2 and 3 of the Chicago Police Department and recommended that the US 'should promptly, thoroughly and impartially investigate all allegations of acts of torture or cruel, inhuman or degrading treatment or punishment by law-enforcement personnel and bring perpetrators to justice, in order to fulfill its obligations under Article 12 of the Convention' (Committee against Torture, 2006).

The legal strategy for the cases developed in 2006 and 2007 when the demand for compensation was linked with the notion of reparations.

Arguably 'the direct linking of Chicago police torture to the brutality of slavery through the concept of reparations – like the previous link to the international scope of torture – was an important step in establishing a true and complete narrative through which torture victims could seek acknowledgment and remedies' (Flint Taylor, 2016: 338).

Survivors of Chicago police brutality sought a $20 million reparations package (Dardick, 2015; Flint Taylor, 2015) and several lawsuits were also filed against the City. In 2007 the Chicago City Council was reported to have approved a $20 million settlement in the cases of Aaron Patterson, Leroy Orange, Stanley Howard and Madison Hobley to settle a lawsuit for police brutality and torture directed at African Americans who were tortured into giving false confessions to the police (Associated Press, 2007). In June of 2010 Burge was convicted on two counts of obstruction of justice and one count of perjury, related to a 2003 civil case in which he denied ever using, or being aware of other officers using, any type of improper coercion, physical abuse or torture with suspects in police custody. However, 'evidence at trial showed that Burge abused multiple victims in Area Two, suffocating them with plastic bags; shocking them with electrical devices; and placing a loaded gun to their heads' (Department of Justice, 2011: np). In 2011 Burge was sentenced to 54 months in prison to be followed by three years of supervised release for lying in a deposition in a civil case about torture and abuse of suspects by Chicago Police Department officers.

In 2012 in *Kitchen and Reeves v Chicago*, two more police torture cases were settled for a total of $12.3 million. In 2015, Chicago City Council passed the Reparations for Burge Torture Victims Ordinance. This provided that:

> the maximum amount that could be paid to each entitled survivor was $100,000, and that those who had received settlements in the past would have the amount of the prior settlement subtracted from the amount of their compensation. Six of the men had previously received settlements ranging from $3,000 to $95,000; after their amounts were adjusted, the remaining fifty-one men each received a full $100,000 share. (Taylor, 2016: 357)

In total a sum of $5.5 million was allocated for payments to each of the approximately 60 living survivors of police torture in Chicago, aimed at African-American citizens who had not received settlements via previous lawsuits. The reparations package also included a full mayoral apology, establishing a centre where victims of police violence could meet and receive professional counselling; and a public memorial dedicated to the survivors of police torture (Rojas, 2020). The City of Chicago is reported to have spent some $20 million in legal fees related to the Burge cases and to have paid civil settlements approximating $64 million (Emmanuel, 2015).

The final case study in this chapter (reparations for the 1921 Tulsa massacre) provides an example of reparations litigation that directly addresses harm that is situated within a specific instance of anti-Black racism as well as addressing the ongoing harm arising from Jim Crow-era racism and present-day racial inequality.

Case study: Tulsa race riot reparations litigation (2003 and 2020)

The 1921 Tulsa incident is generally referred to as a race riot (see for example, Brophy, 2003; Gates, 2004; Messer, 2011; Messer et al, 2018) and has been the subject of two reparations litigation claims aimed at addressing the harm caused in the riot and the subsequent harm and inequality caused to the Black community. The following brief description provides an overview of the riot:

> The Tulsa riot began on May 31 following the arrest of an African American male who was accused of assaulting a white woman. Numerous rumours circulated regarding the details of his arrest. A front page news article sensationalized the story and led to thousands of white citizens gathering at the local courthouse. In addition, rumours of lynching the inmate permeated the city. Following the arrest, a group of armed African Americans arrived on the scene to protect the prisoner and, after a heated confrontation with the white crowd, a shot was fired. Preliminary skirmishes ensued and African Americans retreated back to their district of Greenwood. Angry whites followed, brandishing guns and ammunition that they had stolen from local stores along the way. Guns were also provided to whites by local law enforcement officials. A full-fledged riot ensued, with local police officers and national guardsmen siding with whites in a battle against African American residents. The entire thirty-five city block community of Greenwood, including homes and businesses, was burned to the ground. (Messer, 2011: 1217)

Shortly after the massacre there was an official inquiry, but documents related to the massacre disappeared soon afterwards. Messer and Bell (2010) suggest that the riot was officially attributed to an armed group of Black citizens whose goal was to protect one of its community members from a potential lynching. However, Black residents framed the riot differently in statements of their account of the events. A recurrent theme for both races and a number of media reports was that of inept and incompetent law enforcement officials. In 1997 a Tulsa Race Riot Commission was formed by the state of Oklahoma to investigate the massacre and formally document the incident. Members of the commission gathered accounts of survivors who were still alive, documents from individuals who witnessed the massacre but had since died, and other historical evidence. The Commission's 2001 report noted that following the riot 'Green wood residents and property owners (both Black and White), filed more than one hundred suits against their insurance companies, the city of Tulsa, and even Sinclair Oil Company, that allegedly provided airplanes that were used in attacking Green wood. Not one of those suits was successful' (Oklahoma Commission to Study the Tulsa Race Riot of 1921, 2001: 165–6). The report also noted that 'just as the legal system had failed to provide a vehicle for recovery by Green wood residents and property owners, the legal system failed to hold Tulsans criminally responsible for the reign of terror during the riot', as many of the indictments initially served on riot participants were dismissed (Oklahoma Commission to Study the Tulsa Race Riot of 1921, 2001: 166). The Commission's report recommended reparations for the survivors and their descendants but the City denied legal responsibility for the massacre (Christensen, 2021). However, the Oklahoma State Legislature signed the '1921 Tulsa Race Riot Reconciliation Act' into law in 2001 recognizing the event but arguably failing to provide effective reparations. The Tulsa Reconciliation Education and Scholarship Program subsequently provided 'a scholarship award to residents of the Tulsa School District, which was greatly impacted both socially and economically by the civil unrest that occurred in the City of Tulsa during 1921' (§70–2621). However, such scholarships and the recognition provided by the Oklahoma legislature arguably failed to address the reparations claims, thus further litigation took place.

Reparations litigation was filed in federal district court in Tulsa in February 2003 by way of a lawsuit against the city and state of Oklahoma. At the time of the suit there were 'over 120 survivors of the riots still living' according to the lead attorney (Ogletree, 2007: 455). The lawsuit claimed civil rights violations and argued that the statute of limitations (that is, the state's typical two-year limitation on filing such cases) shouldn't apply because there had been a cover-up in the riot's aftermath. Evidence provided by survivors and their descendants, supported by historians who filed a brief in the case argued that hard evidence of the complicity of the Tulsa Police and National Guard was unavailable until after the special Oklahoma Commission investigated the riot and issued its report in 2001 (Casteel and Marks, 2005). However, the district judge dismissed the case granting a motion filed by the city and the state, and ruled that victims had time between the riot and the commission's report 80 years later to determine the city's responsibility and file claims. The 10th Circuit Court of Appeals upheld the suit's dismissal, and also concluded that there had been ample time to file a lawsuit previously, drawing attention to the fact that Congress passed civil rights legislation in the 1960s and a book about the riot was published in 1982 that raised issues linked to the arguments being raised in the 2003 lawsuit. In May 2005, the Supreme Court rejected an appeal against these dismissals.

In September 2020 a lawsuit was filed against the City of Tulsa, the Tulsa Regional Chamber (a not-for-profit company) the Tulsa Development Board, The Tulsa Metropolitan Area Planning Commission, the Board of Commissioners for Tulsa County, the Sheriff of Tulsa County and the Oklahoma military. The lawsuit sought reparations for the 1921 massacre of African Americans, when a White mob burned down Greenwood, Tulsa's affluent African-American neighbourhood, killing at least 300 residents. One of the plaintiffs, Lessie Benningfield Randle, a 105-year-old woman, is one of two known living survivors of the massacre; other plaintiffs are descendants of Tulsa residents affected by the massacre. The 2020 lawsuit claims that the aftermath of the massacre is still felt by the community and seeks to remedy the 'ongoing nuisance' caused by the 1921 race riot. The lawsuit notes that racial and economic inequality in Tulsa can be traced back to the massacre. It seeks a court order 'to abate the public nuisance of racial disparities, economic inequalities, insecurity and trauma that [the defendants] unlawful actions caused in 1921 and continue to cause ninety-nine years after the Massacre' (paragraph 1, *Randle and Others v City of Tulsa and Others*, 2020). The claim states that authority for such an order is provided by Oklahoma's Public Nuisance Law, Okla. Stat. tit. 50, §1. Nuisance within the statute is defined as unlawfully doing an act, or omitting to perform a duty which:

> First. Annoys, injures or endangers the comfort, repose, health, or safety of others; or
>
> Second. Offends decency; or
>
> Third. Unlawfully interferes with, obstructs or tends to obstruct, or renders dangerous for passage, any lake or navigable river, stream, canal or basin, or any public park, square, street or highway; or
>
> Fourth. In any way renders other persons insecure in life, or in the use of property, provided, this section shall not apply to pre-existing agricultural activities.[4]

The Oklahoma nuisance codes date back to 1910. Thus, notwithstanding the existence of segregation at the time of the riot, the lawsuit arguably situates the 1921 actions as well as ongoing nuisance as being unlawful. The lawsuit describes the 1921 massacre as 'one of the worst acts of domestic terrorism in United States history since slavery' and notes that the large White angry mob, included 'some members of the Tulsa Police Department, the Tulsa County Sheriff's Department, and the National Guard, as well as other City and Council leaders' (paragraph 2, *Randle and Others v City of Tulsa and Others*, 2020). In addition, the lawsuit argues that the defendants added to the suffering of residents by unlawfully detaining survivors, enacting unconstitutional laws that deprived Greenwood residents of reasonable use of their property and have consistently thwarted Black residents from rebuilding while the defendants have 'redirected public resources to benefit the overwhelmingly White parts of Tulsa' (paragraph 3, *Randle and Others v City of Tulsa and Others*, 2020). A further claim of unjust enrichment is arguably being made in the lawsuit. This alleges that since 2016 the defendants have enriched themselves by promoting the site of the massacre as a tourist attraction, obtaining funds to do so while the residents of Greenwood and North Tulsa have gained no direct benefit from the 'appropriation' of the massacre (paragraph 4, *Randle and Others v City of Tulsa and Others*, 2020). The lawsuit documents identify specific harm to Randle noting that:

> Mother Randle at 105 years old is a survivor of the massacre. Defendants looted and destroyed Mother Randle's grandmother's home, rendered her insecure in her health and sense of safety in the immediate aftermath of the Massacre and caused her to have emotional and physical distress that continues to this day. She experiences flashbacks of Black bodies that were stacked up on the street as her neighbourhood was burning, causing her to constantly relive the terror of May 31 and June 1, 1921. The Massacre left her family without sufficient financial resources to provide the needed physical and emotional support needed to overcome the terror of the Massacre. Throughout her life, she has struggled financially, emotionally, and socially as a result of the continued public nuisance and will do so until the nuisance is abated. (Paragraph 22, *Randle and Others v City of Tulsa and Others*, 2020)

At time of writing, this public nuisance reparations claim has not yet been adjudicated. It is unclear whether the claim under public nuisance which arguably situates the potential for a remedy arising from the massacre more clearly within current anti-Black racism and inequality as a public nuisance will be more successful than the 2003 reparations claim. Heath (2020) argues that the Oklahoma legislature should pass legislation that would clearly address any statute of limitations hurdle that civil claims may face and that the state and local authorities should implement a reparations plan based on the Commission's 2001 report. Addressing the human rights issues linked to the massacre and ongoing inequality, she also recommends 'free trauma-informed care as a result of the generational impacts of the massacre' (Heath, 2020). Ogletree, lead lawyer in the original Oklahoma lawsuit, identified that the suit was 'intended to serve as a paradigm by creating concrete cases with actual living victims and by identifying the fact of racial repression as a present and continuing injustice' (2007: 455). He suggests that one benefit of Jim Crow reparations litigation is the relative immediacy of the injury and the reality that both victims of the harm and some people who inflicted the suffering of race riots and attempted to subjugate Black citizens are still alive. Thus, arguably, a case like Tulsa has benefit in giving the lie to a suggestion that 'discrimination is a thing of the past and in tracing the identifiable legal and social effects of slavery and segregation in current society' (Ogletree, 2007: 462). This issue is explored in more detail in Chapter 9's criminological theory of reparations.

Themes arising from litigation

Chapter 2 analyzed some of the neutralization techniques used in contesting the reality of systemic societal and institutional anti-Black racism and in arguments made against reparations. A key component of such arguments is to undermine the harm claims of contemporary citizens while casting doubt on the culpability of present-day citizens, institutions and the state. Thus, while a past injustice can be recognized and there may even be some acknowledgement of its lasting effects and an indirect consequence for subsequent generations and current citizens, the need for any restitution can be denied as can specific responsibility for making such restitution. These arguments are replicated in the litigation examined as part of this research and, in particular in the cases discussed within this chapter. While the decisions in these cases are arguably made in respect of the specific legal arguments raised, they bear some similarity to the neutralizations discussed in Chapter 2. Key themes arising from the cases discussed in this chapter include: denial of injury; denial of responsibility; denial of victims; and condemnation of the condemners (Sykes and Matza, 1957). These are discussed further with reference to the specific cases:

Denial of injury

In *Farmer-Paellmann v FleetBoston* the courts concluded that the plaintiffs had failed to establish that they were *personally* injured by slavery. In the Slave Descendants litigation, the court reached a similar conclusion, noting that the plaintiffs could not establish 'a personal injury sufficient to confer standing [*62] by merely alleging some genealogical relationship to African Americans held in slavery over one-hundred, two-hundred, or three-hundred years ago' (Martin and Yaquinto, 2007b: 670).

It is perhaps important to note that the courts on considering reparations litigation have not denied the reality of injury that was caused by slavery. Indeed, analysis of both legal commentary and court documents identifies that this is acknowledged and largely unopposed within trial discussion. However, what is often disputed is whether a particular plaintiff can establish their direct connection to the injury such that a remedy is required. From a legal perspective, the issues of standing, discussed within this chapter, are highly relevant and set the bar high for cases based primarily on slavery as the cause of the injury. Denial of injury defences are harder to sustain in the case of our second and third classifications of reparations claim, particularly contemporary racism cases like the Chicago Brutality cases.

Denial of responsibility

In *Farmer-Paellmann v FleetBoston*, Judge Norgle is cited as arguing that 'present day Americans are not morally or legally liable for historical injustices, that the debt to African Americans has already been paid, and that reparations talk is divisive, immersing African Americans in a culture of victimhood' (Flaherty and Carlisle, 2004: 6). A criminological perspective might well take issue with Norgle's narrow conception (and apparent lack of understanding) of the nature of victimhood and the manner in which it is socially constructed. But the question of whether a clear link can be established between the harms of slavery and a present-day 'perpetrator' is a valid one. What the slavery reparations cases consistently show is that the courts broadly deny a notion that present-day society is responsible for the harms caused by its predecessors.

Denial of victims and victim blaming

The cases discussed in this chapter provide some evidence of victim criticism albeit the neutralization of suggesting that victims deserved what happened to them is not overtly present. The Court's decision in *Cato* arguably cast doubt on the plaintiffs' status as victims while also raising questions about whether there was an injury that the judiciary rather than the legislature should redress. The conclusion in *Farmer-Paellmann v FleetBoston* contested the notion that there remained a debt to be paid, and its suggestion that the debt to African Americans had already been paid also amounts to a denial of victimhood. An element of victim blaming is also implicit in criticisms of litigants for bringing contemporary cases to address a historical wrong. This criticism can be overt as in the Tulsa case where victims were blamed for not pursuing litigation at an earlier stage (see later discussion of Condemning the condemners). However, it is also implied in the *African-American Slave Descendants Litigation* where the plaintiff's victimhood was challenged. Victim blaming was arguably present in the Burge cases where the criminal status of some claimants was identified as a mechanism to initially deny their claims and undermine the perception of their victimhood. While the initial denial of claims contended that the alleged abuse did not take place, attacking the status of the claimants and highlighting their alleged criminal background also serves to suggest that they are not 'deserving' victims who should be compensated.

Condemnation of the condemners

The cases discussed in this chapter also highlight some resistance towards the lawsuits themselves and the individuals bringing them. Criticism of the Tulsa claimants for not bringing cases earlier and dismissal of this (2003 case) and other reparations claims on statute of limitations grounds arguably represents a form of condemnation of the condemners. These dismissals acknowledge that there is a case to be made in respect of reparations, but raise questions concerning the motives of a plaintiff pursuing a case at this time. Such cases may also be framed in the context of ongoing backward-looking resentment rather than justifiable need for reparations.

Reparations litigation: preliminary conclusions

As this chapter identifies, reparations litigation does not fall into a single homogenous category but instead incorporates several categories of litigation. In the context of this book's discussions of reparations as being about the harms of slavery and ongoing anti-Black racism the classifications are important. But such classifications are also of importance in respect of the likely success of such litigation as well as the identification of appropriate remedies.

While it is acknowledged that the sample of cases directly considered by this book may be limited, analysis of reparations litigation arguably identifies that wider class actions based on the claims of slave descendants seem unlikely to succeed. But cases situated within Jim Crow-era harms or more contemporary notions of personal harm where anti-Black racism can be demonstrated have greater chance of success.

4

Victims of Slavery and Reparations: Who Suffers?

This chapter examines the issue of harm and suffering, one of the issues identified in reparations litigation and policy debates, in more detail. As Chapter 3 identified through its litigation analysis, some reparations claims have been dismissed in part due to the conception that there is nobody alive today who has directly suffered from slavery and thus in one sense there is no surviving victim who should be compensated. This argument distinguishes the 'legacy' of transatlantic slavery as an institution that was directed against Black people who are arguably still feeling its effects, from more recent harms like the persecution of the Jews in the Holocaust of World War II (Rosensaft and Rosensaft, 2002). Holocaust reparations have been paid in part because not only is the Holocaust a more recent memory, but also because several survivors and their children are still alive (Brandler, 2000). As a result, a direct victim who has suffered a tangible injury exists and the harm caused to them can arguably be addressed through reparative approaches that, for example, meet the costs of medical bills and the social care needs and pensions of ageing survivors (discussed further in Chapter 5). The Holocaust was also litigated in an international justice forum in accordance with contemporary international law perspectives (Bassiouni, 1979; Buergenthal, 2003; Bazyler, 2017) whereas transatlantic slavery has not been subject to the same process (discussed further in both Chapter 5 and Chapter 8). Thus, a more coherent legal basis for reparations arguably exists within Holocaust reparations where an identified perpetrator exists whose guilt has been established through normative justice processes.

This chapter considers the notion of harm and suffering from anti-Black racism through a criminological lens, drawing on arguments from race and crime, human rights and victimology discourse that contends that harm and suffering exist in both direct (individual) and indirect (wider community, family and descendants) contexts. In examining this issue this chapter builds towards the criminological theory of reparations as a remedy for wide-ranging harm that is set out in Chapter 9.

The nature of harm

While it is beyond both the scope and purpose of this book to detail the full nature of slavery and its harms, some consideration is given to articulating the extent of the harms caused by slavery and its impacts beyond the initial act of enslavement and the experience of living within a state of slavery. These issues are identified within reparations litigation where the discourse of wider harm is integral to reparations claims that seek more than just lost wages and claim for additional harm to communities and the descendants of slaves. Chapter 2 contained a preliminary discussion of the victimology of reparations, identifying that in part there is a need for a clearer understanding of victimization as an integral part of reparations discourse. In particular, reparations discourse seeks to extend the notion of harm beyond that of just individual perpetrator (for example, plantation owner or other slave owner) and to situate it within the notion of a state-endorsed system. Cohen (2006) talks about the complex psychology of denial as a factor in discussing atrocities such as CAH and genocide. This is particularly the case when states are required to confront the reality of their complicity in an activity such as war crimes, genocide and CAH. Denial is, thus, 'understood as an unconscious defence mechanism for coping with guilt, anxiety and other disturbing emotions aroused by reality' (Cohen, 2006: 5). When practised by states and other institutions, it can serve as a mechanism for minimizing the victimization inherent in slavery and genocide through the use of neutralizations that justify the severity of the harm. Alternatively, in the context of slavery and anti-Black racism, denial can contextualize these harms as things that happened in the past and that have now been resolved or that are confined to isolated 'rogue' elements such as the 'bad apples' that tarnish otherwise exemplary police and criminal justice institutions. Denial thus allows states and governing institutions a means of resisting calls for action over policing and denial of the reality that access to justice is not provided in a uniform manner to all citizens (Nurse, 2020a).

A potential issue with slavery reparations discourse is that it primarily concerns 'harms inflicted by dead people (antebellum whites) on dead people (antebellum blacks)' (Posner and Vermeule, 2003: 692). Thus, arguably the harm caused remains historic and an argument could be made that any required remedy needed to be sought closer to the time. Indeed, the statute of limitations argument has been raised in several reparations cases to denote the harm as a historical one that is beyond the remit or scope of the 20th- and 21st-century courts to remedy. In principle, this argument has legal validity at least in terms of the feasibility of collecting and assessing evidence or of examining first-hand the actions of a perpetrator. But it potentially fails to consider arguments situated in the general inability of Black citizens in the Antebellum and British Empire periods of 'legal' slavery to contest their status as chattels and property as well as the challenges facing emancipated slaves in bringing cases against White former slave owners in the Jim Crow era. However, in the context of examining slavery and anti-Black racism as categories of harm that arguably cannot be justified as being unsuitable for a remedy on the grounds that a historical wrong cannot now be retrospectively remedied in line with modern conceptions, this book's criminological approach suggests there is a need to rethink the conception of harm and how it is considered. In this respect the criminological argument is in sympathy with the notion put forward in *Cato v United States*, the *African-American Slave Descendants Litigation* and the *Tulsa* case(s), that the harms of slavery need to be considered in their wider (criminological) context.

Within criminology, the sub-disciple of victimology accepts that victimization extends beyond the immediate victim (the person who has directly experienced the crime or harm) to family members and friends who also suffer as a consequence of the inflicted harm (Davies et al, 2017). This idea is central to slavery reparations litigation which contends that the harm suffered from slavery extends beyond the point that the historical injustice was committed (Sacerdote, 2006; Miller, 2018; Wenger, 2018). In exploring this idea, first, there is a need to consider both narrow and wider ideas of victimization, and to examine whether and how society has engaged with the needs of slavery victims. The narrow conception on victims relates primarily to those who are direct victims of a wrong or harm and thus applies to slaves living in the Antebellum period and those who experienced race-based discrimination and harm during the Jim Crow era or as a direct consequence of contemporary anti-Black racism. But *Cato v United States*, the *African-American Slave Descendants Litigation* and the *Tulsa* cases contend that descendants of slaves and whole communities should be drawn within the conception of victimization due to the wider nature of the harm they experience.

Criminology (and victimology) already engages with this idea in both theoretical and practical conceptions. The criminal justice conception of a victim primarily relates to a victim of a crime (that is, an illegal act prohibited by law) who has *directly* suffered from the act. Thus, for crime to occur there has to be a perpetrator who commits it, and a victim who experiences it (Xie and McDowall, 2008). However, beyond this perhaps 'traditional' (and potentially outdated) notion of victimhood as being this tightly defined, the perpetrator can be an organization or a state rather than an individual, and the victim may also themselves be an offender, a community or even an entire ethnic group. Criminology also looks beyond the scope of direct victims to incorporate a wider notion of victimhood within criminal justice systems and social policy perspectives that incorporate the conception of *indirect* victims of crime (called secondary victims or co-victims in some cases) as this identifies others who are affected by the crime or event. For example, in the case of *The Prosecutor v Thomas Lubanga Dyilo*, ICC-01/04–01/06 before the ICC, the ICC considered the use of and victimization of child soldiers as a specific crime because it is prohibited under international humanitarian law and international human rights law and constitutes a war crime under the terms of the Rome Statute (Fox, 2005; Breen, 2007; Freeland, 2008). But the ICC also considered whether those who had suffered harm from the actions of the direct victims (that is, the child soldiers) should also be considered 'indirect' victims (Spiga, 2010). Extending the conception of victim to incorporate indirect victimization thus provides a mechanism for considering those such as descendants or other family members who may be negatively impacted.

Within victimization discourse the term 'survivor' is sometimes preferred as being more appropriate and constructive than the term 'victim', in part due to the negative connotations of 'victim' as a term laden with implications of helplessness. Slavery discourse arguably challenges the notion of victimhood and the exercise of White supremacy by appropriating the term 'survivor' and applying it to emancipated slaves. However, the term 'survivor' can also be problematic where those who have experienced victimization may be made to feel somehow inadequate if they do not feel like a survivor or where their suffering is seen as somehow being confined to the past. Thus, in the Jim Crow era of segregation, slavery survivors may well have experienced challenges in relation to perceptions of their emancipation as having addressed their victimization, notwithstanding the existence of ongoing discrimination. Indeed, in respect of contemporary discussions about reparations there have also been criticisms that reparations are linked to an increased notion of victimization linked to America's litigation explosion (see, for example, Flaherty and Carlisle, 2004). Some opponents of reparations also contend that the civil rights reforms of the 1960s and 1970s plus the reality of an African-American male having reached presidential office are signifiers that the harms of slavery and the perceived barriers of discrimination are now things of the past; such ideas arguably also contextualize a subtler kind of victimization (Bonilla-Silva, 2015).

The reality is that victimization does not exist on a straight line from the negative state of victimization experienced in the presence of an offender or solely linked to a specific event, through to the more positive state of survivor. Potentially this creates an impression of the victimization and its impacts as a past event whereas an argument being raised in reparations discourse is that of ongoing victimization and harm. Thus, our conception of harm needs to expand further in line with the arguments of reparations litigation that it is intergenerational.

Intergenerational trauma

A key (and arguably under-explored) element of victimization is trauma (Ajdukovic, 2004). Research suggests that trauma exposure is pervasive to the extent that over 70 per cent of people globally are exposed to at least one traumatic event in their lifetimes and that there is an average of >3 trauma exposures per person (Stenson et al, 2021). Trauma may most obviously be considered in the context of victims of crime or harm who directly experience an event that harms them either physically, psychologically or both. But research indicates that race-based discrimination is detrimental to the mental and physical health of African Americans (Williams-Washington and Mills, 2018). In particular, race-based trauma may be directly experienced in contexts where an individual experiences first-hand abuse at the hands of state authorities or racist discrimination by institutions or fellow citizens. In such cases, repeat incidents (for example, continually being stopped by police or receiving differential treatment in using services) can have a victimizing and traumatic effect that represents a form of harm. However, research has also indicated that trauma can exist on both biological and psychological levels and at an intergenerational level. Arguably this provides an explanation for health inequalities such as hypertension, depression and heart disease in Black communities as a result of colonialism, slavery, Jim Crow laws and segregation (Barlow, 2018). While in the Caribbean, slavery has been cited as having a strong impact on the collective psyche of the people of Jamaica (Longman-Mills et al, 2019). Arguably it can also provide some explanation for how large historical traumas such as war and slavery can have the effect of influencing present-day behaviour and social attitudes even if unconsciously (Walkerdine et al, 2013).

The concept of intergenerational trauma is of value in discussing the harms for which reparations are sought. Arguably:

> slavery did not end the trauma and shame to which blacks were subjected. What followed was Jim Crow (a rigid pattern of racial segregation) lynching, disenfranchisement, an economic system – sharecropping and tenantry, that left little room for ambition or hope, unequal resources ... terrorism, racial caricatures, and every other form of humiliation imaginable. (Graf, 2014: 185)

Thus, Black citizens are conceivably aware of the trauma of their slave past and the historical ordeal of slavery which has left its mark on present-day communities in respect of their economic and social positions and the structural inequalities they need to navigate (Williams, 1985; Mesic et al, 2018). Some scholars also argue that the trauma of slavery and its aftermath has been transmitted from generation to generation in a variety of different ways. The methods of transmission include 'poor parenting, connected to the master-slave relationship as the template for all human relationships, the dominant one parent family structure created by slavery, and transgenerational haunting' (Graf, 2014: 195). Terms like post-traumatic slave syndrome (Leary, 2005) and post-traumatic slavery disorder (or PTSlaveryD) have entered into the psychological language and have been introduced to characterize aspects of the social, emotional and economic dynamics that are considered to impair Black people's ability to self-actualize and capitalize on their own knowledge, information and learning clearly, coherently and independently (Reid et al, 2005). Womack (2016) indicates that Leary's theory of post-traumatic slavery syndrome describes the multigenerational trauma experienced by African Americans that results in them having undiagnosed and untreated post-traumatic stress disorder (PTSD). Thus, it is argued that internalized racism has damaged the self-esteem of African Americans and contributed to a state of cultural trauma (Halloran, 2019). Should this be the case, present-day negative experiences of institutional or structural racism have the capacity to have extreme negative effects, resulting in further harm.

Anti-Black racism and victimization

Chapter 2 provided a brief introduction to the victimology of reparations and identified that the conception of victimization being explored is based on an argument that structural conditions arising from slavery and enduring notions of White supremacy and the subjugation of Black citizens cause victimization. Radical approaches to victimization are of assistance in considering structural conditions that victimize large amounts of people, such as the institutional racism of society that negatively impacts on Black lives. Research from a radical victimology perspective questions the social construction of victimhood, raising questions about how the label of victim is applied as well as who has the power to apply the label (Mawby and Walklate, 1994). Thus, Black people experiencing post-traumatic slave syndrome and being further victimized by their experiences may not be considered to be victims where they are not clearly victims of crime or unlawful acts, but are experiencing repeated incidents of 'minor' harm or trauma. Reparations discourse might argue that disadvantage in housing, education or in terms of income inequality arise from historical injustice and should be compensated, but 'traditional' notions of victimization and harm might argue otherwise. A radical approach to victimization might reject the traditional approach and arguably seeks to expand our understanding of victimization by thinking about how relatively powerless groups in society should be considered, and examining the different types of oppression they suffer. Radical approaches argue that there are a broad range of victims and victimization, and suggest that the state constructs the status of the victim and decides who is 'deserving' and 'undeserving' of the victim label which is 'officially' conferred. Thus, the state's construction of Black citizens as failing to take opportunities when they are due or as having negative attitudes towards contributing to society may negate notions of victimhood. For example, racial realists argue that America has made progress in rectifying racial injustice, the economic divide between Black and White people has been exaggerated, and White Americans have been receptive to, and have addressed, racial equality. Thus, 'racism is a thing of the past' and so 'persistent racial inequalities in income, employment, residence and political representation cannot be explained by white racism' (Brown et al, 2007: 60). Instead, it must be attributable to the failures of African Americans to take advantage of the opportunities afforded to them and represent their cultural and moral failures. Thus, the victimization experienced by African Americans is marginalized.

Arguably, there is also scope to consider ideas about how victims experience the state of being a victim and the exercise of power in reparations discourse (Turvey, 2014). In the case of Black citizens, contemporary justice and human rights discourse identifies that citizens may come to see themselves as 'victims' of policing and criminal justice processes rather than as service users. Anecdotally, Black citizens receive guidance from parental figures on how they should dress and behave when likely to encounter police, and arguably a very real fear exists among Black adolescents that they may become victims of police use of force (Smith and Robinson, 2019). Criminology has long been engaged in critical analysis of the extent to which policing tactics and the use of police powers that arguably target Black citizens or treat them differently on grounds of race or the perception of race, amount to a distinct form of victimization. For example, Bowling and Phillips (2007) examined the use of stop-and-search powers by UK police concluding that the statistics showed that the use of stop-and-search powers against Black people was disproportionate, indicating unlawful racial discrimination. More recent figures indicate that Black citizens in the UK are nine times more likely to be stopped and searched by police than their White counterparts, which generates dissatisfaction with policing and arguably a sense of victimization (Dodd, 2021). In the wake of the killing of George Floyd (and other incidents such as the killing of Eric Garner and Breonna Taylor), questions have been raised again about how police use their powers and whether systematic racism has created a culture of victimization (Rickford, 2015; Ince et al, 2017; Ray et al, 2017). However, criminological victimization discourse also provides a means to consider how victimization can be examined (and addressed) through socio-legal means.

International law sets out some mechanisms to engage with systemic victimization. The United Nations (UN) Declaration on Basic Principles of Justice for Victims of Crime and Abuse of Power (1985) clearly sets out ideas on victims as including those who experience harm from criminal abuse of power. The Declaration's definition of victims is a wide rather than narrow one and specifies that:

- 'Victims' means persons who, individually or collectively, have suffered harm, including physical or mental injury, emotional suffering, economic loss or substantial impairment of their fundamental rights, through acts or omissions that are in violation of criminal laws operative within Member States, including those laws proscribing criminal abuse of power.
- A person may be considered a victim, under this Declaration, regardless of whether the perpetrator is identified, apprehended, prosecuted or convicted and regardless of the familial relationship between the perpetrator and the victim. The term 'victim' also includes, where appropriate, the immediate family or dependants of the direct victim and persons who have suffered harm in intervening to assist victims in stress or to prevent victimisation.

The UN Declaration identifies some interesting points about the nature of victimization. The definition uses the word 'harm' rather than 'crime' and so makes a point about victims being those people that have suffered some form of disadvantage or negative impact. It also talks about 'acts or omissions' and so extends beyond just deliberate criminal acts. The Declaration's definition of victims therefore applies to Black citizens unlawfully killed by policing agencies, even if no perpetrator is identified or if no disciplinary or other action is taken. Arguably it also applies to communities suffering from abuse of power through systematic or institutionalized racism where this violates criminal laws.

Criminology has examined these issues before, and victimology studies in the US and elsewhere have already examined the prevalence of Black citizens in officer-involved shootings, as well as the level of use of force. Studies have also examined how far cultural issues within police forces risk increasing the victimization of Black citizens by law enforcement, with its members potentially considering Black citizens to be more dangerous and more likely to be criminal (Blum, 2020). From a theoretical perspective, we can see society's preference for truly innocent victims and the limited ability of the justice system to avenge them (McShane and Williams, 1992). But as we have already discussed in this chapter, those who may be seen as a threat to society's norms or who historically fell outside of them to be considered as the 'other' (for example, slaves) can be considered to be less deserving victims. As a result, some victims of alleged racist action by policing agencies receive criticism suggesting they are somehow deviant, and somehow to blame for the incidents that led to their deaths.

Contemporary reparations narratives: harm and trauma

In part what reparations discourse does is to draw on some conceptions of narrative victimology; an emergent area concerned with the role of narratives and their relationship to policy. Walklate et al (2019: 200) argue that victimology has been slow to recognize the value of narratives 'both as sources of data for making sense of victims' experiences and policy responses to those experiences, and as forces which act upon such experiences and responses'. This is despite some recognition within criminology (and law) that 'narrative is particularly relevant to the study of how people understand their own experience and actions in relation to their identity and the wider collectives to which they belong (Pemberton et al, 2019 392). Narrative victimology 'focuses on how people experience wrongdoing' (Pemberton et al, 2019: 393) and stories have value both in terms of allowing individuals to make sense of what has happened to them and to articulate this. But they also have value in the context of providing a means for external observers, analysts and policy professionals to understand how victimization has been experienced and understood. But it has been argued that 'some narratives count more than others and the socio-political context in which such "counting" takes place is important to appreciate' (Walklate et al, 2018: 211). Thus, narratives concerning historical injustice for which present-day authorities wish to deny responsibility might be discounted. While consistent with Cohen's (2006) suggestion that states wish to avoid responsibility for atrocities and deny their reality, victimization stories that point to widespread societal problems may also be resisted.

In this respect, there is also value in seeing reparations litigation, such as the cases explored in Chapter 3, within the context of narrative analysis of who has suffered and how that suffering was constructed, experienced and impacted upon present generations. Narrative method is well established as a means through which contested stories can be analyzed and understood within adversarial justice systems and in the context of victimization arguably provides a means through which a victim's voice can be heard (Nurse, 2020b). Wolff (2014: 4) argues directly that 'law is narration: it is narrative, narrator and the narrated'. At its most basic level, legal cases are constructed from a variety of texts that can be read as a series of intertwining stories. Establishing what happened, when, to whom and liability, arguably requires constructing, understanding and assessing a clear narrative to reach a judgement on the facts. Reparations cases are replete with narratives of victimization and trauma and present for consideration by the courts, detail of the harm caused to citizens within a narrative of how that harm occurred and what its effects were. Wolff (2014: 20) identifies that 'narratives are everywhere in law: stories of disputes source the common law; chronicles of efficiency, injustice or unaccountability inspire legislative reform; and debates about the findings, explanations, meanings, scope, influences and impacts of the law inform legal scholarship'. As a result of this, arguably 'law is a narrative medium, particularly within the confines of adversarial trial systems where both prosecution and defence seek to convince jurists of the factual accuracy and adequacy of their "story"' and its implications (Nurse, 2020b: 304). Thus, the competing narratives of criminal trials can lend themselves to analysis understanding and adjudication, whereas the reparations cases considered in this book can incorporate both personal narratives of racialized harm and suffering (as in the Chicago police brutality cases) or can incorporate broader narratives about societal harm often encompassing wider consideration of varied stakeholders including church groups, non-governmental organizations, civil society groups and African-American advocacy groups. Crucially these narratives of harm can serve to challenge a dominant historical wisdom about events.

The recent Tulsa Riot reparations litigation, for example, contains both personal and wider narrative. The personal narrative (outlined in Chapter 3) challenges the notion of the events of 1921 as a one-off event, albeit a tragic one, by constructing its narrative of the ongoing effect of this event and its aftermath on Mother Randle's life chances as well as her mental health. It makes clear that even 99 years after the event, she still experiences its terror while setting out that she will continue to do so until the 'nuisance' is abated (paragraph 22, *Randle and Others v City of Tulsa and Others*, 2020). The wider narrative constructed by the case challenges any notion of the riot as being the actions of an unruly mob and clearly situates it within a Jim Crow-era notion of racial segregation and anti-Black sentiment where state and city institutions were complicit if not actively involved in the persecution of Black citizens who were being denied their human rights. The wider narrative extends to also showing how the persecution of Black citizens continued long after the event and has its present-day resonance in economic inequality and the appropriation of the Tulsa riot for the enrichment of present-day actors at the expense of the poor Black community. Thus, personal narrative and wider narrative combine to generate the case for reparations and articulate the full scope of the harm at issue. Taking these principles into account, the reparations claims of Japanese Americans provide a case study of where the state has accepted the case for reparations in respect of suffering.

Case study: Japanese-American reparations

Reparations have been paid by the US in respect of Japanese Americans who suffered at the hands of the state during World War II. The basis of the reparations claim relates to the internment of approximately 120,000 Japanese Americans in incarceration camps based solely on their Japanese ancestry. Two thirds of those forced to live in the camps were US citizens (Nagata et al, 2015).

The incarceration was arguably a race-based, personal and cultural trauma where individuals suffered directly through being incarcerated while culturally, the status of Japanese Americans was arguably diminished via an extreme form of othering. In the context of this book's discussion of reparations as a remedy for discriminatory practices, the Japanese-American experience provides some insight into how such claims might be accepted by the state. It also marks a successful example of reparations at least in respect of the willingness of the state to provide a remedy.

The cause of the internment was the surprise attack on the US naval base at Pearl Harbor in Hawaii on 7 December 1941. Arguably this prompted widespread fear and insecurity concerning the Japanese threat (heightened by the state of war between Japan and the US that followed the attack). Thus President Roosevelt, responding to concerns that Americans of Japanese ancestry might pose a threat to the US, signed Executive Order 9066, which ultimately paved the way for the forced repatriation of 120,000 American citizens and legal residents of Japanese descent from their homes into US internment camps throughout the western US. Executive Order 9066 was strengthened when Congress passed Public Law 77–503, which authorized a civil prison term and fine for a civilian convicted of violating a military order. While these legislative acts were challenged as being unconstitutional in two cases before the US Supreme Court, *Hirabayashi v United States,* 320 U.S. 81 (1943) and *Korematsu v United States,* 323 U.S. 214 (1944), the actions were considered to be constitutional, and thus internment of Japanese Americans was legal.

Reparations for Japanese Americans ultimately garnered broad political support (Henry, 2007: 364–5). Executive Order 9066 was rescinded in April 1976 by President Ford, and in 1980 President Carter signed legislation creating the Commission on Wartime Relocation and Internment of Civilians. This body was charged with investigating the impact of Executive Order 9066 and the internment camps on the citizens and residents of Japanese ancestry. Between July and December 1981, the Commission held 20 days of hearings and took testimony from more than 750 witnesses including Japanese Americans and Aleuts who had lived through the events of World War II. The Commission's 1982/83 report, 'Personal Justice Denied', ultimately concluded that the government's wartime internment policies were not justified by military necessity. Thus, the report also called for a Congressional joint resolution apologizing for the injustices against Japanese Americans and also made recommendations for remedies to be provided to the surviving internees and their families.

Subsequently the Civil Liberties Act 1988 was passed which 'provided for an official apology payments of $20,000 to each surviving detainee, and the establishment of a public education fund' (Saito, 2001: 1). In 1990, the government distributed the individual redress payments of $20,000 to an estimated 60,000 surviving Japanese Americans who were affected by the internment, along with its apology for the treatment of Japanese Americans during World War II.

Japanese-American redress has been cited in relation to African-American redress 'sometimes as legal precedent. Sometimes as moral compass. Sometimes as political guide' (Yamamoto, 1998: 481). In respect of precedent, it establishes the notion that reparations can be made (and paid) for a harm that was considered legal at the time but subsequently considered to be unjust. The internment's legal status was originally provided by Presidential Executive Order and supported by action from the legislature. Its constitutionality was challenged but upheld by the Supreme Court. Thus, although the harm caused by the internment arguably infringed human rights principles developing in customary international law of the time (at least a principle of no punishment without first committing a crime) it had its basis in a perception of legality. However, internment had public support and was potentially considered to be normal wartime practice and those who opposed it were considered to be unpatriotic (Miksch and Ghere, 2004). Thus, much like slavery, it required a change in the social and political climate before it became recognized as unjust. Henry (2007: 363) cites Hatamiya (1993) as labelling civil rights legislation 'as special interest legislation and argued that Japanese American redress had to be presented as a constitutional issue rather than a racial issue'. Henry partially contests this issue noting that Japanese Americans (as a group) were interned because of their race rather than on any notion of individuality. Thus, the racial nature of any reparations claim is relevant, notwithstanding the subsequent reconsideration of the necessity of internment as a military necessity and a (misguided) public safety issue.

In potentially comparing African-American reparations to Japanese-American reparations, the Japanese-American case highlights what a strong reparations case looks like while also indicating some of the hurdles that African-American litigation needs to overcome. One point to note is that only 'certain' Japanese Americans were provided with reparations. Thus, the reparative approach was confined to 'only those Japanese Americans who actually suffered in the internment camps during World War Two as opposed to all Japanese Americans as a collective' (Corlett, 2007: 186). In this respect it differs from African-American or Caribbean reparations claims that seek reparations for an entire ethnic group. Arguably the Japanese-American reparations claim was successful as a social movement in ways that African-American reparations have yet to achieve despite some vocal support for the African-American claim. Grassroots groups assisted in making the case for the claim and Yamamoto (1998) identified that framing the claim in respect of it being a claim made by a 'model minority' was an integral part of its success. Arguably how the claim is framed is important to the context in which it may or may not succeed or be acceptable in a policy sense (Howard-Hassmann, 2004). There are several important distinctions between the African-American claims and the Japanese-American claims. Accordingly, African-American claims face challenges the Japanese-American claims did not. First, while the treatment of African Americans over a long period of time potentially makes a case for a greater level of reparations than the Japanese-American cases, in the Japanese-American cases the perpetrator is clearly the state and the state apparatus was used as the mechanism for internment. Thus, issues of liability and causation are clear, provable and crucially are accepted. The state determined that Japanese Americans should be incarcerated and set about creating the means to do so. Secondly, the Japanese-American claims like Holocaust claims involved still-living survivors of internment rather than an entire class; that is, it was confined to some Japanese Americans who had suffered a particular, specific and clearly documented injury rather than all Japanese Americans who might be seeking compensation for their overall diminished status. Thus, the issue of standing to pursue a claim or receive restitution is easily identifiable in a way that claims made by descendants of slaves and Black society more generally might not be. Finally, the relatively narrow scope of the claim arguably served the government's practical and policy interests (Henry, 2007: 365). The government was able to award compensation to a relatively small, defined class of 'deserving' Japanese Americans without opening the floodgates to any other racial groups (Yamamoto, 1998). Thus, Japanese-American reparations can be distinguished from African-American or other claims on the uniqueness of the circumstances, the claimants and the specific focus of the reparations provided.

Some conclusions on 'who suffers?'

This chapter's discussion of victimization and harm identifies the reality of victimization as existing in both narrow and wide contexts. Accordingly, it identifies that for reparations discourse, the consideration of 'who suffers' needs to examine the nature of any harm caused to citizens as well as how that harm and victimization was created, experienced and understood. It also needs to consider both the short- and long-term effects of any harm, recognizing that secondary victims such as family members, descendants and communities may experience the harm long after the initial event has taken place. Criminological and reparations discourse has begun to embrace this idea, and within reparations litigation of various types, the narratives of victimization and harm are integral to identifying and articulating the impact of anti-Black racism in both direct and indirect contexts.

These ideas on harm and suffering are further explored in Chapter 5's discussion of reparations claims.

5

A Comparative Analysis of Reparations

The previous chapter identified that reparations have been considered by the US government in cases where the state acknowledged an obligation to pay reparations for harms attributable to government action; namely the harms caused to native Americans and Japanese Americans. In this case, state acceptance of the case for reparations is arguably linked to direct action that harmed citizens and amounted to an infringement of human rights.

This establishes an important consideration in reparations discourse; the notion that where states can tangibly be determined to be culpable for harm to an identifiable group or individuals within a group then reparations may be due at a state level. Such reparations amount to a form of compensation for the harm caused and 'damages' owed to the affected group or collection of individuals. This chapter expands on Chapter 4's discussion of this principle via an in-depth case study of another reparations case; restitution for the Holocaust and the losses suffered by Jewish people during World War II. The nature of these reparations is well documented, and a robust legal and administrative process was created to allow for the making of claims, the administration of payments and review of the operation of the scheme. Records exist concerning the nature of reparations owed and of the affected individuals. Reparations were also given to native Americans where the state has accepted the necessity of providing federal aid and redress as a consequence of state exploitation, and to Japanese Americans for internment following the Pearl Harbor attack.

This chapter conducts a comparative case study of Holocaust reparations and anti-Black/slavery reparations noting that while the Holocaust reparations claims were arguably successful, the case for reparations was not without its problems. Securing reparations from Germany for survivors of the Holocaust was arguably an ordeal that for some survivors lasted for decades after the formal end of hostilities. As this chapter shows, not all who were arguably eligible or deserving of reparations were compensated and thus questions could be raised about the extent to which the reparations paid amounted to an adequate remedy for the harm caused. Thus, Holocaust reparations provide for a useful comparison from which to consider how slavery and anti-Black reparations might be pursued.

Genocide reparations in principle

Holocaust reparations are situated within international law's recognition of war crimes. In contemporary law, the 1998 Rome Statute which set up the ICC recognizes CAH, genocide and war crimes as threats to international peace and security and matters that can be prosecuted under international law (Nadya Sadat, 2013). An important principle for such international criminal law is that those who perpetrate such crimes against the international community should be brought to trial so that justice can be done and seen to be done. That victims should be able to provide testimony and evidence is also important in allowing survivors to confront their tormentors and for witnesses to give evidence (Jackson and Brunger, 2015). Increasingly, international law provides for legal accountability for human rights violations and, where possible, that some form of remedy or restitution is provided. The prosecution of Nazi leaders for CAH at the Nuremberg trials identified that 'all states are bound to protect fundamental rights, and that the vitality of these rights depends upon the assurance of their enforcement through legal process' (Orentlicher, 1994: 425). Arguably Nuremberg commenced the process of bringing leaders of a criminal state to account for genocidal actions. Weitz (2009: 357) identified that following World War II 'the international community came to acknowledge victims as a distinct group, deserving of reparations for their physical and emotional damage' with a reparations movement developing in response to the Holocaust. Ellis and Hutton (2002) identify the Nuremberg and Far East trials (concerning wartime atrocities committed by Japan) as legal landmarks in establishing the principle that government officials could be held legally accountable for the atrocities they had committed. Contemporary human rights treaties and international criminal law mechanisms further develop these principles. Human rights treaties applicable to mass harms and violations of international norms emphasize the role of punishment and remedy in securing rights. Arguably, 'human rights treaties also affirm the importance of civil redress for violations of protected rights, and in recent years international responses to gross violations have placed increasing emphasis on enforcement of states' duty to compensate victims' (Orentlicher, 1994, 425–6).

Thus, important principles are established through prosecution via international law and reinforcing human rights in this way. It ensures that effective legal safeguards exist against a breach of rights as well as providing a means of securing justice beyond the confines of national courts who may be ill-equipped to do so. Prosecution through the ICC for one of the international crimes contained in the Rome Statute is the main contemporary mechanism although ad hoc tribunals such as the International Criminal Tribunal for the Former Yugoslavia have also been used. The principle underlying these duties is straightforward: the only way to assure that rights are protected is to maintain effective legal safeguards against their breach. In particular, those who commit atrocious human rights crimes must be punished, and victims must be assured appropriate redress. Thus, Holocaust reparations arguably show post-war West Germany as an exemplar of a state being forced to take accountability for its crimes, in part through payment of reparations.

Case study: Holocaust reparations

Reparations for the Holocaust were originally proposed and submitted to Allied powers just three months after the end of World War II when the Jewish Agency submitted a memorandum for restitution and indemnification due to the Jewish people from Germany for its part in the Holocaust. This initial request did not meet with much progress but in 1951 Israel's Foreign Minister, Moshe Sharett, claimed global recompense of $1.5 million from the German Federal Republic (West Germany) via the four Allied governments of the UK, US, USSR and France. The claim was based on Israel meeting the cost of rehabilitating those Jews that had survived or escaped the Nazi regime and were now part of the newly created Jewish state. In 1951 the West German Chancellor, Konrad Adenauer, indicated that Germany would be prepared to compensate Israel for material damage and losses and would also negotiate with Israel for other reparations.

The original compensation treaty between Germany and Israel was signed by Sharett and Adenauer in September 1952 after six months of negotiations. Under the agreement, Germany agreed to pay a total of $845 million, $100 million of which was to go the US-based Conference on Jewish Material Claims against Germany (Claims Conference) that had been established to deal with individual claims. The remainder was paid to Israel. The direct compensation was to be paid over a period of 14 years (a period commencing 1 April 1953 and ending 31 March 1966). In 1988 The German government allocated an additional $125 million for reparations to provide a monthly payment of $290 to remaining Holocaust survivors that was intended to last for the rest of their lives. Rising (2012) identified that compensation continued to evolve since the 1952 agreement and that in 2012 Germany provided increased compensation by agreeing to provide compensation payments to a new category of Nazi victims; around 80,000

Jews who fled ahead of the advancing German army and mobile killing squads and eventually resettled in the former Soviet Union. This new class of compensatable survivor became eligible for one-off payments of $3,253 in an amendment to the compensation agreement (Rising, 2012). The amendment also formalized an increase in pensions for Holocaust survivors living in formerly communist Eastern Europe to the same as those living elsewhere so that they would receive $382 per month, an increase from the $255 to $331 they had been receiving. In July 2018 the Claims Conference and German government announced an $88 million increase in social welfare funding for Holocaust survivors. The aim of this increased funding was to provide for better and more frequent home care for ageing survivors. It brought the total funding from Germany through the Claims Conference for Holocaust survivors to over $967 million (Claims Conference, 2019). In addition to state compensation, reparations have also been achieved through individual lawsuits.

The nature of Holocaust reparations

Crucially, Holocaust reparations did not go to the victorious powers in World War II but were intended to provide some form of redress for Nazi atrocities. Woolford and Wolejszo (2006) suggest that critical victimological lessons can be drawn from the study of the victims of genocide and mass violence. In this case, post-World War II reparations primarily consist of monetary reparations or 'compensation' as a value-based payment. Arguably these payments amount to recognition of the harm caused by Nazi state-sponsored violence where it is accepted that millions died at the hands of the criminal state. It is also accepted that the state apparatus engaged in systematic disenfranchisement of a particular ethnic population; Jewish businesses had their property and assets seized. Notwithstanding the existence of some Holocaust deniers (Kahn, 2004) who contest the scale of state-sponsored killing and, in some cases, that the Holocaust took place at all,[1] there is also general acceptance that the German state engaged in genocide. Accordingly, there is a case for reparations linked to a recognized class of victim that includes: those who suffered at the time (for example, *direct* victimization at the hands of the state); those in fear of victimization (indirect victims such as those who fled as a consequence of impending or feared victimization and wider family members and relatives of those who suffered direct persecution); and those affected by the wider trauma (for example, the Jewish state). The direct victimization also includes harms that took place after the event to include the ongoing psychological and medical needs of an ageing population of Holocaust survivors. The post-World War II monetary reparations, or compensation, demands made against the West German state by Jewish and Roma survivors of Nazi state-sponsored violence, illustrate the organizational, social and discursive conditions that either enabled or obstructed victim mobilization and help to understand 'victim movements' and the trauma narratives they construct.

Weitz identifies that while large sums of money have been paid out in Holocaust reparations, the amounts given to individuals are relatively small and the initial reparations may not have covered the monetary losses that victims actually suffered (2009: 362). Rising (2012) notes that an elderly population with health conditions arguably caused or made worse by their treatment during the war has a set of complex medical and social care needs that require periodically revisiting the amounts paid out. Nathan (2016: 218) identifies that key issues in the reparations programme administered by the Claims Conference were to secure reparations for the harm that Jewish people experienced during the Holocaust, and to provide survivors with the necessary conditions to live with dignity. This is not to suggest that the Claims Conference always proceeded smoothly. While it is beyond the scope of this book to discuss the Claims Conference scheme in any detail, it is worth noting that litigation has been brought against the Claims Conference over alleged mismanagement of funds. In *Revici v Jewish Material Claims* (1958) 174 N.Y.S.2d at 827 'Tullio Revici, a Holocaust claimant, brought suit in New York state court alleging that the Claims Conference had shown improper favoritism among the beneficiaries entitled to relief' (Bazyler, 2000: 27). The Court dismissed Revici's claim on the grounds that the nature of the Israel-Germany agreement and the Protocol that established the Claims Conference's authority to determine how the funds allocated to it should be spent meant that individuals were barred from questioning in court the manner in which the Claims Conference discharged its duties. This meant that Revici was also barred from questioning why he was not receiving money from the scheme or indeed whether he might never receive money from the scheme. Bazyler (2000: 27–8) notes that several similar claims were raised in the 1990s but were unsuccessful when the courts upheld the view that plaintiffs lacked standing to pursue such claims in US courts.

In addition to state-provided compensation agreed to by the German state, compensation has also been paid as a result of litigation against private entities for Holocaust-era harms. Bazyler (2002: 11) identified the existence of a 'Holocaust restitution movement in the United States, whose aim is to obtain financial restitution from European and American corporations for their nefarious wartime activities', noting that the majority of the Holocaust-era lawsuits of the late 1990s and early 2000s were successful. This contrasted with the lack of success of lawsuits filed in American courts between 1945 and 1995, most of which were dismissed. Bazyler noted that between 1995 and 2001, 75 lawsuits had been filed in US courts compared to approximately 12 between 1945 and 1995. He cited a number of factors in the relative 'popularity' of US Holocaust litigation:

- The history of American courts to accept jurisdiction over cases where other courts may not.
- The American discovery system that allows lawyers to develop a case through information gathering practices such as depositions, requests for document discovery and requests for admission as part of a pre-trial process rather than being required to have a fully formed case before initiating proceedings.
- The guarantee of jury trials in civil cases and the expansive nature of jury verdicts within a legal culture where juries can award millions of dollars (sometimes billions) as compensation and punitive damages.
- The existence of class actions within the civil justice system allowing cases to be taken on behalf of a group ('class') of plaintiffs, a mechanism that can facilitate the award of large damages.
- American legal culture and the willingness of US lawyers to take on cases on a contingency basis (no win no fee) which can allow victims to bring claims more often and allow lawyers to take cases that might otherwise be deemed risky. (Adapted from Bazyler, 2002: 12–13)

The majority of the private law Holocaust litigation involved corporations, although Bazyler (2000: 22) notes an attempt by elderly Holocaust survivors from Yugoslavia to pursue a class action against Andrija Artuković, a former pro-Nazi Croatian official who emigrated to the US after the war, and who the plaintiffs claimed had persecuted them during the Holocaust. The claims raised in the four causes of action raised in the class action were all based on international law or foreign law. The plaintiffs 'alleged violations of the Geneva and Hague Conventions, war crimes in violation of international law, crimes against humanity in violation of international law, and violations of the Yugoslavian Criminal Code' (Bazyler, 2000: 22). The court dismissed the international law claims both for lack of subject matter jurisdiction and due also to statute of limitation reasons given that the claims related to historical matters. The court reinforced the idea that enforcement of international law is left to nation states and thus there was a requirement for the claims to be admissible under US law before they could be considered.[2]

Litigation was also used to pursue claims for artworks stolen by the Nazi regime. While this topic is possibly tangential to the core issue of this book it is worth a brief mention in the context of later discussions concerning property theft, and how policies of destruction and extermination can also be combined with looting as a policy of benefitting one group at the expense of another (Keim, 2003). Kreder (2017: 4) identifies that 'despite internationally accepted rules of law forbidding the theft of art and cultural property, some dating back to Roman times, pillaging an enemy's cultural heritage during times of warfare is often seen as a symbol of the conqueror's total victory' and that theft of art was a widespread practice of the Nazi regime.

The beginning of late 1990s' wave of litigation was arguably the October 1996 federal class action lawsuit filed by Holocaust survivors and their heirs in New York 'against the three largest Swiss banks stemming from the defendant banks' alleged failure to return monies deposited with them during World War II' (Bazyler, 2000: 6). For example, Jacob Freidman along with four other named plaintiffs sued Union Bank of Switzerland, Swiss Bank Corporation and Credit Suisse. The Friedman complaint alleged:

> that Swiss banks have withheld Jewish assets deposited prior to and during World War II, laundered Nazi regime money, accepted looted or cloaked assets stolen by the Nazis, accepted profits from Nazi Regime forced slave labourers and participated in a conspiracy to conceal and prevent the recovery of these assets. (Bilenker, 1997: 252)

Bilsky (2012) argued that the civil class action provided an appropriate legal tool to deal with the liability of bureaucratic institutions for participation in gross civil rights violations. Where the actions of and harms caused by a corporation were arguably incidental to the German state's actions in the Holocaust, criminal law tools might be ineffective in bringing actions against a corporation whose activities might not fit neatly within criminal law processes. The state's actions were arguably framed in the context of criminal harm such as genocide, forced labour (as a form of cruel and unusual punishment inflicted by the state) and CAH. By contrast the action against private corporations began in the form of seeking restitution for money held by Swiss banks and then 'the litigation expanded to include claims against banks in other countries, as well as claims for life insurance plans and for compensation for slave and forced labour from German and other private corporations' (Bilsky, 2012: 350). Bilsky (2012) notes that while there had previously been libel trials linked to Holocaust denial and a few attempts to sue Germany and private corporations in restitution for looted property and forced labour, the reparation programme was mainly administrative in nature and attempts to use private law were sporadic and unsuccessful. Accordingly, 'the restitution litigation of the 1990s therefore represents the first significant instance of the use of civil litigation and private law doctrines in relation to the Holocaust' (Bilsky, 2012: 350). Bush (2009) noted the challenges of establishing criminal liability against corporations for Holocaust-era actions. He identified that no corporation had ever been charged with or convicted of an international war crime or similar offence, and only individuals were charged in the first trials at Nuremberg and Tokyo as well as in the four subsequent trials at Nuremberg that focused on managers, directors and owners of giant German enterprises such as Krupp, Flick and I.G. Farben (Bush, 2009: 1098). Bush (2009) concluded that in the Nuremberg trials conspiracy was seen to be a vital part of international law, albeit mainly for its evidentiary advantages, and that criminal charges against corporations were considered entirely permissible, though ultimately not used.

The Swiss bank cases were grouped together and collectively titled In re Holocaust Victim Assets Litigation (2000). The court summarized the claims as follows:

> Plaintiffs alleged that, before and during World War II, they were subjected to persecution by the Nazi regime, including genocide, wholesale and systematic looting of personal and business property and slave labour. Plaintiffs alleged that, in knowingly retaining and concealing the assets of Holocaust victims, accepting and laundering illegally obtained Nazi loot and transacting in the profits of slave labour, Swiss institutions and entities, including the named defendants, collaborated with and aided the Nazi regime in furtherance of war crimes, crimes against humanity, crimes against peace, slave labour and genocide. Plaintiffs also alleged that defendants breached fiduciary and other duties; breached contracts; converted plaintiffs' property; enriched themselves unjustly; were negligent; violated customary international law, Swiss banking law and the Swiss commercial code of obligations; engaged in fraud and conspiracy; and concealed relevant facts from the named plaintiffs and the plaintiff class members in an effort to frustrate plaintiffs' ability to pursue their claims. Plaintiffs sought an accounting, disgorgement, compensatory and punitive damages, and declaratory and other appropriate relief. (In re Holocaust Victim Assets Litigation, 105 F. Supp. 2d 139 (E.D.N.Y. 2000))

Cabraser (2004) notes that on 26 July 2000 'final approval was granted on a landmark $1.25 billion settlement of the claims of an international class of Holocaust victims against Swiss banks that engaged in massive looting and misappropriation of assets entrusted to them by hundreds and thousands of Jews and other groups' who were victims of the Nazi regimes (2004: 2211). The Court noted that in accepting the settlement, the plaintiffs:

> have agreed irrevocably and unconditionally to release, acquit and forever discharge certain releasees from any and all claims relating to the Holocaust, World War II and its prelude and aftermath, victims or targets of Nazi persecution, transactions with or actions of or in connection with the Nazi regime, treatment by the Swiss Confederation or other releasees of refugees fleeing persecution, or any related cause or thing whatever. (In re Holocaust Victim Assets Litigation, 105 F. Supp. 2d 139 (E.D.N.Y. 2000))

This settlement 'waiver' was introduced because as the court noted, the defendant banks were trying to settle not only the causes of action alleged against them but were also seeking to resolve legal claims against Swiss governmental and business entities so that further claims of a similar type would not be pursued. Bazyler (2000: 32–3) identifies the Swiss Class action as important in three core respects. First, it was the first successful Holocaust-era class action lawsuit, although it was the second such case filed in the US. Second, the Swiss banks filed several motions to dismiss the case and 'presented every conceivable reason why a Holocaust-era suit should not be adjudicated in US courts' (Bazyler, 2000: 32). While this issue was not fully resolved due to the settlement of the case, it arguably identifies a range of legal arguments that might benefit further cases. Third, the Swiss bank action resulted in what was at the time 'the largest settlement of a human rights case in the history of American litigation' (Bazyler, 2000: 32). The Swiss bank settlement as the first Holocaust-era case to be settled had the benefit of exposing issues surrounding how to allocate and distribute funds to elderly Holocaust survivors and other victims of World War II. It is also worth noting that the settlement was not confined only to Jews but also included four other groups persecuted by the Nazis: '(1) homosexuals; (2) physically or mentally disabled or handicapped persons; (3) the Romani (Gypsy) peoples; and (4) Jehovah's Witnesses' (Bazyler, 2002: 16).

Fourth, Baumgartner (2005) notes that all of the assets' litigation cases against Swiss, German, Austrian and French corporations were settled but questioned whether the litigation supported the theory that granting individuals standing to sue for human-rights violations in national courts improves enforcement of human rights.

Holocaust reparations and slavery reparations: a comparative analysis

While the Jewish movement for reparations was successful, Africans have been unable to gain similar reparations for the slave trade and the harms of colonialism. Howard-Hassmann and Lombardo (2007) suggest that the success of reparations claims depends to a large extent on how the claim for reparations is framed. Arguably it is now acknowledged that past treatment of Africans by the West violated key contemporary norms of bodily integrity, equality and private property, notwithstanding the fact that the institutions of slavery and its operation were supported by legal structures. However, Craemer (2019) argues that neither the injustice of the German Holocaust nor the transatlantic slave trade was legal at the time according to international common law notwithstanding the existence of state-supported structures that allowed both to happen. He identifies that this line of legal reasoning was successfully applied at the Nuremberg trials although it did *not* directly lead to Holocaust reparations. Instead, the reparations were agreed afterwards when representatives of the perpetrator side reached out to representatives of the victimized side (Craemer, 2019). Thus, potentially Holocaust reparations provide a template for slavery and anti-Black racism reparations in the context of the state acknowledging its role in genocide and the subjugation of citizens on the grounds of ethnic or racial difference. Yet there are notable differences between Holocaust reparations and slavery reparations. First, the direct victims of slavery are no longer living, the perpetrators are diffuse, some of the harms were legal when they were committed and the causal chain of harm is long and complex (Jordan, 2003; Howard-Hassmann and Lombardo, 2007). Not all living victims of the Holocaust were compensated while alive and arguably owed compensation. Thus, the 'living victim' argument that is sometimes used to deny reparations to slave descendants might be brought into question using Holocaust reparations as a template. As outlined earlier, Holocaust reparations contain recognition of the harm and suffering caused by the state. An important factor in the initial reparations' agreement is their close proximity to the events that caused the harm. As outlined earlier in this chapter, the Holocaust reparations claim was raised by Israel shortly after the end of World War II and continued to be pressed for several years afterwards. Thus, events were fresh in the minds of both the aggrieved state (Israel) and the aggressor (Germany). A clear judicial process followed in the form of the Nuremberg trials and the Far East trials, which endorsed notions of guilt and the demands of justice that there should be some form of reparation.

While the notion of reparations for slavery followed the emancipation proclamation and the reconstruction periods that followed, in practice it was only at later stages that reparations for slavery was pursued in a dedicated way via litigation and political pressure. Jordan (2003) identifies defects in the focus of slavery as the case for racism reparations (discussed later in Chapter 9) noting that 'the time line of potentially reparable injury extends to well before the period of any person now living' (Jordan, 2003: 557).

This potentially raises a question concerning the scope of intergenerational justice. The principle identifies that those who pay reparations for significant injustices 'must be the ones directly guilty and at fault for the harms and wrongs done to the group for which reparations are at justice' (Corlett, 2007: 177). This is arguably clear in the notion of Germany as a criminal state in World War II and of post-war Germany as the logical successor.

Conclusion

Bazyler identifies that 'the new trend by governments and corporations to finally "come clean" about the wrongs committed by them in the past would not be occurring without the spotlight being shined on their activities through the lawsuits in the United States' (2002: 34). Arguably this applies most easily to the activities of states and corporations engaged in human rights abuses and activities that have occurred within living memory and where there are victims and direct descendants for whom reparations might be due. That said, Bazyler identifies that the (then) ongoing claims for victims of Japanese wartime corporate misfeasance and what he called 'the spark in the debate about reparations to African-Americans for slavery' as well as payments to descendants of the Armenian genocide were all 'direct consequences of the Holocaust restitution litigation' (2002: 34). Thus, the principle of reparations for historical injustices is an important one that might inform debates and litigation for other types of reparation. This is not, however, without its challenges; Jordan notes: 'If reparations are to become a successful legal strategy, the fact that slavery ended more than 130 years ago presents formidable obstacles and conceptual challenges that require careful consideration' (2003: 557). This is not least in respect of correlative arguments; that there must be a nexus (or relationship) between the two parties (Weinrib, 2000) and that the plaintiff should be entitled to receive any sum that the defendant is liable to pay. Weinrib's focus was primarily based on a discussion of corrective justice within private (civil) law within common law jurisdictions. He argued that corrective justice as a private law tool connected two parties and provided a means for resolving disputes between them where a clear relationship was established between the harm caused. He stated that 'restitutionary damages are available when the potential for gain is an incident of the right that the wrongdoer violated. Hence the availability of restitutionary damages depends on the defendant's violation of a property (or property-like) right held by the plaintiff' (2000: 37). In the context of slavery reparations this raises some questions about the existence of rights that were 'legally' denied while slavery was lawful. Given that laws generally cannot be applied retrospectively Weinrib's principles may be problematic to apply. However, in this respect, Weinrib's arguments link to the direct relationship between a person who has been wronged and the person (or group) that has benefitted from that wrong and needs to make restitution. Arguably this relies on a direct relationship, and Weinrib notes that restitutionary damages are not:

> occasions for the promotion of social purposes extrinsic to the relationship between the parties. Purposes such as punishment or deterrence (or broader purposes such as the promotion of economic efficiency or of other goods), even if they otherwise seem desirable, cannot be accommodated to the correlative nature of private law justifications and therefore cannot explain the most characteristic and pervasive features of private law. (Weinrib, 2000: 37)

Thus, Holocaust claims have the 'benefit' of establishing a clear relationship between the actions of state institutions (for example, the army, the administrative bodies that oversaw transportation and execution of Jewish citizens) and the use of state resources (methods of transportation, the running of concentration camps and employment of the manufacturers of gas ovens and so on). The nexus is established by the testimony of survivors and the judicial process of the Nuremberg trials that assesses evidence and determines the guilt of living officials and the later acceptance of the German state for paying compensation. The same cannot now easily be said of the US state in respect of slavery, although using Holocaust reparations as a template, there is arguably some merit in preserving slavery as the root cause of claims against the state when pursuing a mass tort claim. As a legal strategy, the involvement of state institutions and legislative frameworks to support slavery can be clearly established during the period of transatlantic slavery. So too can the nature and type of harm caused and relatively straightforward claims of unjust enrichment and unpaid wages.

Later chapters of this book examine the contemporary reparations movement including legal mechanisms and litigation efforts that seek to provide reparations for specific aspects of anti-Black racism that are arguably a legacy of slavery. Hylton (2004) notes the distinction between tort suits and social welfare suits; reparations claims based on a 'doing justice' model of repairing uncorrected harms or uncompensated injustice, versus claims that seek to change the distribution of wealth. Holocaust claims arguably fit within the former category.

6

Unjust Enrichment and the Socio-Legal Case for Reparations

This chapter examines questions of who benefits or benefitted from slavery as well as further examining the nature of disadvantage and inequality. It examines the arguments raised in reparations litigation concerning the benefit gained by companies and other institutions (discussed in Chapter 3) but explores this within the context of specific arguments about enrichment, specifically the legal concept of unjust enrichment. Central to these arguments are questions concerning whether the present-day status of some institutions and even wider society is built on their participation in historic injustices and arguably whether they could be said to have benefitted from participation in discriminatory practices.

As outlined in this chapter and elsewhere in this book it has been argued that reparations should not be paid by present-day institutions for harm caused by their predecessors due to an activity that was ostensibly legal albeit distinctly harmful to a specific community or section of a society. This chapter challenges this notion in part by examining the unjust enrichment argument from a contemporary criminological and zemiological perspective, contending that ideas of the need to remedy contemporary injustice and social harm, arising from the legacy of slavery can be applied to the concept of unjust enrichment. Thus, it argues that the concept of unjust enrichment should be applied not just in the strict context of whether institutions can be said to have acted legally or illegally at the time of slavery, but adopting the Roman Law principle that no one should benefit at another's expense. In part, this chapter makes an argument for institutions to recognize that their existing wealth and social prestige amount to unjust enrichment, irrespective of any legal arguments that the doctrine should not apply.

In examining this issue this chapter argues for a wider articulation of unjust enrichment accepting that it is a civil rather than criminal doctrine and is concerned with addressing harm rather than directly engaging with issues of punishment. However, some of the slavery reparations cases to date arguably are concerned with issues of punishment rather than redress and might be considered to be backward-looking in respect of failing to address or prevent future harm.

Defining unjust enrichment

Unjust enrichment occurs when one person is enriched (or profits) at the expense of another in circumstances that the law sees as unjust. Where an individual is unjustly enriched, the law imposes an obligation upon the recipient to make restitution, subject to defences such as change of position. In this respect the definition of the victim and the 'unjust' injuries visited upon them must comport with the experiences of those who are raising the demand for reparations (Aiyetoro, 2003: 465). Thus, generalized claims for unjust enrichment have some legal hurdles to overcome although unjust enrichment remains a valid legal strategy for reparations claims.

Birks (2005) identifies the modern law of unjust enrichment as being primarily concerned with the following questions:

- Was the defendant enriched?
- If so, was it at the claimant's expense?
- If so, was the enrichment unjust?
- What kind of right does the claimant have?
- What if any defence does the defendant have?

Sherwin (2001: 2084) argues that the principle of unjust enrichment can be understood first as part of the principle of equity that provides correction when 'normally sound rules produce unjust results in particular cases'. Secondly, unjust enrichment can be 'characterised as a "legal principle" incorporating a broad ideal of justice, from which courts can deduce solutions to particular restitution problems'. Finally, Sherwin contends that the principle of unjust enrichment provides a means of 'expressing a common theme of restitution cases' such that the notion of unjust enrichment can shape judicial decision-making and provide for consideration of the extent to which a person or group has profited at the expense of a claimant and the extent to which this gives rise to a right to restitution. Birks (2005) indicates that the right to restitution is arguably a right to the gain received by the defendant. This may be straightforward to ascertain in the context of a contemporary private law dispute where it may be relatively straightforward to establish that a debt is owed in the context of a tangible benefit gained by one person at the expense of another. But this may be more problematic in the context of 'intangible' interests such as labour where it may be difficult to prove that a legal right or title to the interest exists.

However, unjust enrichment has been used in Holocaust litigation and has potential as a basis for claims against multinational corporations 'by indigenous peoples who have been displaced or harmed by environmental damage to their land but have thus far been unable to obtain judicial relief' (Armstrong, 2002: 775). Unjust enrichment claims have been successful in international law because they provide a means of examining how particular groups have been disadvantaged and examining how that disadvantage might be linked to the benefits gained by others. Feagin (2000) argues that unjust enrichment claims could also incorporate consideration of unjust impoverishment. This notion 'describes the condition of those who have suffered from those being unfairly enriched' (Feagin, 2000: 2) and could extend to harms suffered by a group (for example, African Americans, Black Caribbeans). Unjust enrichment claims can also be directed towards redress for injuries to the person, or human dignity although arguably there is a risk that 'reparations based on unjust enrichment theory devalue or misrepresent the harms of slavery, treating them as if they were equivalent to claims for "backpay"' (Dagan et al, 2004: 1136). This may represent a sound legal strategy in respect of arguing the merits of a claim but may be counterproductive in the wider context of using reparations litigation to remedy issues of contemporary inequality and anti-Black racism.

Birks' (2005) five questions provide a means for exploring how unjust enrichment can be examined in the context of both narrow (that is, direct) claims for harm, as well as in the wider context of considering enrichment. This is discussed next.

The first two questions: was the defendant enriched and, if so, was it at the claimant's expense?

Taking Birks' five questions into account it is possible to construct a narrative around reparations which determines that either specific individuals or (perhaps more challengingly) society as a whole has benefitted from the labour or contribution of Black citizens in a manner that is unjust. In considering slavery as a starting point it becomes clear that this was at the expense of Black citizens who provided unpaid labour and lived in indentured servitude where they were denied the benefits of their labour and indeed were denied full participation in the society they laboured to support. Thus, the enrichment becomes unjust because it involved the exploitation of one group to serve the needs and interests of another while denying Black citizens rights automatically afforded to those in White (mainstream) society benefitting from their labour. Arguably, one could also include reference to the discriminatory practice that meant that Black labourers and White labourers were treated differently with regards to their pay, conditions and ability to participate in society. Perhaps more challenging to address are Birks' fourth and fifth questions. In respect of the kind of right the claimants in a reparations case have, arguably a right equivalent to the value of the unpaid labour exploited during the slavery period serves as a starting point. Perhaps more challenging is the notion of a right to the gain that has been received by the defendant against whom reparations are claimed via an unjust enrichment claim. Yet both approaches raise questions concerning the extent to which a claim can realistically be applied in respect of historical injustices. Birks (2005) identifies that the law of restitution is primarily the law of gain-based recovery while the law of compensation is the law of loss-based recovery. Thus, the right to restitution relied on in an unjust enrichment claim would need to identify the benefit accruing from the unjust enrichment, perhaps making it most suitable for direct claims against companies and other institutions where a benefit from slavery can potentially be calculated. This still does not automatically address the question of whether the claimant has suffered and thus has standing to bring a claim or an identifiable right requiring a remedy.

More challenging in this context is moving beyond direct restitution for a tangible gain (for example, a company's profits that are in part owed to slavery) and compensation for the wider social disadvantage and ongoing anti-Black racism identified in earlier chapters of this book. Arguably, the principle of unjust enrichment can apply to the retention of income and wealth derived from past actions and thus seek restitution for 'the current, the present value and distribution of the benefits from past transactions' (America, 1988: 414). For example, evidence and analysis show that there is consistent disparity between Black and White income. While a range of different factors such as age, occupation, sex, family structure, education, culture, genetics and geographic location might be cited as explanatory variables there is also some evidence that racial discrimination and exclusion can also account for some differences. Where this can be proved and it might be shown that non-Black citizens have benefitted, an argument could conceivably be made that there has been unjust enrichment. Potentially this is problematic at the level of the individual but may be invoked in the context of arguing that discrimination and difference has allowed a wider social benefit that is unfair. Again, this is potentially problematic; arguably persons who are *direct* descendants of those whose labour and ideas were stolen can bring an unjust enrichment claim based on the notion that 'their families were denied the right to the benefits of their labour and creative ideas while others were, and continue to be, enriched by this appropriation' (Aiyetoro, 2003: 468–9). A question remains on whether this logic can be applied more widely but Feagin's unjust impoverishment argument contends that the racialized advantages enjoyed by White people in US society 'has conferred advantages for whites across some fifteen generations' (2000: 2). He further contends that 'the exploitation and oppression of African Americans have redistributed income and wealth earned by black labour to generations of white Americans, leaving the former relatively impoverished as a group and the latter relatively privileged as a group' (Feagin, 2000: 3). Applying Birks' principles (2005), a wider conception of enrichment can be applied.

The third question: was the enrichment unjust?

In addressing this question, issues of fairness and lawfulness are raised. In the context of slavery reparations this may seem straightforward; slavery was wrong, the brutalization of Black people within slavery was also wrong, thus any profit derived from slavery must surely be unjust. But 'unjust' and 'unfair' are arguably different terms to consider and reparations discourse potentially indicates that contemporary notions of unfairness (for example, present-day human rights norms) arguably should not apply in an historical context where societal norms were different than they are today. Potentially this raises arguments about slavery as a human rights violation invoking claims that corporations involved in and benefitting from slavery either knew, or should have known, that their activities amounted to a crime against humanity (see, for example, specific claims made in the *African-American Slave Descendants Litigation* discussed in Chapter 3).

The fourth question: what kind of right exists?

Priel (2014: 856) suggests: 'A familiar argumentative strategy in private law theory is to first try to identify, fairly independently of the law, what we owe to each other as a matter of morality. It is then assumed that the law should be shaped to match what morality requires.' Invoking this theory, the rights of claimants in unjust enrichment cases based on claims of anti-Black racism can be both narrow and wide.

The law of unjust enrichment is in part concerned with the right to restitution which is based on ideas of gain-based recovery (Birks, 2005). Thus, where a defendant has received a gain, the right to restitution applies to that gain, whereas a right to compensation arguably applies to the idea that the defendant makes good on a loss suffered by the claimant. This is an important distinction in determining the rights claimed by those arguing they have been affected by slavery and/or its legacy and potentially reparations cases may pursue claims of restitution and compensation as if the two were interchangeable. From a criminological perspective concerned with assessing the nature of victimization, restitution and compensation serve two different aims. A claim for restitution could be argued in the wider sense of unjust enrichment considered by this chapter; that of addressing the gains made by White society at the expense of Black society. Or perhaps, the restriction of Black society and the perpetuation of Black citizens as second-class citizens to the benefit of White society. This is not to automatically suggest a deliberate effort of present-day White society to suppress Black citizens and thus to argue that all White society is culpable for systemic racism. On the contrary, such a claim for restitution could acknowledge that much of White society is blameless for contemporary racial inequalities while nonetheless benefitting from structural conditions that are geared towards a normative view of Whiteness as the dominant position. Thus, the restitution claim is focused on the effect of the wrong and is arguably forward-looking to how it may be addressed rather than being backward-looking towards the cause of the difference. It is also linked to the zemiological conception, identifying that restitution is required for social harm caused to Black citizens (Boukli et al, 2020).

The compensation claim, by contrast, arguably focuses on the narrower conception of unjust enrichment in terms of a loss experienced by Black citizens. Thus, the loss of wages, loss of property and potentially even loss of rights can be conceptualized as something that can tangibly be compensated. The question to consider is whether there is a right to either restitution or compensation.

In the narrow sense of unjust enrichment, the right being claimed can arguably be the right to fair and equal treatment. Thus, Black citizens who have been denied the same economic and social benefits as their White counterparts may claim that they have a right to these. Such claims may invoke specific claims such as particular types of employment, access to financial profits that have been unfairly taken from them and also perhaps access to education. The narrow right may also include a right to fair payment for labour, even where that relates to the labour of an ancestor. Thus, a claim may obviously be made where corporations have benefitted from slave labour or lost property, although as *Cato* and other cases have demonstrated, the courts may contest any assumption that a claimant would automatically have received this benefit.

The wider conception of a right may include the right to restitution for the human rights harms caused by discrimination and ongoing anti-Black racism. Thus, wider reparations discourse argues for exploration of the extent to which society is unfair and the reparations claim could argue that part of the remedy is formal investigation of societal unfairness of this en route to assessing the precise nature of the enrichment (and the detriment).

The fifth question: what kind of defence exists?

Within slavery reparations discourse the issue of defences has arguably proved to be problematic as defences can be raised that challenge both the standing of a plaintiff to pursue a claim, and the notion that a present-day corporation (or wider society) can be held liable for past injustice. The *African-Descendants* case dealt squarely with the latter issue in relation to potential challenges to the notion that a contemporary corporation bears responsibility for the actions of a long-dead predecessor. Arguments can be raised, for example, that the claim is being raised against the wrong corporate entity or one that is so far removed from the business practices of the alleged predecessor that it would be unreasonable to pursue the present-day corporation for the alleged wrong. A litany of other issues such as changes in accounting practices, changes of business, the ability to trace the alleged profit or gain and to directly attribute it to gain caused by slavery can all be invoked in the context of arguing that the corporation should not be liable.

A defence arguably also exists in relation to statute of limitations issues where restitution is being sought from a company for actions that arguably took place in the distant past. In addition, holding individual corporations responsible for 'generalized' societal ills is potentially problematic and difficult to prove. The reparations cases thus far illustrate this point.

Contextualizing unjust enrichment

Arguably 'the principle of unjust enrichment draws on sentiments of resentment that victims feel towards those who have gained at their expense and it provides a remedy akin to retaliation' (Sherwin, 2004: 1465). Thus, unjust enrichment can be thought of as being wider than just its technical legal meaning as outlined earlier in this chapter and can extend to a much broader social and moral meaning. For the purposes of reparations litigation, the narrow legal meaning might be relied upon and this can depend, for example, on calculations of the amount of unpaid labour and the benefit perceived as (unfairly) deriving from that labour. However, in the context of reparations for slavery and its legacy of anti-Black racism that is the focus of this book's discussion, arguably a wider conception of unjust enrichment should be explored.

One potential criticism of unjust enrichment claims as framed by a focus solely on the harms of slavery is that the issue is usually conceived as compensation for Past Injustices. However, arguably:

> The problem is to define and correct a current, not a past, injustice. The current injustice concerns the receipt and retention of income and wealth wrongfully produced in the past. The key is to focus on the current, the present value and distribution of the benefits from past transactions. (America: 1988, 414)

Thus, the conception of unjust enrichment might be thought of in its broader social and moral sense concerning the manner in which White society has enriched itself to the detriment of Black society. In the process of doing so, Black society has been marginalized in a variety of different ways. This argument is partially raised in the most recent Tulsa Riot reparations claim (discussed in Chapter 3) where part of the claim relates to how the Tulsa Riot has been appropriated and Tulsan society has enriched itself at the expense of those who suffered as a consequence of the riot. The increased tourism revenues derived from the Tulsa museum and associated activities can arguably be said to have been obtained unfairly if there is little to no benefit provided to the Black community who are arguably being exploited. Thus, the claim seeks to contend that the appropriation of the riot as a cultural event and the subsequent appropriation of profits derived from exploiting this event are to the detriment of the Black community and the benefit of the White community and city authorities who are not entitled to them.

Tulsa provides a straightforward example of where the wider claim of enrichment may be linked to specific activity. But for this approach to gain traction in a wider sense arguably requires moving beyond the confines of strict legal arguments that are predicated on a linear conception of event leading to profit or consequence and detriment.

The nature of restitution

Restitution is arguably the restoration of something that has been lost or stolen, that is, the making good on something that has been displaced. But while restitution and reparation both concern something having been lost and some action being taken to address that loss restitution and reparation are not the same thing. Arguably 'reparation can only occur after some losses or damage due to a prior wrongdoing. But though restitution can only occur after some loss or damage, that loss or damage need not be due to a prior wrongdoing' (Boxill, 2016).

Webb (2009) acknowledges that while there is widespread acceptance that unjust enrichment plays some role within the law of restitution there is a lack of clarity over its precise role and importance. This issue is explored in slavery reparations litigation where unjust enrichment claims are inextricably linked to arguments that if a defendant has unfairly enriched themselves, then it follows that there should be some form of restitution. In this context, unjust enrichment is discussed in the context of corrective justice (Priel, 2014) and is arguably a means through which private law can be used to address or remedy harm. In traditional unjust enrichment cases this may serve to embody restorative justice principles that seek to put the claimant back into the position they would have been in had the harm not occurred, or to bring them as close to that state as is possible within the confines of the situation they find themselves in. Thus, where a claimant finds themselves at a financial disadvantage such as where a corporation or individual has obtained profit or gain that is rightfully theirs or is unfairly derived from their efforts, a straightforward accounting of the gain can identify the remedy. For example, an indigenous tribe whose knowledge has been unfairly appropriated to develop and patent an energy drink, may claim part-ownership of the product and a share of the profits. While this does not entirely address the harm and cultural appropriation, it at least provides a form of restitution. However, in a wider case of enrichment at the expense of an entire community, this becomes more problematic.

Preceding chapters have identified that part of the restitution being claimed in slavery reparations and racism cases is a recognition of the harm that has been caused and of the contemporary reality of the disadvantage suffered. *Cato v United States*, for example, specifically requested an apology as well as acknowledgement of racial discrimination (see discussion in Chapter 3). However, *Cato* also sought compensation of $100 million, identified as restitution not only for the original removal of Africans and their forced repatriation to America, but also for the subsequent claimed discrimination and inequality that successive generations of African Americans suffered. Thus, the notion of restitution was arguably backwards-looking and based on past harm, albeit past harm impacting on present-day communities.

Unjust enrichment in reparations litigation

Unjust enrichment was an element of the Holocaust litigation and the *Farmer-Paellmann* reparations lawsuit (Seebok, 2003). America (1988: 413) advances the core of the unjust enrichment argument as being that 'income has been coercively diverted interracially by means of slavery and past discrimination' thus producing an unjust enrichment. Following this logic, there is a need for a remedy that estimates the amount of the benefits from slavery (and arguably ongoing discrimination and social injustice) and to identify the class of beneficiaries (that is, those profiting from the unjust enrichment) and then to 'redistribute income from the wrongful beneficiaries to the classes, if not the individuals, who have been exploited, excluded and discriminated against' (America, 1988: 413). While this may appear to be straightforward, it raises complex questions concerning liability and concerning how best to achieve restitution and reparations for 'victims'.

Sherwin (2004: 1444) argues that 'at its core, an unjust enrichment claim seeks to right a wrong not by alleviating the adverse consequences to the victim, but by diminishing the position of others' thus being retaliatory rather than focusing on recovery from harm and the paying of compensation. Seebok (2003: 652–3) identifies that in reparations litigation such as the slavery and Holocaust cases, unjust enrichment has the 'tactical' advantage of the plaintiffs being 'able to evade defenses based on statutes of limitations' and arguably to widen the scope of arguments concerning the extent to which respondents have benefitted at the expense of others. Yet as Chapter 3 explored, one challenge for such claims concerns the linkage between the past and present. From a legal perspective, the attenuated nature of the harm claims in reparations suits potentially draws criticism on the grounds that modern claimants are not (directly) connected to slaves and also that modern payers are not connected to slave owners. It can also be debated whether the harms suffered by modern Black citizens can be directly connected to slavery in a manner that is provable within litigation to satisfy the requirements of an unjust enrichment claim (Wenger, 2006).

Goodin (2013) suggests that disgorgement potentially provides a means of addressing historical wrongdoing as it primarily requires that 'the fruits of wrongdoing be relinquished' correcting the wrong of unjust enrichment if not actually ensuring that others are actively enriched (2013: 478). In this context 'for disgorgement, we need only know that current holdings are seriously tainted by grievous past wrongdoings' (Goodin, 2013: 478). Thus, the focus potentially shifts to considering the consequences of any unjust enrichment and addressing this through the benefit accrued to present-day actors. Goodin uses one example of a present-day building that was originally constructed in part using lumber and slave labour to suggest how disgorgement could be applied. He notes that in making other forms of reparations for the heirs of slaves, knowledge of who they (the labourers) were and also who their descendants were would be essential. But 'for purposes of disgorgement, however, it does not matter' given that knowledge that the building stands in part because of the anonymous victims of the slave trading. While it is by no means straightforward to identify and remove the 'fruits' of unjust enrichment Goodin identifies the potential of a redistributive tax as a means to achieve disgorgement. Thus, Goodin (2013) identifies disgorgement as one of the potentially 'least demanding' ways of seeking reparations in a context where present-day actors are arguably innocent beneficiaries of historical wrongdoing.

Unjust enrichment claims that are targeted at present-day corporations are in part facilitated because (US) corporations are susceptible to successor corporation laws. Accordingly, corporations that have been sold or merged multiple times arguably are still at risk of unjust enrichment claims where their lineage can be established and where their own corporate records may assist in determining this. Thus, the *African-American Descendants* case sought to examine corporate records and required the production of these as a means of establishing the link between victim and wrongdoer and the causation of injury through past corporate action (for example, slave ownership or insuring slaves).

The National legal and Policy Centre suggested that activist lawyer Robert Block 'wants the government to pay $500,000 to every slave descendant' noting that since 'the large majority of the 35 million African Americans have a slave ancestor that would amount to more than $15 trillion and require a surtax of roughly $50,000 on each non African American man woman and child' in the US (Flaherty and Carlisle, 2004: 1). Olson comments on work by the Reparations Assessment group which *Harper's* magazine estimated 'that it could require $97 trillion to pay for the hours of uncompensated work done during the slavery era' (2008: np). However, Massey (2004: 165) indicates that 'in connection with the claim for wrongful confinement, the present value of the profits derived from slavery by any given contemporary defendant is virtually impossible to calculate'. In the context of harm caused to present-day descendants one legal argument is that reparations claims point to an injury which is not 'fairly traceable to slavery through a chain that contains no links of independent causation' (Massey, 2004). Massey further argues that any assessment could only be guesswork, noting that 'few corporate defendants will have records adequate to prove such profits, and no individual will have such records' (Massey, 2004) although as later chapters of this book illustrate, some institutions have attempted such calculations. In addition, arguably reparations claims should not fail or be abandoned solely because of the difficulties of precisely calculating the value of reparations. Indeed, one aspect of the unjust enrichment claims is establishing the principle of unjust enrichment by present-day respondents (whether individual or corporate) and that reparations should be made (or paid) notwithstanding complex debates about the precise value of any such reparations. From the criminological viewpoint that this book adopts, one core consideration is a linkage between the harm caused to the victim, including the notion of indirect victimization from those caused harm beyond the initial event (Spiga, 2010).

However, unjust enrichment may apply more readily in the context of claims specifically situated within Jim Crow harms or within present-day claims. Tulsa again serves as an example, particularly in respect of the Jim Crow-era harms where claims made by the direct descendants of Black businesses that were destroyed in the race riot or of those few remaining survivors can arguably now be litigated. Although Tulsa's claim is primarily based on nuisance law, it contains aspects of unjust enrichment that clearly indicate unfairness in the benefit accrued to identifiable actors (City of Tulsa, the Tulsa Regional Chamber (a not-for-profit company) the Tulsa Development Board, The Tulsa Metropolitan Area Planning Commission) for whom enrichment is claimed, with the unfairness of such enrichment as arising from an alleged 'terrorist' incident and identifiable public nuisance also clearly identified.

Some conclusions on unjust enrichment

Arguably, unjust enrichment has potential to go beyond legal technicalities and to focus on the essence of wrongdoing by considering the nature of the alleged enrichment. Once it has done so it can then redistribute or correct for unjust gain and provide either restitution or compensation. In this respect, unjust enrichment claims linked to reparations litigation provide for a form of corrective justice that integrate notions of addressing unjust enrichment and unjust impoverishment (Feagin, 2000).

What the Slavery reparations litigation arguably shows is that the courts have been reluctant to decide cases on a wider conception of unjust enrichment (that is, to a class such as the descendants of slaves) when arguably the principle being relied upon in making a claim is that of the past wrong that is based on a narrow conception of unjust enrichment. Thus, while in a case like *Cato v United States*, the claim that was being made illustrates that claims for reparations can be well served by restitutionary law and theory, a wider conception of unjust enrichment that situates it within a social and moral conception of harm and enrichment is arguably required.

7

The 'Value' of Reparations

This chapter applies a criminological perspective to questions surrounding what is owed by way of reparations, combined with a critical examination of how value is assigned in respect of the harm caused by slavery and anti-Black racism.

Litigation and political arguments suggest that one mechanism for assessing the value owed to the descendants of slaves and their communities is by way of calculating the amount of wages that should have been paid in respect of unpaid labour carried out by slaves. Thus, a straightforward calculation can provide a notional value to serve as the basis for reparations. However, this chapter also extends the discussion of 'value' to consider the wider 'cost' of slavery and anti-Black racism and its relevance to the reparations debate in both narrow and wide sense. Calculating the wages of slaves and African Americans retained in indentured servitude following emancipation in the US provides for a straightforward mechanism for assigning value to the loss incurred to African Americans and/or their descendants or to Black Britons (and/or their descendants) who contributed to the British Empire but were marginalized in the process. The wider cost debate employs a zemiological approach that considers 'cost' in the wider sense of economic loss through social harm, missed opportunities and ongoing disadvantage. Wider conceptions of cost and value examine how Black citizens generally remain in the lower socio-economic brackets in both the US and UK and are arguably still denied access to some of the tools of social mobility.

This chapter also highlights how some aspects of inequality in some African and Caribbean states is arguably a consequence of slavery. Thus, this chapter argues for both narrow and wide conceptions of cost and value to be deployed in reparations discussions.

Criminological conceptions on value

This book's criminological perspective on reparations contends that the question of value extends beyond purely financial concerns and should also consider social justice and victimization issues (Magarrell, 2003; Miller and Kumar, 2007). Reparations can have an economic, legal, political and social or moral value, and arguably these objectives can also apply to the justification applied to reparations (Corlett, 2011). Accordingly, how value is ascribed may be a complex calculation that should consider a range of factors including the nature of the initial harm, the ongoing nature of that harm or any long-term consequences, and the perspectives of victims and survivors on how any proposed remedy effectively deals with their needs. These principles are already embedded in criminal justice reparations discourse. For example, in the UK, the Victims' Code and Witness Charter provides guidance on support for victims of crime and criminal conduct in England and Wales. Since October 2001, the Victim Personal Statement scheme (VPS) helps victims to provide evidence on how they have been affected by a crime. The VPS provides a mechanism to:

- give victims the opportunity to state how the crime has affected them – physically, emotionally, psychologically, financially or in any other way;
- allow victims to express their concerns in relation to bail or the fear of intimidation by or on behalf of the defendant;
- provide victims with a means by which they can state whether they require information about, for example, the progress of the case;
- provide victims with the opportunity of stating whether or not they wish to claim compensation or request assistance from Victim Support or any other help agency;
- provide the criminal justice agencies with a ready source of information on how the particular crime has affected the victim involved. (www.gov.uk/government/publications/victim-personal-statement)

A VPS gives the court discretion to take into account the consequences of the crime on the victim and the victim's perspective on compensation when passing sentence on an offender. Thus, in assessing the value of any sentence as a tool to address the victim's harm, it considers a victim's perspective, subject to the Police having taken a VPS and the Crown Prosecution Service drawing it to the attention of the court. While this is a criminal justice mechanism, its principle of considering a victim's perspective clearly incorporates corrective justice principles to issues of punishment and reparation.

The legal value of reparations is arguably that when reparations are determined according to law they may provide a binding form of settlement that addresses the claimed wrong. Thus, the reparation is considered an appropriate settlement according to a set of tightly defined criteria. From a legal perspective, reparations may serve to draw a line under a historical injustice or claimed injury, amount to an agreement that there will be no further claims from others in the same class of injured party, or indeed to create a framework to compensate others similarly affected without the need for further litigation. Reparations mandated by legislation also have the benefit of affording legal recognition of the harm and the justification of a settlement, often in a public and transparent manner. Legislation setting out the basis for a reparations scheme (such as that relating to the Japanese-American reparations discussed in Chapter 4) or court judgments that determine the basis for reparations also have the benefit of clarifying the logic behind any decisions to award reparations to particular groups and, by inference, the justification for denying it to others.

Reparations also have value in a restorative capacity as opposed to their corrective or compensatory value. By applying principles of restorative justice to reparations, value is potentially added by allowing victims to achieve closure from events and perceptions of injustice. Appropriate application of restorative principles also provides potential to restore relations via a social and political process rather than a solely legal one (Walker, 2006). The ideal for effective restorative justice is that perpetrators are held to account for what they have done, realize the harm that they have caused and are persuaded or compelled to repair that harm. Successful restorative justice also avoids the escalation of legal justice and its associated costs and delays (Marshall, 1999) by engaging both offender and victim in finding a resolution to crime and social harm problems. While various different conceptions on restorative justice exist, the UK's Restorative Justice Council provides the following broad definition:

> Restorative justice gives victims the chance to meet or communicate with their offenders to explain the real impact of the crime – it empowers victims by giving them a voice. It also holds offenders to account for what they have done and helps them to take responsibility and make amends. Government research demonstrates that restorative justice provides an 85% victim satisfaction rate, and a 14% reduction in the frequency of reoffending. (Restorative Justice Council, 2014)

As this definition indicates, a core aspect of restorative justice is the involvement of victims of crime (or harm) who are often powerless within justice systems, and for there to be some form of mediation or contact between victim and offender. In one sense, this 'pure' notion of restorative justice, predicated on victim/offender meeting and mediation creates an alternative justice system, one where redress and resolution of harm is directly in the hands of the participants in a crime (victim and offender) rather than wider criminal justice agents such as the police or courts. Effective victim/offender meeting and mediation can lead to:

- an apology;
- a chance for victims to get answers to questions;
- a chance for victims to tell offenders the real impact of their crimes and for offenders to understand this impact;
- a chance to achieve some form of reparation;
- a chance for victims to achieve some form of closure from events.

Thus, the ideal for effective restorative justice is dialogue that allows for offenders to be held accountable for their actions and gain greater understanding of the harm they have caused. Personalizing the victim prevents offenders from distancing themselves from the consequences of their actions and may mitigate the use of neutralization techniques (Sykes and Matza, 1957) such as the denial of injury or victim-blaming techniques discussed earlier. In successful restorative justice, victims are often able to confront offenders, personalizing the harm, expressing in detail the long-term consequences of a crime and ensuring that offenders understand the social and long-term consequences of seemingly 'minor' crime incidents such as the theft of small items which may be replaceable in principle but which hold considerable sentimental value. A core aspect of restorative justice in a criminological context is victim/offender conferencing or the mediation meeting where victims are also often able to make sense of what has happened to them and to achieve some form of closure (Marshall, 1999).

The 'pure' notion of restorative justice contained within mainstream criminal justice including 'standard' victim/offender conferencing is arguably unsuitable to some forms of reparation claim thus partial or modified restorative justice may be required (Nurse, 2016). Where harms such as mass human rights violations have been caused the full menu of restorative justice techniques may not be possible or desirable but a modified or partial form might be attempted. Braithwaite (2002) describes restorative justice as 'a process whereby all the parties with a stake in a particular offence come together to resolve collectively how to deal with the aftermath of the offence and its implications for the future'. But in the slavery reparations cases discussed in this book this can only occur in a modified sense; for example, between representatives of a corporation and the descendants of slaves, or via community or civil rights groups and representatives of the state. Llewellyn has argued that 'restorative processes are founded on a conception of justice as fundamentally concerned with restoring relationships' (2002). There need not be any face-to-face meeting between victim and offender, and in the case of slavery reparations this is no longer possible where both victim and perpetrator are long dead. But as long as there has been some mechanism through which the victim or 'wronged party' (for example, descendants) is able to communicate with the offender, even if via a third party or mediator, restorative principles have arguably been applied. For example, the South African Truth and Reconciliation Commission (TRC) and international tribunals such as the International Tribunal for the Former Yugoslavia, employ restorative principles by allowing victims of the regimes to be heard and in some cases confront perpetrators of harms. Extending this principle to the type of Commission on slavery envisaged by the Congressional proposal contained in H.R.40 in the US (discussed further in Chapter 9) would allow descendants of slaves and other African Americans to make representations on how they have been affected by anti-Black racism or the intergenerational trauma of slavery, and potentially provide for the kind of victim/perpetrator dialogue considered integral to a restorative approach. Thus a modified indirect form of victim-offender mediation/conferencing is applied with the victim being given an opportunity to identify the harm and injustice they have suffered, with the 'offender' given an opportunity to respond and apologize or otherwise provide a remedy.

Braithwaite (2004) argues for 'reintegrative shaming', disapproval of the crime act within a continuum of respect for the offender, as a means of preventing crime through forgiveness. Thus restorative justice serves to assist the offender. Braithwaite (2004) identifies restorative conferences as a means through which offender and victim discuss the consequences of a crime and draw out the feelings of those who have been harmed. But in accordance with Foucault's conception that power exists only when it is put into action, one aspect of restorative justice is to give power back to the victim (Dreyfus and Rabinow, 1982). This is potentially problematic in reparations cases where the rights of descendants might be contested or may not be formally recognized in respect of harms from which they are arguably removed. However, it offers potential to empower slave descendants by allowing them to articulate their ongoing disadvantage and trauma, and several mechanisms exist through which restorative justice, both 'pure' and partial, can be applied to reparations claims, particularly in the area of human rights abuses.

In larger reparations claims, such as the slavery descendants reparations claims and mass human rights violation claims discussed in this book, value is arguably achieved when reparations are examined in the context of several goals, namely recognition, civic trust and social solidarity; goals that are inextricably linked to the idea of justice (De Greiff, 2006). Thus, a broader social value of reparations is that they protect the rights of those who either have or would suffer at the hands of perpetrators (whether individual, organization or the state). Reparations have value in that they amount to a declaration from society that the harm caused was wrong and can arguably prove as a corrective to past failures of law and policy to protect citizens from state or corporate abuses. Reparations 'can express sympathy, benevolence, and concern, but, in addition, it is always the acknowledgement of a past wrong, a "repayment of a debt," and hence, like an apology, the redressing of the moral balance of the restoring of the *status quo ante culpum*' (Feinberg, 1970: 76). Thus, the Japanese-American reparations have value as a form of corrective justice; addressing not just the wrong of the actual internment, but also the failure of a legal system that declared the internment to be constitutional. The consequence of this decision was a failure by the courts to prevent what was arguably an abuse of power and human rights violation by the state. Reparations served as acknowledgement by the state of this error and an attempt to address the harm it caused. In this context, reparations served in part to separate present-day society from its corrupt or discriminatory past and to both reassert the contemporary ideals of fairness and equity and to absolve society of its historical ills (at least partially). Thus, when considering slavery reparations, there is arguably a conception that reparations could serve a similar purpose, the value of clear separation from a colonial past where slavery had become a normative practice, and the broad value to be provided in this context is one of recognition and redress. This does, however, raise questions concerning the value of what is owed. The broader canvass of possibly providing reparations for *all* slavery descendants brings with it the challenges of calculating what may be owed in both a narrow and wider sense. In contrast to the finite nature of the Japanese-American reparations a wider class of claim raises questions concerning how best to calculate what is owed and the dual challenge of avoiding reparations that might be considered to be tokenistic, and determining how best to adequately compensate all who might reasonably claim to be disadvantaged by slavery and its legacy.

What is 'owed'

Reparations claims arguably fall into two differing conceptions on what is 'owed' to Black citizens. One conception is based on the notion of correcting historical injustice, the second is driven by social justice goals and notions of equity and distributional justice (Hylton, 2004: 1). Thus, the perspective of what may be owed or at least what is being claimed may vary according to the defined objective of any reparations claim. For example, the reparations claims arising from the Tulsa riot case (discussed in Chapter 3) are arguably reasonably self-contained as they are directly linked to the harm suffered only by residents of Tulsa, both identified individuals and the wider Black

Tulsan community. Thus, a calculation on what is owed in both monetary and social justice terms is arguably relatively straightforward and potentially has a finite value. By contrast, the reparations claims that arose in South Africa following the end of the apartheid regime (discussed further in Chapter 8) are much wider in scope and arguably defy a finite monetary and social justice calculation. In this case, reparations extend beyond the financial redress of individual claimants who were affected by the regime, and extend further to consider what may be owed in terms of the impacts of racial segregation and how legal classifications of race impacted on life chances for Black citizens in South Africa. Other costs include the value and emotional calculations that might be made in respect of the loss of loved ones and the fear of living under an oppressive regime. Thus, the calculations on what is owed extend into broader considerations of how redress can engage with both the lost past experienced by Black South African citizens and also what is owed in terms of securing a future of equality and an effective human rights regime (see further discussion in the next chapter).

In respect of African-American citizens and Black Britons, various calculations have been presented to identify both specific and societal losses which would then inform discussion of what is 'owed' by way of reparations. One calculation noted:

> Relative to Whites, Blacks fall on the negative side of a wide array of important social indicators, with infant mortality rates 146% higher; life chances of imprisonment – state or federal facility! 447% higher; rate of death by homicide 521% higher; lack of health insurance coverage 42.3% more likely; median income rate 55.3% lower; poverty rates 173% higher; and proportion with a college degree or beyond 59.5% lower. Strikingly, the average White American will even live five and one-half years longer than the average Black American – seven years for males! (Mazzocco et al, 2006: 263)

More recent figures from the Brookings Institute showed that:

> At $171,000, the net worth of a typical white family is nearly ten times greater than that of a Black family ($17,150) in 2016. Gaps in wealth between Black and white households reveal the effects of accumulated inequality and discrimination, as well as differences in power and opportunity that can be traced back to this nation's inception. (McIntosh et al, 2020: np)

Analysis of contemporary racial inequality in the UK by *The Independent* newspaper identified various measures considered to reveal the ethnic disparities in the UK. These included:

- Stop-and-search rates between 2018 and 2019 which show that black people are now nearly 10 times more likely to be stopped and searched by police than white people.
- Not a single police force in England or Wales registered an arrest rate of less than 20 for every 1,000 black people. But by contrast, not a single police force in England and Wales registered an arrest rate of *more* than 20 for every 1,000 white people.
- White British people have higher than average home ownership rates – nearly double that of black Caribbean people and more than treble that of black African people.
- Inequality exists in education. At A-levels, white British students are more than three times as likely to achieve high grades than black Caribbean students.
- Black people had at least double the unemployment levels as white people between 2004 and 2018 and the UK's Annual Population Survey revealed that black people in employment are also paid less on average than white people.
- Data reveals that people from BAME backgrounds are up to twice as likely to die from Covid-19 than people of white British ethnicity. (Cuthbertson, 2020: np)

While these figures provide a baseline for discussing inequality, caution should be exercised in drawing too much by way of conclusions from these figures. McIntosh et al (2020) draw on work from economists Hamilton and Darity to comment that White families on average receive higher inheritances than Black families and note Hamilton and Darity's conclusion that inheritances and other intergenerational transfers 'account for more of the racial wealth gap than any other demographic and socioeconomic indicators' (Hamilton and Darity, 2010). While arguably the higher levels of inheritance could be linked to relative positions in society and wealth that are determined in part by racial factors, this may not be a simple evidence-based conclusion that lends itself to a simple calculation. But the points raised by these figures denote that complexity is possibly added to the reparations debate by the need to first define how any reparations are to be calculated.

Even where there may be agreement that the value to be assessed relates solely to the issue of lost wages, arguably there are difficulties in identifying the precise calculation to be used. Two core problems arise in estimating the cost of multigenerational reparations: legal obstacles caused by the passage of time and economic difficulties in obtaining realistic present value estimates (Craemer, 2015). The legal question in part relates to establishing what amounts to unpaid labour and the nature of any legal relationship under which unpaid labour was carried out. In the case of slaves as property this may be relatively straightforward if it is possible to calculate average amounts of labour based on the historical records of plantations and other holdings where slaves worked and were in servitude. It arguably becomes more problematic in post-emancipation cases where wages or other remuneration has been provided, but the claim of loss also relates to disparity in the remuneration provided to Black and White people due to racial discrimination.

The 'narrow' cost of reparations

Calculating the wages of slave labour and the cost of slaves as property is arguably the narrow cost calculation that places financial value on slave labour and the indentured servitude that followed emancipation in the US.

An analysis of different calculations suggested in reparations discourse identifies the range of labour reparations costs that might be claimed. Dependent on which formula is used, including the type of adjustments that might be made for inflation and whether and how interest is calculated, reparations in the US alone can come to billions, if not trillions. Researcher Larry Neal calculated the 1983 value of slave labour 'expropriated by whites from 1620 to 1865 ranges from about $963 billion to as much as $97,064 billion', noting that the variation in part depended on the rate of interest chosen for the long intervening period (Feagin, 2004: 53). Economist Marketti (1990) estimated the dollar value of labour taken from enslaved African Americans from 1790 to 1860 to range from $7 billion to as much as $40 billion. Marketti further suggested that if the stolen income from wages was multiplied by also taking into account lost interest from then to the present, the 1983 estimated economic loss (income diverted) for Black Americans would then range from $2.1 to $4.7 trillion. Craemer's analysis (2015) was based on the French spoliation claims, which were paid over a period of 123 years, and also on the basis of Haiti's independence debt, which was paid over 156 years. To arrive at a present-day (2015) value estimation, he compared existing slavery reparations estimates based on slave prices as expected future income to alternative estimates based on the number of unremunerated work hours multiplied with historical free labour market wages. Arguably this provided for a value to be attributed to slave labour, which Craemer estimated to range from $5.9 to $14.2 trillion at 2009 prices.

These initial figures provide some guide to the 'value' of slave labour during recognized periods of the Atlantic slave trade. But these examples draw on different time periods, with Neal's analysis covering the longest period of time but Craemer's the most high value in attempting to cover a period of the slave trade spanning almost 200 years. Swinton (1990) also noted that in the post-civil war period of legal segregation income and other economic losses for Black Americans linked to labour market discrimination were high, with one study estimating the cost of labour market discrimination for 1929–69 to be as high as $1.6 trillion in 1983 figures (Feagin, 2004: 54). In addition,

Feagin (2004) notes that calculating the cost of anti-Black discrimination from the end of slavery in 1865 to the year 1968, the end of legal segregation would make the wage-loss calculation amount to several trillion dollars.

Social harm and the wider cost of reparations

A zemiological approach to reparations considers not just the lost wages of Black citizens but also the wider social harm that they have experienced through discrimination, poor housing and continued anti-Black racism. These are arguably more challenging issues to ascribe a financial value to, and part of this book's contention is that reparations discourse which arguably began in the context of reparations as primarily financial compensation and apologies also needs to extend towards other forms of reparations.

Darity (1990) argues that since the end of official segregation, Black Americans have suffered additional economic losses. A number of economic studies have suggested how much African-American workers annually lose from continuing discrimination and informal segregation in employment. For example, 'just for one year in the 1970s, the cost of continuing racial discrimination in employment has been estimated at about $94 to 123 billion' (Darity, 1990; Feagin, 2004: 54).

From a utilitarian perspective, the wider conception on reparations could be approached by providing for a programme of social reforms that benefits Black citizens by directly addressing any continuing issues of discrimination. For example, affirmative action policies implemented by private and public institutions as a means to address racial and sexual discrimination have been conceptualized as a means of compensation for historical injustice. Thus, arguably, affirmative action can be conceptualized as a form of reparations, where the aim of such action is to level the playing field of disadvantage (Mosley, 2003). This perspective is not without its disadvantages or criticisms, particularly where affirmative action becomes less about engaging with discrimination and disadvantage and instead become about quotas and a restricted notion of diversity.

The social harm cost also extends to the harm caused to Caribbean and African nations from slavery. The CRC continues to call for slavery reparations to address the harm caused to Caribbean communities and the CAH endemic to the slave trade that have impacted negatively on African and Caribbean nations. However, on a visit to Jamaica in 2015, former UK Prime Minister David Cameron responded to calls from Jamaica's Parliament for reparations by asking them to 'move on' and 'continue to build for the future'. Yet inequality continues to be felt across the Caribbean, and access to the wealth available to White Caribbeans, as well as the luxury of the islands' tourism industry and produce resources, continue to be denied to large portions of the Black and indigenous population who are segregated from the benefits of island economies that have arguably been made possible by slavery and the wealth made for Britain by its slave plantations (González-Pérez et al, 2016). This issue is explored further in Chapter 9.

Conclusions on value

As this chapter identifies, value is more than just a financial consideration and reparations should be valued according to the extent to which they serve different objectives. Legal, political and social and moral considerations are all relevant to this consideration, and the extent to which a reparations programme or claim may be determined according to any or all of these considerations is integral to identifying its notional value. Thus, the case for reparations should not only be considered in the context of there being a homogenous conception of 'value'. Instead, value should be considered according to the specific criteria for harm and restitution set out in any reparations claim while the restitution or compensation response should also determine value according to specific criteria and a clear articulation of what the reparative programme is intended to achieve.

For 'traditional' class-based claims (for example, all descendants of slavery, Holocaust victims) some notion of value is arguably achieved through recognition of the historical wrong that serves to recognize the legitimacy of the claim and perhaps by way of an apology. But by itself this may not have sufficient value to satisfy claimants if it is not also supported by some form of restitution or compensation that in some way seeks to address the historical wrong. This raises questions concerning the extent to which it is possible to do so, given the nature of such claims which are inextricably linked to historical loss of life and persecution. For example, the compensation claimed in *Cato v United States* (1995) was set at $100 million. Clearly this has value by virtue of being a substantial sum, but arguably it is a small amount when set against calculations of lost labour discussed in this chapter. Thus, if paid, it potentially raises questions about the extent to which such reparations diminish the value of overall harm caused to Black citizens (discussed further in Chapter 9). However, its value is arguably in part symbolic; recognition by the state that a substantial sum is required as recognition of the wrong. Arguably should that claim have been settled in Cato's favour, its true value would have been in the judicial recognition of the claim's merits and the precedent setting nature of the payment as establishing the state's culpability for the harms of slavery and their consequences for present-day generations of African Americans.

The wider social and moral aspects of reparations potentially provide higher value in respect of upholding human rights and satisfying the needs and concerns of victims. Reparations have value in signalling to victims that a remedy exists for harms visited upon them and that the reparative and compensatory justice principles of human rights law can operate effectively. Thus, for victims, reparations have value in identifying that mechanisms of redress work, are effective and can be deployed against states and institutions who have committed either mass or individual rights violations. In this respect, reparations have an expressive function, providing an apology on behalf of the perpetrator and society, and articulating in a public way, the wrong of the action that caused the harm and a recognition of its gravity. The extent to which reparations achieve this to the satisfaction of victims is dependent on the nature of any remedy and its applicability to the harm (for example, an apology by itself would be inadequate where there has been loss of life). However, reparations also serve as a reminder of violations, and where a remedy of appropriate value has been determined may also serve as a deterrent to ensure that it is not repeated.

Chapter 8 discusses this issue in more detail and examines the value and scope of reparations as a remedy for gross human rights violations.

8

The Nature of Reparations

This chapter further examines the case for reparations through a restorative justice and human rights lens. In doing so, it also applies a critical criminological perspective to examining the nature and type of reparations and the purpose of reparations. This chapter draws on contemporary human rights and international criminal law to critically evaluate conceptions on repairing harm.

The chapter's discussion identifies and conceptualizes reparations as a human rights issue and draws on selected case law and judicial principles from the ICC, the ECtHR and the International Court of Justice (ICJ) to discuss issues surrounding remedying international crimes such as war crimes, genocide, unlawful discrimination and other human rights abuses including modern slavery, with a focus on how these might be remedied within contemporary justice systems.

While acknowledging that contemporary law cannot be retrospectively applied, this chapter identifies that reparations can take many forms from apology and state recognition of the harms caused by CAH like slavery, through to financial compensation, affirmative action or social rebuilding that contributes to social justice. The chapter also contains analysis using contemporary examples of reparations mechanisms to discuss how international principles could arguably be applied to the issue of ongoing reparations for slavery and its legacy of anti-Black racism.

Reparations and international law

Reparations arguably have a strong basis in international law since World War II. Governments may agree to reparations through political settlements in order 'to draw a line under the past and provide new opportunities for victims' (Moffett and Schwarz, 2018). Reparations, as a legal mechanism for resolving a dispute have the potential to provide for a practical remedy to an identified social or political need while also resolving individual or group rights to a remedy for harm directly caused to them. Du Plessis (2007) identifies that the language of international law (state responsibility, CAH, genocide) can also be invoked in respect of questions concerning state responsibility for restitution, compensation or 'just satisfaction'.

> International law is broadly a product of cooperation and collective agreement between states and sets out the obligations on states in respect of the legal standards they should adhere to. These have generally been agreed and identified via treaties and conventions as the core international law mechanisms; these signed agreements arguably, reflects areas considered to be of such importance that only a consensus between states and formalization of them in written agreements can deal with the subject matter which includes areas such as crimes against humanity. However, in practice, international law is a combination of 'hard' law in the form of such written agreements or principles which are directly enforceable by national or international bodies; and 'soft' law which incorporates a range of different measures including codes of conduct, resolutions, agreements commitments and joint statements. A core problem in the enforcement and application of international law is that there is no general 'world court' able to enforce international law, albeit international courts like the ICC exist, and the ICJ as the UN's main court is sometimes referred to as the World Court (Rosenne, 1989). Thus, it largely remains for states to choose whether to agree with the relevant provisions of international law or to disregard them in the interests of sovereignty, as the ICJ states: 'In international law there are no rules, other than such rules as may be accepted by the State concerned, by treaty or otherwise' (Military and Paramilitary Activities in and against Nicaragua (*Nicaragua v United States of America*) ICJ Rep 1986, 269).

Thus, states arguably will comply with international law only to the extent to which doing so serves national interest and may depart from international norms where they consider it expedient to do so. Accordingly, flexibility exists in how states approach their international law obligations, even in respect of areas such as human rights law. This is especially true of 'soft' international law which is not directly enforceable, but which sets out shared standards or aspirations for states, albeit these may be subject to varied interpretations commensurate with state interests. But it is also true of 'hard' international law, particularly where the enforcement mechanisms might be considered to lack teeth and rely on states accepting any sanctions that are imposed.

Earlier chapters of this book have highlighted the existence of the ICC, the permanent criminal court that considers matters of international crimes such as war crimes, genocide and CAH. The UN General Assembly on 9 December 1948 adopted a resolution reciting that 'in the course of development of the international community, there will be an increasing need of an international judicial organ for the trial of certain crimes under international law' (United Nations, 1948). The ICC came into being with a clear definition of the international crimes falling within its jurisdiction and with the detail of the Rome Statute setting out general principles of international criminal law. While the potential for the court to provide robust mechanisms to deal with mass harms like CAH should arguably be welcomed, the ICC has not been without its criticisms. Simmons and Danner (2010) suggested that the ICC represented a serious intrusion into state sovereignty, namely the right to administer justice to one's nationals. The court has also been accused of being a colonial court and of pursuing cases against African nations rather than Global North states that are arguably guilty of war crimes, complicit in genocide and in perpetuating discriminatory practices and racial discrimination (Clarke et al, 2016; Mutua, 2016). Indeed, several African states have threatened to leave the ICC over its possible investigation into historic CAH (Agence France-Presse, 2017), risking the prospect of the court having a crisis of legitimacy in respect of African states (Vilmer, 2016; Mbengue and McClellan, 2018).

A range of international human rights mechanisms and international human rights law are relevant to discussion of providing principles of reparations in areas of racial discrimination and inhumane treatment of Black citizens. As these measures are mostly contained in international law introduced after the abolition of slavery in the UK and the US, they are of limited use as tools to address historical harms of Antebellum and British Empire slavery. But they are arguably applicable in terms of being the international law principles that were in place during parts of the Jim Crow era and Britain's racially turbulent periods of the 1950 and 1960s. Some key elements of international law that provide the international law basis to contest systemic racism and race-based state abuses of power are briefly set out in this chapter.

International human rights law

The Universal Declaration of Human Rights, for example, was adopted by the UN in 1948 while the ECHR entered into force in 1953; thus both measures provide some guidance on human rights norms applicable to the 1950s and 1960s periods of discrimination. Table 8.1 outlines the core anti-discrimination provisions of the Universal Declaration.

Table 8.1: The Universal Declaration of Human Rights, core anti-discrimination, justice and equality provisions

Article	Text	Equality and justice considerations
Article 2	Everyone is entitled to all the rights and freedoms set forth in this Declaration, without distinction of any kind, such as race, colour, sex, language, religion, political or other opinion, national or social origin, property, birth or other status.	Establishes the incompatibility of racial discrimination as non-human rights compliant and identifies that citizens' reliance on human rights is not restricted by virtue of race or other factors.
Article 3	Everyone has the right to life, liberty and security of person.	Protects against arbitrary state interference with the right to life and liberty, thus requiring justification for any interference with these rights. Restrictions on liberty (e.g. imprisonment) cannot be arbitrary (see also Articles 9 and 11).
Article 5	No one shall be subjected to torture or to cruel, inhuman or degrading treatment or punishment.	Prohibits state use of torture, also applies to conditions of imprisonment and the nature of punishment for criminal offences.
Article 6	Everyone has the right to recognition everywhere as a person before the law.	Provides for legal recognition and application of the law to all citizens (e.g. preventing discrimination or marginalization of vulnerable groups).
Article 7	All are equal before the law and are entitled without any discrimination to equal protection of the law. All are entitled to equal protection against any discrimination in violation of this Declaration and against any incitement to such discrimination.	Prohibition on discrimination in criminal justice matters as well as providing for equal access to and protection of the law. Discriminatory criminal justice practices arguably require remedy (see Article 8).
Article 8	Everyone has the right to an effective remedy by the competent national tribunals for acts violating the fundamental rights granted him by the constitution or by law.	Provides for access to justice and the provision of a remedy where fundamental rights are violated. Linked to this are ideas that the remedy must be *effective* i.e. capable of repairing the harm or achieving some form of redress.
Article 9	No one shall be subjected to arbitrary arrest, detention or exile.	Prohibits arbitrary application of criminal justice sanctions. Thus, these must be according to law which should arguably be understandable to all those subject to arrest, detention or exile. In principles, also provides for consistency in the application of these punitive powers.

Table 8.1: The Universal Declaration of Human Rights, core anti-discrimination, justice and equality provisions (continued)

Article	Text	Equality and justice considerations
Article 10	Everyone is entitled in full equality to a fair and public hearing by an independent and impartial tribunal, in the determination of his rights and obligations and of any criminal charge against him.	Provides for a fair hearing and independent adjudication on criminal matters (see also Article 11). Also indicates that justice should be public and transparent.
Article 12	No one shall be subjected to arbitrary interference with his privacy, family, home or correspondence, nor to attacks upon his honour and reputation. Everyone has the right to the protection of the law against such interference or attacks.	Provides for protection against unnecessary interference with private life, limiting the exercise of criminal justice interference in these areas.

Source: Universal Declaration of Human Rights (OHCHR, 2019)

Several of these provisions have scope to be invoked in the context of systemic racism perpetrated by the state. The Declaration also sets out the idea that these are fundamental rights that citizens should be able to rely on, thus any interference with these rights can only be carried out for specified purposes and can only be done in accordance with the law (discussed elsewhere in Chapters 7 and 8). Article 3 of the International Covenant on Civil and Political Rights (ICCPR) was adopted by the UN in 1966 and requires that each State that is a Party to present Covenant undertakes:

- to ensure that any person whose rights or freedoms as herein recognized are violated shall have an effective remedy, notwithstanding that the violation has been committed by persons acting in an official capacity;
- to ensure that any person claiming such a remedy shall have his right thereto determined by competent judicial, administrative or legislative authorities, or by any other competent authority provided for by the legal system of the State, and to develop the possibilities of judicial remedy;
- to ensure that the competent authorities shall enforce such remedies when granted.

Article 26 of the ICCPR states that:

> All persons are equal before the law and are entitled without any discrimination to the equal protection of the law. In this respect, the law shall prohibit any discrimination and guarantee to all persons equal

and effective protection against discrimination on any ground such as race, colour, sex, language, religion, political or other opinion, national or social origin, property, birth or other status.

Taken together, the ICCPR and the International Covenant on Economic, Social and Cultural Rights (ICESCR, also enacted in 1966) form the UN's 'International Bill of Rights' (Humphrey, 1976; Arat, 2006). Potentially they provide mechanisms through which reparations claims might be pursued under international law. Simmons (2009: 438) argues that the two treaties 'have come to be thought of as international society's clearest expression of a core set of human rights commitments with "constitutional" status in international law' as they are binding on parties to the treaties in a way that the Universal Declaration on Human Rights was not. Thus, the provisions of these two treaties, taken together, arguably enshrine realization of fundamental rights within state law and represent customary international law by establishing agreed upon human rights standards to be implemented in domestic law. Each of the treaties contain principles requiring states to positively uphold human rights and to provide for enforcement of the rights contained within the ICCPR and the ICESCR respectively. Thus, states abusing their criminal justice powers, implementing draconian policing powers or failing to provide for protection of the rights contained within the treaties, for example for Black citizens, may be subject to legal action in respect of alleged breaches of their international obligations.

Yet the extent to which such legal and political measures of reparations can address the past is strained, due to the size of the victim population and how long ago some historic violations were committed. But other measures provide for action to be pursued in respect of race-based discrimination and racism by state policing agencies as the ECHR illustrates.

European Court of Human Rights

Article 4 of the ECHR concerns slavery and forced servitude which are outlawed under the Convention. The case law considered by the ECtHR in this area frequently involves individuals forced into slavery, servitude or prostitution. Its definition of 'servitude', for example, identifies that what is prohibited is 'particularly serious form of denial of freedom'; this includes 'in addition to the obligation to perform certain services for others … the obligation for the "serf" to live on another person's property and the impossibility of altering his condition' (European Court of Human Rights, 2020, 7/18). While the Court's jurisdiction applies specifically to the ECHR, its decisions are discussed in the context of identifying principles for engaging with issues of harm.

In its consideration of servitude, the Court has concluded that servitude was a specific form of forced or compulsory labour that has an aggravated element to it. It concluded that 'the fundamental distinguishing feature between servitude and forced or compulsory labour within the meaning of Article 4 of the Convention lies in the victims' feeling that their condition is permanent and that the situation is unlikely to change'. In *C.N. v the United Kingdom*, § 80 the Court concluded that domestic servitude is a specific offence, distinct from trafficking and exploitation and which involves a complex set of dynamics, involving both overt and more subtle forms of coercion, to force compliance. The court has also identified that under the ECHR, 'forced or compulsory labour' means 'all work or service which is exacted from any person under the menace of any penalty and for which the said person has not offered himself voluntarily' (*Van der Mussele v Belgium*, 1983).

These examples obviously link to modern conceptions on slavery and thus are of little use to the descendants of slaves (except where they suffer such activities in a contemporary setting within a European State). The European Court has noted that, with regard to certain Convention provisions, such as Articles 2, 3 and 8, the fact that a State refrains from infringing the guaranteed rights does not suffice to conclude that it has complied with its obligations under Article 1 of the Convention (§ 77). In this connection, it held that limiting compliance with Article 4 of the Convention only to direct action by the State authorities would be inconsistent with the international instruments specifically concerned with this issue and would amount to rendering it ineffective (§ 89). It has therefore held that States have positive obligations under Article 4 of the Convention. Article 4 requires that member States penalize and prosecute effectively any act aimed at maintaining a person in a situation of slavery, servitude or forced or compulsory labour. In order to comply with this obligation, member States are required to put in place a legislative and administrative framework to prohibit and punish such acts.

Contemporary international law reparations mechanisms

It is a principle of international law that the breach of an international obligation involves an obligation to make reparation in an 'adequate' form. Reparation to individuals for damage caused by gross violations of international human rights law and serious violations of international humanitarian law have become features of the international law landscape. As a result, reparations are now part of the practice of States, international organizations and international tribunals. In part, this reflects contemporary conceptions on the increased status of individuals under international law, especially since World War II. One of the principles of international law on reparations is that so far as is possible, reparations should aim to wipe out all the consequences of the illegal act and to re-establish the position that would have existed had the illegal act not taken place. This is obviously problematic in the case of mass harms such as genocide and CAH. But the ICJ confirmed this principle in its decision in the case of Armed Activities on the Territory of the Congo (*Democratic Republic of the Congo v Uganda*) where the Democratic Republic of the Conga sought reparation for acts of intentional destruction and looting and the restitution of national property and resources that had been appropriated in the conflict. The ICJ confirmed that a State that has violated a rule of international law causing damage to persons has the obligation to make reparation for the damage caused, and in its judgement stated that in accordance with customary international law, Uganda should:

- make reparation for all types of damage caused by all types of wrongful act attributable to it, no matter how remote the causal link between the acts and the damage concerned;
- accordingly, make reparation in kind where this is still physically possible, in particular in regard to any Congolese resources, assets or wealth still in its possession;
- failing this, furnish a sum covering the whole of the damage suffered;
- further, in any event, render satisfaction for the injuries inflicted upon the Democratic Republic of the Congo, in the form of official apologies, the payment of damages reflecting the gravity of the violations and the prosecution of all those responsible. (Case concerning Armed Activities on the Territory of the Congo (*Democratic Republic of the Congo v Uganda*) 2005, paragraph 184)

Accordingly, the conception of reparations identified in the judgement seeks to address all of the harms of the conflict. At the domestic level, individuals should be able to bring claims for the violation of international human rights law or international humanitarian law in national courts. The principle enshrined in the rules of international law is that domestic mechanisms are supposed to provide an *effective* remedy for affected individuals, and this should include appropriate reparation if the violation is proven. Where possible local remedies should ideally be exhausted before resorting to international law mechanisms, although international and domestic mechanisms may complement each other as is arguably the case in respect of the relationship between the UK's Human Rights Act 1998 and the ECHR. However, the right to an effective remedy at domestic level is enshrined in international law as indicated in the earlier discussion of Article 8 of the Universal Declaration of Human Rights. The ICCPR also contains this principle in its Article 2(3), and of relevance to this book's discussion on reparations for anti-Black racism is also Article 6 of the International Convention on the Elimination of All Forms of Racial Discrimination (1969). The American Convention on Human Rights (invoked to a certain extent in the Chicago police brutality cases, albeit unsuccessfully) also contains provisions on the right to an effective remedy.

International mechanisms such as these are arguably removed from direct reparations claims in US or UK courts which employ specific legal arguments to which international law may not be directly applicable. Challenges may also exist where international law cannot be directly invoked in domestic courts. The UN's Working Group of Experts on People of African Descent in its 2016 report recommended that US '[f]ederal and state laws should be adopted that incorporate the International Covenant on Civil and Political Rights and other international human rights treaties, as well as regional treaties' (2016: 19). But the tribunals established to enforce these conventions have developed varied and useful criteria to establish what constitutes full and appropriate reparation within the confines of particular cases, and their principles could be relied upon to develop reparations criteria for mass harms like racism and anti-Black racism, notwithstanding the obvious issues concerning the historical nature of some harms that give rise to reparations claims and jurisdictional differences. Domestic laws and the decisions of national courts may also draw on international perspectives and regulate reparations owed to individuals for violations of international law.

Case study: the international commission of inquiry on systemic racist police violence against people of African descent in the United States

In March 2021 the Commission of Inquiry on Systemic Racist Police Violence (the Commission) published its report on its examination into whether widespread and systemic racist violence in policing against people of African descent in the US 'has resulted in a continuing pattern of gross and reliably attested violations of human rights and fundamental freedoms' (Commission, 2021: 13). The Commission reports that it was established following the death of George Floyd after which the families of Mr Floyd, Breonna Taylor, Michael Brown and Philando Castile together with 600 rights groups petitioned the UN Human Rights Council (UNHRC) to appoint a UN Commission of Inquiry to examine alleged systemic racist policing and human rights violations against people of African descent in the US. The UNHRC declined to do so but instead directed the Office of the High Commissioner of Human Rights to report on systemic racism and human rights violations committed by police against Africans and people of African descent throughout the world. As the UN declined to hold the requested inquiry, the independent Commission of Inquiry was established and held public hearings from 18 January to 6 February 2021.

The Commission examined 44 cases of Black people; all but one had been killed by police. The cases selected involved the killing or maiming of Black citizens including:

> (1) the killing of unarmed individuals who posed no threat of death or serious bodily harm; (2) the killings of individuals fleeing the police who posed no serious threat of death or serious bodily harm to the officers they were fleeing or others; (3) the use of, or threat to use, physical or psychological intimidation to extract confessions; and (4) the maiming of individuals fleeing the police and/or who posed no serious threat of death or serious bodily harm to others. (Commission, 2021: 13)

The Commissioners concluded that the cases they examined identified breaches of international human rights law, including the right to life, security, freedom from torture, freedom from discrimination, mental health, access to remedies for violations, fair trial and presumption of innocence. The Commissioners concluded that 'the use of force against unarmed people of African descent during traffic and investigatory stops is driven by racial stereotypes and racial biases resulting in US law enforcement agencies routinely targeting people of African descent for questioning, arrest and detention based on racist associations between Blackness and criminality' (Commission, 2021: 14). The Commission report argued that there is a case of CAH that warrants an investigation by the ICC, suggesting that systematic racism against Black citizens by US policing agencies appears to meet the definition of a widespread or systematic attack against Black citizens that would bring it within Article 7 of the Rome Statute of the ICC. The Commission recommended that the Office of the Prosecutor of the ICC should initiate an investigation and that the Executive Branch of the US government should accept the jurisdiction of the ICC to conduct such an investigation. The Commissioners also urged the US government to make provision for reparations including that the US Congress should pass H.R.40 to establish a commission to examine enslavement and racial discrimination in the US and to recommend appropriate remedies (see discussion of H.R.40 in Chapter 9). The Commission also recommended that the US should pass an Atonement, Reparation and Justice Act 'with the objective of correcting structural racism in US society' (Commission, 2021: 136). Recommendations were also made for the US to ratify and implement international human rights norms by fully ratifying the treaties that it is not a party to and also removing any reservations relating to the treaties that it has signed or ratified.

At time of writing, it seems unlikely that the ICC will conduct the formal investigation that the Commission is requesting. However, were the ICC to do so or were the UN to accept and respond to the Commission's recommendations, there is potential for reparations for contemporary systemic racism to be pursued at an international level.

The work of truth commissions and other transitional justice bodies is also relevant in identifying how mass harms might be adjudicated and reparation provided. While these may be domestic mechanisms, they can incorporate international law perspectives to arrive at a remedy for mass harms. The following example of reparative justice in South Africa illustrates this.

Case study: reparations in South Africa

Apartheid was a system of institutionalized and racial segregation that existed in South Africa from 1948 until 1994, following the election of Nelson Mandela's African National Congress party (ANC) and the subsequent dismantling of the apartheid system.[1] Miller (2016: 1) identifies how the President of Zambia had declared that 'the philosophy of Apartheid denies to the Black people the right to be, it forces them to conform to an image which the so called Master Race has created of them to prove Black inferiority and White superiority' via a system that Miller identifies as classifying all South Africans by race. Thus, their positions in society, future prospects and societal rights were all determined by the classification.

The apartheid system reflected the ideology of the South African National Party that there should be separate development in South Africa and a distinction between the races. Thus, apartheid created a legislative basis for racial segregation and the separate development of the races. This included the Prohibition of Mixed Marriages Act 55 of 1949, which prohibited marriage between White people and people of other races. The Immorality Amendment Act 21 of 1950 (as amended in 1957 by Act 23) also forbade 'unlawful racial intercourse' and 'any immoral or indecent act' between a White and a Black, Indian or Coloured person. Black people were denied voting rights despite being a majority in the country. Racial segregation in South African cities was also a consequence of legislative processes as places of residence were also dependent on racial classification, and between 1960 and 1983 an estimated 3.5 million Black Africans were removed from their homes and forced into segregated neighbourhoods (Christopher, 1990). A repressive state security and policing apparatus also reinforced the racial separation (Gottschalk, 2002), and the apartheid regime was marked by political violence between 1960 and 1994 (Foster et al, 2005). Apartheid ended following negotiations between 1990 and 1993 between the governing National Party, the ANC and other political parties. The election of the ANC to power in 1994, gaining 252 seats of the possible 400 in the country's first election held under universal suffrage, resulted in changes in the South African constitution and a drive by the new ANC government to try and redress the problems of South Africa's past and its eventual dismantling.

The right to reparations is contained in South African law, which specifies that 'the right to reparations for persons who suffered gross human rights violations is contained in the Promotion of National Unity and Reconciliation Act 34 of 1995 (the TRC Act)' (Fernandez, 1999: 210). While the Act does not specify the form that reparations should take, it identifies the committee established to make recommendations on reparations (Sarkin, 1996; 1997; 1998). The objectives of the Commission were outlined in a government booklet entitled *Justice in Transition*, which set out the provisions on the interim Constitution of South Africa, the final clause of which specified that:

> This Constitution provides a historic bridge between the past of a deeply divided society characterised by strife, conflict, untold suffering and injustice, and a future rounded on the recognition of human rights, democracy and peaceful co-existence and development opportunities for all South Africans, irrespective of colour, race, class, belief or sex. (Department of Justice and Constitutional Development, 2021)[2]

The final clauses of the interim Constitution also specified that gross violations of human rights and the transgression of humanitarian principles:

> can now be addressed on the basis that there is a need for understanding but not for vengeance, a need for reparation but not retaliation, a need for ubuntu but not for victimisation.
>
> In order to advance such reconciliation and reconstruction, amnesty shall be granted in respect of acts, omissions and offences associated with political objectives and committed in the course of the conflicts of the past. To this end, Parliament under this Constitution shall adopt a law determining a firm cut-off date which shall be a date after 8 October 1990 and before 6 December 1993, and providing for the mechanisms, criteria and procedures, including tribunals, if any, through which such amnesty shall be dealt with at any time after the law has been passed. (Chapter 15 of the Constitution of the Republic of South Africa, Act No. 82 of 1993)

The TRC made a series of recommendations in the areas of: promoting a culture of reconciliation and unity; the prevention of gross human rights violations in the future; accountability (which included considering prosecution for individuals who had committed gross human rights violations where amnesty had not been sought or had been denied); healing and rehabilitation; reparations and rehabilitation; organization, administration and management of a human rights centred culture.

The Commission contended that the case for reparation awards to victims of gross violations of human rights added value to the 'truth-seeking' phase or the truth and reconciliation process by 'enabling the survivors to experience in a concrete way the state's acknowledgement of wrongs done to victims and survivors, family members, communities and the nation at large' as well as 'restoring the survivors' dignity' and 'affirming the values, interests, aspirations and rights advanced by those who suffered' as well as 'raising consciousness about the public's moral responsibility to participate in healing the wounded and facilitating nation-building' (Truth and Reconciliation Commission, 1998: 312). The Commission recommended that financial awards would be appropriate in some cases and that the reconciliation process would also require other measures including:

- issuing of death certificates by the appropriate ministry;
- expediting exhumations and burials by the appropriate ministry;
- facilitating the expunging of criminal records where the political activism of individuals was criminalised;
- facilitating the resolution of outstanding legal matters;
- the Government declaring a national day of remembrance. (Truth and Reconciliation Commission, 1998: 312–13)

The TRC's recommendations were not immediately implemented and Colvin (2006) notes that it was not until 2003 that a reduced version of the reparations policy was enacted while many claimants still waited for their individual payments (Daly, 2003). The TRC had originally recommended that victims of apartheid should receive a monthly payment of R2,000 for a period of six years but during (former) President Mbeki's term, this was altered to a one-off payment of R30,000 to victims who claimed reparations. Bond and Sharife (2009) also identified that claims against corporations that benefitted from the apartheid regime were also pursued in US courts acknowledging that banks including Barclays, Standard Bank, Anglo American and other firms provided corporate support for apartheid policies, thus arguably supporting the regime.

In principle, the South African experience provides a clear model for reparations in respect of a mass wrong linked to racial discrimination. There were clear and gross violations of human rights, still-suffering victims, an acknowledgement of the state's role in perpetrating human rights abuses and racial discrimination as well as constitutional and legislative mandates for reparations. The TRC also examined the role of businesses in supporting the apartheid regime and concluded that some businesses were culpable by having benefitted by operating in a 'racially structured environment' (Nattrass, 1999). Yet despite the process of a transparent and rigorous fact-finding commission of the type arguably being sought in the US via measures such as H.R.40 (discussed further in Chapter 9) the reparations agreed in principle were not easily implemented. Thus, there is a risk that reparations, as in the South African case, become susceptible to political instrumentalization, and where this happens there is a need to consider what mechanisms can be used to challenge inadequate redress programmes although arguably international law mechanisms may fail to protect victims' rights to reparations from political manoeuvring (Pradier et al, 2018).

Reparations and international perspectives

The reparative principles enshrined in the human rights law discussed in this chapter illustrate the basis on which reparations might be sought. They also clarify some aspects of the rights that citizens have under international law as well as the scope of reparative principles to be incorporated into reparations proposals that can achieve an effective remedy for those aggrieved by historical and present injustice.

Both the 2016 Report of the Working Group of Experts on People of African Descent on Its Mission to the United States of America and the 2021 Commission of Inquiry argued that the US still needed to take further action to give full effect to international human rights law. Both reports also recommended improvements to the possibility of securing remedies for police brutality and discriminatory practices. The Working Group recommended:

> urgent action to ensure accountability for police violence against African Americans: by improving the reporting of violations involving the excessive use of force and extrajudicial killings by the police, and ensuring that reported cases of excessive use of force are independently investigated; by ensuring that alleged perpetrators are prosecuted and, if convicted, are punished with appropriate sanctions; by ensuring that investigations are re-opened when new evidence becomes available; and by ensuring that victims or their families are provided with remedies.
> (UN Human Rights Council, 2016: 20)

The reparations examples discussed in this chapter arguably identify how the 'traditional' notions of restitution or compensation can now be combined with restorative ideas to provide for more effective reparations. This is explored further in the final chapter.

9

Reparations in the 21st Century: Contemporary Debates and Issues on Reparations

This concluding chapter examines contemporary debates in reparations and the reparations movement and returns to the earlier discussion of legal, political and social conceptions on reparations. Differences exist in reparations discourse in the US and UK where different reparations movements and considerations are at play. But the US has experienced a greater level of reparations litigation than the UK and arguably has a more advanced conception on the nature of reparations claims.

This chapter's core focus is on constructing a criminological theory of reparations, building on discussions in the previous chapters. It sets out the case for reparations as linked to notions of justice, forgiveness and repairing harm even though in one sense this may not be possible from a criminological perspective where those who died as a direct consequence of slavery and anti-Black racism cannot now directly receive a remedy. But reparations can reflect not just the harm caused to those who have died, but also the wider suffering caused to affected groups and their intergenerational trauma. Corrective justice is often about repairing harm with the ideal being that of restoring the aggrieved person to the position they would have been in had the wrong not occurred. There are challenges in doing so for a person who has died or, for example, the victims of a genocide. But some form of reparation can be provided via a form of redress if only by way of an apology or consideration of the harm caused to their family or descendants. Reparations can thus be made indirectly via compensation payments to descendants and can be either 'pure' reparation in the form of direct compensation to an aggrieved individual or group, or can be a wider reparative approach incorporating restorative justice principles (as outlined in Chapter 8). Examples of contemporary reparations initiatives are contained within this chapter's discussion.

In constructing its theory on reparations, this chapter examines some of the arguments against reparations set out by governments and objectors and which draw on the neutralization techniques discussed earlier in this book. This chapter's theory of reparations argues for a menu of reparative tools to be deployed to provide a holistic approach to reparations.

Contemporary international perspectives on reparations

While much of this book's discussion relates to specific reparations claims or initiatives in the UK and US, the contemporary reparations movement is situated within wider discourse on reparations in an international context. As Chapter 8 indicated, this includes discussion of reparations within the framework of international law and human rights mechanisms, as well as claims being pursued by nation states in respect of the harm that they allege has arisen from the transatlantic slave trade.

Franklin (2013) identifies that the contemporary global movement to demand reparations from Western industrialized nations and for the international slave trade began in 1993 with the first Pan-African Congress on Reparations, held in Nigeria. Subsequently, the UN World Conference Against Racism, Racial Discrimination, Xenophobia and Related Intolerance which took place in Durban, South Africa, 'declared slavery and the slave trade a crime against humanity and suggested reparations in 2001 over the objections of the US, UK, Spain, and Portugal' (Scruggs, 2013: 2).

Torpey and Burkett (2010) identified that the notion of reparations for the transatlantic slave trade, slavery, sexual slavery, genocide, colonialism, apartheid, disenfranchisement and other forms of racial discrimination and exploitation is now an embedded part of global anti-racist advocacy but with particular relevance in the US (see also Biondi, 2003). As Chapter 8 illustrates, reparations are firmly embedded in the language of international law and international human rights law. Thus, international law provides for individuals and states to claim for reparations through recognized legal routes. However, states may also pursue reparations discourse through wider political campaigns as the following example illustrates.

Case study: the CARICOM Reparations Commission

In 2013 Caribbean Heads of Governments established CRC, providing them with a mandate to prepare the case for reparatory justice for the region's indigenous and African descendant communities who are the victims of CAH in the forms of genocide, slavery, slave trading and racial apartheid. The CRC produced a ten-point reparations plan intended to deliver the case for reparative justice, arguing that victims and descendants of CAH are owed reparatory justice from those enriched by the proceeds of CAH. In particular, the CRC argues that European governments were owners and traders of enslaved Africans and instructed genocidal actions upon indigenous communities. In addition, CRC claims European states created the legal, financial and fiscal policies necessary for the enslavement of Africans and characterized African enslavement and native genocide as being in their national interest (CRC, 2021). Thus, European governments not only failed to take action to eliminate slavery but also actively supported the continuation of slavery and refused compensation to the enslaved when slavery ended.[1] Accordingly, Caribbean and African states arguably have a claim for reparations because European governments:

- refused compensation to the enslaved with the ending of their enslavement;
- compensated slave owners at emancipation for the loss of legal property rights in enslaved Africans;
- imposed a further 100 years of racial apartheid upon the emancipated;
- imposed for another 100 years policies designed to perpetuate suffering upon the emancipated and survivors of genocide;
- and have refused to acknowledge such crimes or to compensate victims and their descendants.

The CRC has set out a ten-point plan for reparations which consists of: Full Formal Apology; Repatriation; Indigenous Peoples Development Program; Cultural Institutions; Public Health Crisis; Illiteracy Eradication; African Knowledge Program; Psychological Rehabilitation; Technology Transfer; and Debt Cancellation. The detail of these specific claims is briefly discussed further as follows.

The notion of a full apology is considered integral to achieve reparation. The CRC argues that the healing process for victims and their descendants can only take place where governments make a sincere formal apology. While some governments have issued statements of regret, CRC maintains that this is insufficient to address the harms caused by slavery. In restorative justice discourse, an apology and clear recognition of the victim's claim is an integral part of ensuring that the victim can gain understanding of what has happened to them and can achieve some form of closure. The CRC also notes that over 10 million Africans were 'forcefully transported to the Caribbean as the enslaved chattel and property of Europeans' (CRC, 2021). Thus, the transatlantic slave trade is arguably the largest forced migration in human history and has placed citizens in an environment that is not of their choosing. CRC suggests that the descendants of African slaves have a legal right to return to their homeland but contends that the European countries should be responsible for facilitating this using all available channels of international law and diplomacy used to resettle those persons who wish to return.

The CRC also argues that the governments of Europe committed genocide upon the native Caribbean population and that military commanders were given official instructions by their governments to eliminate these communities and to remove those who survived pogroms from the region. The CRC notes that a community of over 3,000,000 in 1700 had been reduced to less than 30,000 by 2000 and that survivors remain traumatized, landless, and are the most marginalized social group within the region.

The CRC also identifies areas of cultural disadvantage comparable to some such claims raised in the US and UK. It argues that European nations have invested in the development of community institutions such as museums and research centres in order to prepare their citizens for an understanding of CAH. But while such facilities support European citizens in understanding their role in history as rulers and change agents, there is a lack of investment in comparable institutions in the Caribbean where the CAH were committed. Thus Caribbean educators do not have the same opportunity for cultural engagement and their experience is not told. The CRC argues that this should be remedied within a reparations programme.

The CRC also argues that the African descended population in the Caribbean has the highest incidence in the world of chronic diseases in the forms of hypertension and type two diabetes. It claims that this is the direct result of the nutritional experience, physical and emotional brutality and overall stress profiles associated with slavery, genocide and apartheid. The CRC claims that this, together with issues such as high levels of illiteracy among Caribbean peoples are direct legacies of slavery. Slavery in the US also restricted access to education for African-American citizens, and levels of illiteracy and lower levels of educational attainment continue to be concerns for Black citizens in the US and UK (Buttaro et al, 2010; Levine and Levine, 2014; Mcduff et al, 2018). It would perhaps be too simplistic to link these issues solely to slavery without examining further discourse on the causes and dimensions of illiteracy and education attainment gaps. Research, for example in the UK, has indicated that even where they are entering into higher education Black and Minority Ethnic students experience obstacles that inhibit their ability to achieve their full potential (Bunce et al, 2019). The CRC argues that widespread illiteracy has a negative effect on social and economic advancement and contends that Caribbean governments allocate 'more than 70 percent of public expenditure to health and education in an effort to uproot the legacies of slavery and colonization' (CRC, 2021). The CRC view is that European governments have a responsibility to participate in this effort within the context of a reparations programme.

However, despite expressing sympathy for the Caribbean Community's (CARICOM) position, thus far both UK and US governments have rejected repeated calls for reparations from Caribbean nations (Scruggs, 2013; Clegg, 2014).

The political reparations movement

Reparations discourse has developed as a political movement supported by politicians and political actors as well as activists and advocacy groups. In 1989 Congressman John Conyers first introduced a proposal for a Commission to Study Reparations for African Americans. The bill was intended to 'investigate differing options to resolve the issue of the effects of slavery' (Henry, 2007: 359–60) and was initially unsuccessful but was reintroduced by Conyers every year until he left Congress in 2017. After its initial introduction the bill was reintroduced as House Resolution 40 (H.R.40) which would establish a federal commission to examine the impacts of slavery (Martin and Yaquinto, 2007a: 12). The designation of Resolution 40 was intended to reflect the original (unfulfilled) promise made to freed slaves that they would receive '40 acres and a mule' as a form of reparation after the civil war (Darity, 2008).[2]

Shifts in public attention and support, measured by media coverage in the US, were arguably a factor in encouraging support for reparations legislation to expand beyond Black members of Congress to embrace increasingly large numbers of non-Black Congressional Democrats. Wider acceptance of the case for reparations has arguably been influenced by recognition of the enduring racial divide in contemporary society.

The current version of H.R.40 was introduced into the US House of Representatives sponsored by Sheila Jackson Lee on 3 January 2019. Its text specifies H.R.40 as a bill:

> To address the fundamental injustice, cruelty, brutality, and inhumanity of slavery in the United States and the 13 American colonies between 1619 and 1865 and to establish a commission to study and consider a national apology and proposal for reparations for the institution of slavery, its subsequent de jure and de facto racial and economic discrimination against African-Americans, and the impact of these forces on living African-Americans, to make recommendations to the Congress on appropriate remedies, and for other purposes. (US Congress, 2019)

Thus, if passed, H.R.40 would establish an expert federal commission to study the legacy of slavery in the US and its ongoing harm and develop proposals for redress and repair, including reparations. The current bill's wording reflects the purpose of the Commission as being to determine whether the US government 'should offer a formal apology to African slaves and their descendants on behalf of the nation; whether African-Americans still suffer from the lingering effects of slavery; whether any form of compensation is warranted; and if compensation is warranted, the amount of such compensation' (Concepcion, 2001: 2). H.R.40 has been described as 'a legal mechanism which would arguably move America forward by making this country confront its past' (Muhammad, 2020: 45). While the bill was mostly stuck in Committee during Conyers' period, hearings were held in 2019 and 2020. H.R.40 was approved out of Committee in April 2021 with the potential for it to head to the House floor. However, according to Govtrack (2021) despite a Democrat-controlled legislature (House and Senate) in 2021, H.R.40 has only a 56 per cent chance of being enacted according to the following factors: 'The bill's primary sponsor is from the state/territory: TX. The bill's primary sponsor is a Democrat. The bill is assigned to the House Judiciary committee. The bill's primary subject is Civil rights and liberties, minority issues'[3] (Govtrack, 2021).

The bill now 'has 180 co-sponsors in the House, the most ever' and if brought to the House floor is arguably likely to succeed (King, 2021: np). But the likelihood of the bill achieving legislative success beyond passing the House 'would require votes from all 50 Senate Democrats and 10 Republicans, who are almost certain to oppose it' (King, 2021: np).

Renewed interest in reparations is arguably a combination of various factors. The success of the US Holocaust litigation arguably highlighted the potential for reparations claims to succeed in the courts (Martin and Yaquinto, 2007a). In addition, the changing landscape of public support and the increased contemporary push to draw attention to and address ongoing racial (in)equality also created the conditions under which reparations discourse attracts media and political attention. The argument that racial inequality is a continued legacy of slavery draws focus in establishing it as a longstanding problem with deep ideological and social roots. Jordan (2003: 557) argues that the reparations movement's strategic litigation focus and rhetorical effort has been flawed by focusing upon the institution of slavery. She contends that while slavery is the root of modern racism, it suffers many defects as the centrepiece of a reparations litigation strategy. By contrast, Waterhouse (2011) argues for preserving slavery as the root focus of reparations discourse in part to ensure that the relationship between public memory, rectificatory justice and reparations is preserved. Waterhouse acknowledges that legal theories on reparations have examined the doctrinal bases of reparations for slavery (and its continuing legacy) 'in tort law, contract law, criminal law, civil-rights law, corporate law, tax law, civil procedure, international law, and constitutional law' (2011: 2). But he contends that 'the federal government, through the United States Congress, has the legal authority and responsibility to remedy specific acts of governmental discrimination against large numbers of African-Americans in the Jim Crow Era' (2011: 2) and argues that a specific goal of the reparations movement should be to ensure that the memory of slavery is a collective one. Jordan (2003) argues instead for a focus on lynching as being the root cause of reparations, noting that federal authorities did little to stop these extra-judicial killings and that the widespread nature of lynchings was indicative of a 'pattern of racial atrocity in the relatively recent past' which has arguably disappeared from memory but is one for which 'the conventional lawsuit or legislative reparations might serve as an appropriate vehicle for redress' (Jordan, 2003: 559).

The positions of Jordan and Waterhouse are not mutually exclusive as each serves to preserve the memory of racial atrocity and to identify it as a cause of harm that should be remedied by reparations. Such arguments and others do, however, come up against objections.

The case against reparations

As earlier chapters of this book have identified, African-American reparations in the 'traditional' category of a 'class' claim have generally been unsuccessful, whereas some Jim Crow-era reparations and individual private tort reparations claims have arguably been more successful.

The reparations movement is arguably gaining political momentum and reparations have become an accepted part of contemporary political, legal and social justice discourse (Coates, 2014). But while the ideal of reparations is noted and there is general acceptance of the harms of slavery and the existence of ongoing injustice of racial discrimination, conceptual problems exist concerning 'whether the court system is the best (or even an appropriate) place to look for redress and, at a higher level of generality, whether the dominant liberalism of American law is equipped to deal with such claims' (Brophy, 2003: 497). At a more fundamental level, there is political and even ideological objection to reparations in both the UK and US. Consideration of the objections is integral to the later discussion of a criminological theory of reparations.

Judge Norgle's decision in the *African-American Slave Descendants Litigation* articulated three objections to reparations on procedural grounds: standing, the political question, and the statute of limitations. However, while these issues are addressed in the context of their legal relevance, they are also engaged in wider socio-legal and political discourse that objects to reparations. Thus, not only are they procedural grounds they are also conceptual grounds worthy of consideration.

Legal objections

The issue of standing, considered as a direct issue in relation to the justiciability of a claim before the courts is also worthy of wider consideration. Thus, the legality of paying reparations and the legislative basis for doing so requires some examination. Bittker (1973) favoured a legislative programme of Black reparations arguably similar to that put forward in respect of Japanese-American reparations. The legislative grounding has the benefit of codifying the nature of any reparations programme. But an objection to a legislative case for reparations can arguably be made on the grounds that traditional class claims are not justified and that rather than making reparations on behalf of all descendants of slaves, arguably each case should be determined on its merits in respect of the particular injury claimed by a group. This argument challenges the merits of a generalized legislative approach and instead might contend that a case such as Tulsa is justiciable, even 100 years after the event because there are survivors claiming ongoing injustice arising from a harm they directly experienced. There is also a Black community tangibly affected by activities arising from that event (its appropriation for tourist purposes) in a way that is arguable in respect of slavery activities dating back beyond the experience of living survivors. Thus, the objection is based on the requirement for cases to be considered individually on their legal merits.

The political question

Political considerations on reparations are arguably more problematic as they involve not just the reality of whether reparations will pass through the legislative and political process, but also political calculations concerning whether there may be negative consequences of supporting reparations. The judgement in slavery reparations litigation in the US has thus far been that whether the state should pay reparations should be a matter for Congress (that is, a political [and legislative] decision rather than a judicial one). But as is discussed elsewhere in this chapter, contemporary measures such as H.R.40 have been unable to make it beyond the first stage of the legislative process. Ostensibly the main cause of this is lack of political will and support to progress the matter. This contrasts with the clear political will to make reparations for Japanese Americans, native Americans and in the case of Holocaust claimants.

The political objection arguably also relates to the issue of standing and the nature of the reparations being claimed. The Japanese-American and Holocaust claims were linked to an identifiable class of victim, survivors of the respective harms of internment and the Holocaust. Thus, while there may have been political considerations in respect of the financial amount of the reparations claims, these could be addressed via arguments that the reparations were directly relatable to a proven injury and harm rather than one of a generalized nature. Thus, the claims were considered on their own merits and any complaints that they would open the floodgates to further claims might be contested. Arguably Japanese-American, Holocaust and even Native American reparations claims also had the 'benefit' of being situated in a specific conception of the state's involvement as perpetrator of the harm, without accepting any contemporary responsibility for further claims, consistent with the international humanitarian law perspectives discussed in Chapter 8. Thus, the German authorities were able to acknowledge responsibility for the harms visited upon the Jews during the Holocaust by the (former) Nazi regime. The American government of the 1970s and 1980s was also able to acknowledge complicity in the wrong of Japanese-American internment by the 1940s administration. In doing so, neither government bound the state to make reparations for wider harms or be liable for further reparations claims, although as noted previously, the German government has reviewed the level of Holocaust reparations payments and authorized further payments. But even so, such demands on the public purse can be justified on the grounds of their (relatively) limited scope and the political expediency of making such payments.

Politically, payment of large-scale anti-Black reparations opens up claims of innocent citizens meeting the cost of harms for which they should not be held responsible. Thus, arguably White society in general is being penalized for a notion of White supremacy and ongoing racism that might be contested. In a response to Ta-Nehisi Coates' 2014 article on the case for reparations, Williamson (2014) contested the necessity and validity of claims of racial disadvantage. Invoking several neutralization techniques, he argued that economic realignment policies are either intended to improve those who are socially disadvantaged and that these tend to be African Americans, or they are part of a symbolic political process; thus reparations are not meaningful. The notion of White supremacy as the primary factor in racial difference is arguably contested on the grounds that this argument relies on acceptance of 'the facts of *aggregate* advantage and disadvantage with their roots in historical injustice' but contending that 'the aggregate cannot be converted into the *collective* inasmuch as neither advantage nor disadvantage is universal on either side nor linked to a straightforward chain of causality' (Williamson, 2014). Green (2019) also noted that some Black citizens are opposed to reparations and might consider these to be an insult.

The statute of limitations

The statute of limitations argument also has a wider conception in argument against reparations. Brown (1993) argued that left-wing identity politics equated to Nietzschean *ressentiment*, thus a notion of relative weakness could be used to assume moral or ethical supremacy. Brown's conception of 'wounded attachments' was used to describe a form of politics that allows suffering to establish an advantaged perspective and group identity. But Brown raised questions concerning the kind of political recognition that identity-based claims could reach 'given the subjectivizing conditions of identity production in a late modern liberal, capitalist, and disciplinary bureaucratic social order' (1993: 390). The notion of embracing a victim-centred identity as a distinct political tool has been raised by others in respect of slavery-based reparations claims (Flaherty and Carlisle, 2004). Such objections allege that identity politics risk becoming a tactic such that 'progressives' become attached to identity politics as a mechanism to push against the status quo. Brown acknowledges that in some circumstances an oppositional relationship does exist such that some groups are genuinely disadvantaged (for example, the poor and oppressed in developing countries who face real political oppression, or LGBTQ citizens who still experience discrimination in the workplace and in the provision of services). But contemporary opponents of Black reparations dispute that the same level of disadvantage still exists for Black citizens, notwithstanding the existence of specific instances of racism or discrimination. Thus, campaigns such as the movement for reparations might be challenged on the grounds that they are intended to progress a particular ideological agenda of discrimination rather than being situated in a genuine (or at least justified) notion of inequality that requires reparation or restitution. Such arguments might be articulated in the context of suggesting that considerable strides have been made by Black citizens as a consequence of equalities legislation and the gains of the civil rights movement. Alternatively claims that deny the link between slavery and present-day circumstances or even deny the reality of systematic racism as a tangible factor in today's society are part of the neutralizations that might be used to contest both the validity and necessity of contemporary reparations claims.

In this respect, the issue of statute of limitations is raised in the context of questioning whether the time for reparations has passed as well as contesting whether the claim of continuing injustice and disparity is such that there is a case for a mass claim as opposed to individual or specific claims, for example the Tulsa riot, albeit Tulsa also faced statute of limitations challenges (see Chapter 3). When the US House Judiciary Subcommittee on the Constitution, Civil Rights, and Civil Liberties held a hearing on reparations in 2019, objections to reparations included arguments that to provide reparations now would be an insult to African Americans and that the time for such payment had passed (Lockhart, 2019). However, the case for reparations has been accepted by some sectors as the following section discusses.

Contemporary reparation efforts

While previous chapters and, in particular, the analysis of Chapter 3, identify that litigation efforts have broadly failed to achieve reparations for slavery, other reparations efforts have been successful in persuading corporations to engage with their historical links to slavery. In particular, banks, other financial institutions and universities forced to confront their past engagement with slavery have accepted the need for reparations in recent years. Jolly

(2020) identifies that several UK banks including Barclays, the Royal Bank of Scotland, HSBC, Lloyds Banking Group and Lloyds of London had links to the slave trade. The links included: directors of predecessor companies owning slaves and predecessor banks giving loans and other support to plantation owners; managers or directors of predecessor banks having received slave compensation; predecessor companies receiving compensation for ceding plantations in the Caribbean and for their perceived losses in doing so. The UCL project that tracked compensation to former slaveholders and created publicly accessible details of slave ownership and other links to the slave trade in the UK (Hall et al, 2014; Hall, 2016) was instrumental in bringing details of former corporate slavery links into the public domain. Allied to UK Black Lives Matter protests and increased public and journalistic scrutiny of links to slavery, corporations in the UK, like some of their US counterparts, arguably had little choice but to acknowledge such links and to consider or reconsider their stance on paying reparations. This includes some US banks and other financial institutions who had resisted making reparations in the initial *Farmer-Paellmann* case and subsequent *African-American Slave Descendants Litigation*, modifying their positions to make reparations outside of the court process. Universities in both the UK and US who have also examined their historical links to slavery have agreed to make reparations.

These reparations initiatives falling outside of the confines of traditional reparations litigation arguably represent a recognition by such institutions of a shifting social landscape in which corporate denial of reparations signified by challenges to *Farmer-Paellmann*, the *African-American Slave Descendants Litigation* and other reparations cases is no longer sustainable.

Businesses may previously have resisted paying compensation or making reparations but the contemporary climate is arguably one in which racism and historical links to slavery will become entwined with concepts of ethical operations and human rights compliance and thus will engage corporate social responsibility (CSR) policies. CSR is arguably integrated into a business model that theoretically provides for adherence to the law, ethical standards and international norms of business behaviour and accountability (Nurse, 2015). Thus, CSR provides a means for corporations to promote their brand as ethically and socially responsible and operates mainly on the basis of self-regulation, where corporations are trusted to voluntarily adhere to non-legally binding standards of ethical behaviour, with no single commonly accepted definition of the principle (Mazurkiewicz, 2004).

Harris (2011) highlights that corporations may adopt CSR for a variety of reasons, principally:

- acting ethically is the right way for the company to behave;
- doing what is right and fair is expected of an organization;
- acting ethically is in the organization's best interests. (Harris, 2011: 39)

The extent to which one (or all) of these reasons applies and provides the corporation's motivation for integrating CSR (and the wider notions of corporate environmental responsibility that can incorporate human rights perspectives) can have an effect on whether CSR is adopted as part of operational practices. This influences corporate consideration of the impact and wider implications of its activities, or whether CSR becomes solely an aspect of marketing and brand management, or simply a PR tool. The need to combat negative publicity or damaging perceptions of a corporation (that is, as a former slave owner or engaged in other discriminatory practices) and to protect its valuable brand may, for example, lead to the adoption of specific CSR initiatives purely to obtain benefits for a major corporation's public image. There may even be inconsistency within a Multi-National Enterprise (MNE) or major corporation about the extent to which CSR should be observed or apply to its operations, especially where there is no clear chain of CSR ownership at board (strategic) level and CSR reporting is outside of core corporate governance, external scrutiny or stakeholder audit.

Thus, historical links to slavery and any calls for reparations may now become a CSR issue, integral to maintaining a brand image (particularly a 'non-racist' image). In response to identification of their historical links to slavery, the majority of the financial institutions mentioned earlier issued statements deploring the evils of slavery, expressing regret for their past or predecessor companies' actions and reaffirming their commitment to equality, diversity and their opposition to racism. Several companies went further and initiated reparations programs or anti-slavery initiatives as the following examples illustrate.

Financial institution reparations

As the *African-American Descendants* litigation identified, several present-day financial institutions have historical links to slavery that make them susceptible to reparations claims. Despite resisting such lawsuits, a number of finance houses have now developed or entered into reparations schemes.

In 2005 JP Morgan Chase filed a disclosure statement with the City of Chicago and acknowledged that between 1831 and 1865 two of its predecessor banks, Citizens Bank and Canal Bank in Louisiana, had accepted approximately 13,000 slaves as collateral for loans. The Bank ended up owning approximately 1,250 following defaults on these loans (Magill, 2005). The company subsequently issued an apology and confirmed that it would provide $5 million to fund scholarships for African Americans from Louisiana to attend college.

In 2020, insurance company Lloyd's of London said it would provide reparations by way of funding and investing in charities promoting diversity and opportunities for minority ethnic groups. The UCL data identified that

Simon Fraser, a founding member of Lloyd's of London, owned at least 162 slaves. He received reparations of about £400,000 (US$508,407) in today's value to cede the plantation. Also in 2020 the Bank of England apologized for its historic links to slavery after it emerged that the Bank 'had 27 former members, including 11 former bank governors and 16 directors, who owned slaves or profited directly from the slave trade' (Kahn, 2020).

University reparations

In 2019, Glasgow University (UK) agreed to pay £20m in reparations to atone for its historical links to the transatlantic slave trade in a partnership with the University of the West Indies (Carrell, 2019). The agreement will fund a programme of restorative justice after Glasgow University discovered that it had benefitted financially from Scottish slave traders in the 18th and 19th centuries by between £16.7m and £198m (equivalent 2019 value). Also in 2019, Georgetown University confirmed that it would raise about $400,000 a year to benefit the descendants of the 272 enslaved people that were sold to benefit the college nearly 200 years ago (Swarns, 2019). In September 2015 Georgetown's president convened the Working Group on Slavery, Memory and Reconciliation with a remit to: make recommendations on how best to acknowledge and recognize Georgetown's historical relationship with the institution of slavery; examine and interpret the history of certain sites on the Georgetown campus; and convene events and opportunities for dialogue on these issues. The Working Group's report documents the sale of 272 men, women and children valued at a price of $115,000 (roughly $3.3 million today when adjusted for inflation) to be paid over ten years (Georgetown Working Group on Slavery, Memory and Reconciliation, 2016: 15). The Committee recommended an apology from the University president offered jointly with the provincial superior of the Maryland Jesuits, considering this to be a prerequisite for reconciliation. It also recommended the renaming of Mulledy Hall (Freedom Hall) to Isaac Hall in recognition of the first named slave in the sale of the 272, plus the renaming of McSherry Hall to Anne Marie Becraft Hall (a woman of colour). It also proposed the University should meet with the descendants of slaves and descendant communities and should commission an oral history project and explore the feasibility of admission and financial aid programmes as well as erecting a permanent memorial to the enslaved peoples. Hamilton (2020) identifies that in 2018 the Isaac Hawkins Legacy Group, composed of Hawkins' direct descendants, requested that Georgetown repay them for their enslaved ancestors' labour. In 2019 the Student Senate passed a resolution for formal reparations (Cuccia, 2019).

These are by no means the only university reparations initiatives, but they do illustrate the localized and individualized nature of reparations.

Both Glasgow and Georgetown are arguably elite educational institutions with considerable financial resources and a prestigious reputation, thus the reputational damage they might incur by being perceived as being linked to slavery is considerable, particularly in the context of current societal interest in institutional and systemic racism.

The changing landscape of reparations

Fagan and Thompson identify class actions as being the primary legal mechanism feared by US corporations, which Hodges (2008: 2) identifies as being based on a model where 'one individual claim is asserted to represent a class of others, whose owners are bound by the result of the single claim unless they opt out of the class and procedure'. The class action procedure allows for punitive damages and requires parties to meet their own costs (Fagan and Thompson, 2009: 56–7). Yet arguably past corporate resistance to slavery reparations litigation illustrates the difficulty of achieving effective social justice in the area of reparations where major institutions are able to exert considerable economic and political power to resist such claims. Such cases also demonstrate the difficulties facing communities and activists attempting to enforce equality and social justice perspectives where the domestic judicial system, legislature and regulatory enforcement mechanisms are perceived as inadequate to deal with human rights abuses committed by major corporations and where strictly speaking corporate non-compliance and past engagement with slavery and anti-Black racism may not be classified as criminal. But the university and financial institution cases outlined earlier show how public perception and threat of public censure can motivate different types of reparation initiatives.

Repairing harms from anti-Black racism: a criminological perspective

Set in the context of restorative or reparative justice discourse, reparations assess the goals of reparationists, such as apologies and truth commissions, accounting for past wrongs, and addressing those wrongs through programmes of community empowerment (Brophy, 2004).

From the criminological perspective adopted by this book, critical race theory (CRT) is relevant in respect of its commitment to treating the social construction of race as central to the way that people of colour are ordered and constrained in society (Treviño et al, 2008). CRT argues that American law (and policy) including anti-discrimination laws are structured in ways that maintain White privilege. Capers (2014: 26) identifies five key themes and debates in this area of CRT:

- Equality laws frequently have the effect of marginalising and obscuring social, political and economic equality.
- The principle of 'interest convergence' in reality means that legal reforms that should benefit ethnic minorities only happen and do so when such reforms benefit the interests of the white majority.
- Race is socially and legally constructed and so biological constructions of race are insignificant.
- CRT scholars recognise that oppression and subordination operate on multiple axes and thus they reject crude essentialism.
- Reference to race is often neglected within the law and thus CRT tries to make race visible by incorporating personal narratives or 'legal storytelling' within CRT methods.

Thus, within a CRT context while efforts may have been made to legislate for equality and to end race discrimination, these efforts are potentially unsuccessful not only because they fail to engage with the reality of discrimination on grounds of race but also because the mechanisms that are used to monitor and serve as checks and balances are not always available to those from marginalized groups. As an example, Ashworth (2004) has argued that the response and treatment that victims receive within the criminal justice system is something of a lottery, in addition to any secondary victimization that might be caused by having to relive the ordeal of the crime itself. Bowling and Phillips in their discussion of *Racism, Crime and Justice* (2002) identified the social and political context that determined the reality that different ethnic groups experienced policing, offending and victimization. Thus, for Black citizens, the experience of policing may be different from that experienced by White citizens in part because racism in policing and criminal justice practices adversely impacts on the safety and liberty of minority ethnic groups. This is irrespective of the fact that scrutiny mechanisms exist in the form of anti-discrimination laws or conduct laws (for example, the UK's Police and Criminal Evidence Act 1984 and conduct or procedural rules) that are designed to prevent abuses of state policing powers. As the Burge reparations case (discussed in Chapter 3) and various police brutality and racially motivated abuse cases show, while successive attempts have been made to eradicate racial difference in policing and criminal justice, it remains a contemporary problem (Lammy, 2017). From a criminological perspective, reparations are an integral part of addressing harm. As earlier chapters of this book have identified, where crime exists, the state usually metes out punishment as part of its contract with its citizens to keep them safe and to secure reparation or revenge where it has failed to do so and crime has occurred. This logic applies to the failure of states to end discrimination and protect citizens. Thus, state obligations to uphold human rights and comply with international norms provide a compelling case for providing reparations.

Justice and forgiveness: reparations in the 21st century

As this book's prior discussion establishes, the case for reparations and the manner in which they should be provided is complex. First, there are issues of standing and who is entitled to reparations. Second, there is the question of who should make reparations, whether the individual or the state. Third, there is the question of what form reparations should take and how they might be calculated or implemented. Finally, there is the question of equity in reparations. Arguably, before consideration of any of these issues there should be a clear consideration of what purpose reparations are intended to achieve.

To return to an earlier discussion on the nature of reparations, these are arguably framed in a context in which reparations:

> (1) provide payment (in cash or in kind) to a large group of claimants, (2) on the basis of wrongs that were substantively permissible under the prevailing law when committed, (3) in which current law bars a compulsory remedy for the past wrong (by virtue of sovereign immunity, statutes of limitations, or similar rules), and (4) in which the payment is justified on backward-looking grounds of corrective justice, rather than forward-looking grounds such as the deterrence of future wrongdoing. (Posner and Vermeule, 2003: 691)

These issues are clarified in some of the reparations litigation discussed in Chapter 3 and elsewhere in this book, and arguably Posner and Vermeule's definition provides an accurate articulation of the focus of slavery reparations litigation, based largely on past harms even where these may also consider some ongoing activity. However, this book's theory of reparations seeks to extend beyond the narrow confines of this definition, particularly in extending the ideals of reparations to encompass ongoing anti-Black racism and the disadvantage experienced by Black citizens. Thus, its consideration of reparations identifies that these should apply in respect of three categories of reparations: first, the 'traditional' claims relating to the harms and unpaid labour of slavery; second, in respect of Jim Crow segregation; and third, in respect of contemporary anti-Black racism which includes institutional practices. Miller (2004) sets out three pre-requisites for establishing right to claim reparations: enduring social harm; psychological harm; 'unlawful, unfair or fraudulent business practice' (110). While Miller primarily considers these issues in respect of standing to bring a suit, they are arguably core elements of the criminological approach to reparations.[4] The issues of standing, liability, the form of reparations and equity are more expansive and each is considered further in the following section.

Standing

As the case discussions in Chapter 3 identify, the issue of standing to bring a claim is potentially a problematic one, particularly in respect of historic injustice. A core issue in (legal) discussions of standing is the notion of a plaintiff having 'sufficient interest' to bring a case. In contemporary human rights discourse this is relatively straightforward. Measures such as the ECHR identify that a person identified as a 'victim' can seek a remedy for a breach of their rights by way of an unlawful act, because they clearly have an interest in their victimization (Miles, 2000). But in the case of historical injustices such as slavery the courts have shown some unwillingness to widen the notion of a victim to descendants who are arguably far removed from the events (that is, slavery and the status of being property) that caused the harm, even though arguments are presented that the consequences of the original harm are far-reaching and impact on present-day citizens. Jim Crow-related reparations claims and individualized claims (such as the Chicago police brutality cases) arguably provide for a clearer application of standing where individuals can demonstrate their sufficient interest by virtue of having experienced a personal (that is, direct) injury and thus a clear interest in the harm visited upon them. The success of the Chicago cases illustrates the capability for reparations claims to be brought in other cases of *direct* anti-Black racism although such claims are not without their challenges. But considering such issues, a conception of standing based on tangible individual harm arguably provides a basis for a reparations claim that links discrimination-based harm to social attitudes held by institutions.

Thus, from a criminological perspective, the existence of discriminatory practices within substantive law, policies and practices such that it can be proved that communities are marginalized according to race-based criteria arguably provides for a wider notion of standing where individuals or groups can demonstrate their interest in both the harm caused and that they have been somehow affected. In accordance with human rights principles that require states to provide for an effective remedy where rights have been infringed, and discourse on addressing state crime, individuals in this category should be eligible for reparations.

Liability and responsibility

In reality, 'reparations claims sometimes fit within the framework of identifiable victims and perpetrators, but they usually do not. Often the perpetrators cannot be identified with specificity or are no longer alive' (Brophy, 2003: 503). Again, the slavery reparations cases discussed within this book identify some of the challenges of linking historical injustices to present-day individuals and corporations that should be held liable. Further problems exist in respect of determining that the state should be liable although here, international criminal and human rights law is helpful and, in particular, discourse on remedying CAH even where conducted under the (possibly dubious) umbrella of legality. The state bears responsibility to take action even if only to explore the nature of harms via the kind of commission envisaged by H.R.40.

The form of reparations

In respect of the form that reparations should take, this book's perspective is that they should be applied along the restorative principles outlined in Chapter 8 and should incorporate a menu of reparations that are applicable to the harm caused. Accordingly this book's theory of reparations is situated within the criminological perspectives of restorative justice (that is, repairing harm) while also incorporating transitional justice principles of promoting healing and confronting and addressing state crime and state-corporate crime (broadly defined to incorporate mass wrongs that amount to human rights violations that may not be strictly defined as crimes). Accordingly, this book adopts a broad notion of reparations that can include:

- an apology;
- fact-finding or truth and reconciliation-style investigations of the harm;
- formal declaration or recognition of harm and the associated injustice;
- financial compensation for individual or group harm;
- settlement of legal claims and grievances;
- restorative penalty;
- compensation or restitution in the form of scholarships, provision of services to affected communities;
- memorials and renaming of buildings, streets or other infrastructure;
- wiping out of debt.

The key to determining which mechanism is appropriate is based on the harm that is claimed. But the overriding principle should be a restorative one, that seeks to repair harm, heal relations and bring some form of closure to affected citizens. As CARICOM identify, an apology is an essential step in addressing the harm caused through enslavement and anti-Black racism (CRC, 2021) and should be an integral aspect of considering reparations claims or providing reparations outside of any legal claims. Apologies have already been provided by some institutions such as the US Senate and House of Representatives (Wenger, 2009) and by some states (for example, the UK in 2006) in respect of their past involvement in slavery (Smith, 2006). Support for Black Lives Matter protests and some 'official' recognitions of the reality of racism, discrimination in criminal justice processes and of specific or individualized wrongdoing in policing practices also arguably amount to an apology.

This book's discussion of reparations identifies a case for reparations to be considered within a conceptual framework that incorporates several different notions on what reparations are and how they might be achieved. Thus, it makes the case for reparations within a notion of equity and fairness in which reparations incorporates restitution, compensation and restoration. These are not easy principles to combine within a reparations programme, and arguably before detailed consideration of any of these issues there should be a clear consideration of what purpose reparations are intended to achieve.

Appendix: Reparations Litigation and Settlements

The following table provides an overview of key reparations litigation, settlements and initiatives in the US and UK.

Year	Case detail
1878	Former enslaved person Henrietta Wood sued for damages and lost wages, and won restitution of $2,500.
1916	*Johnson v McAdoo* (D.C. Cir. 1916): The plaintiffs were former slaves (and descendants of slaves) who argued for an equitable lien on US Treasury funds acquired during slavery from cotton taxes.
1974	A $10 million out-of-court settlement was reached between the US government and the Black Tuskegee victims.
1994	The Florida legislature passed the Rosewood Compensation Bill and the state of Florida approved $2.1 million for the living survivors of the 1923 Rosewood racial pogrom, the cause of multiple deaths and the decimation of the town's Black community. Nine survivors were each entitled to $150,000 dollars in compensation; a $500,000 pool of funds was established for their descendants; and individual $4,000 scholarships for the youngest generation of Rosewood family members were established.
1995	*Cato v United States*, 70 F.3d 1103 (9th Cir. 1995)
1999	*Pigford v Glickman* (1999): Class action for racial discrimination in farm loans and assistance between 1981 and 1996.
2001	Oklahoma legislature passed a bill intended to pay limited reparations for the destruction of the Greenwood, Oklahoma community in 1921. Reparations were to be paid as low-income student scholarships in Tulsa.
2002	*Farmer-Paellmann v FleetBoston Fin. Corp.*, No. 02-1862 (E.D.N.Y. 26 March 2002).
2004	State of Florida declares Rosewood a Florida Heritage Landmark and subsequently erects a historical marker that names the victims and describes the site's destruction.

Year	Case detail
2004	*re African-American Slave Descendants Litigation* 304 F. Supp. 2d 1027 (N.D. Ill. 2004): Class action on behalf of the descendants of slaves, targeted at specific corporations.
2008	Burge reparations: $19.8 million settlement of lawsuits by Aaron Patterson, Leroy Orange, Stanley Howard and Madison Hobley as a combined settlement to address discrimination and torture claims by African Americans who were tortured into giving false confessions.
2010	Pigford II: Settlement for the second stage of the farm loans class action.
2012	*Kitchen and Reeves v Chicago*: Two more police torture cases settled for a total of $12.3 million.
2015	Chicago City Council approved (Burge reparations) payment of $100,000 to each of the approximately 60 living survivors of police torture in Chicago, aimed at African-American citizens who had not received settlements via previous lawsuits. In addition, the reparations ordinance made provision for creation of a public memorial and the Chicago Torture Justice Center.
2017	All Souls College Oxford (UK) established an annual scholarship for Caribbean students and paid a £100,000 grant to a college in Barbados in recognition of its financial benefit from the slave trade.
2019	The Virginia Theological Seminary establishes a $1.7 million reparations fund for the descendants of African Americans who were enslaved to work on their campus during the 1800s.
2019	Glasgow University (UK) set up a £20 million restorative justice initiative in conjunction with the University of the West Indies in recognition of its historical links to the transatlantic slave trade and the financial benefit it gained from Scottish slave traders in the 18th and 19th centuries.
2019	City of Evanston, Illinois, voted to allocate $10 million in tax revenue to fund reparations initiatives aimed at addressing the gaps in wealth and opportunity of Black residents.
2019	Georgetown University announced a commitment to a $400,000-a-year fund for reparations to the descendants of 272 slaves sold by the college in the pre-civil war.
2019	Princeton Theological Seminary announces a $27 million reparations fund to recognize and address its benefit from Black slavery including scholarships and doctoral fellowships.
2020	*Randle and Others v City of Tulsa and Others* (2020): Tulsa Reparations Lawsuit based on a claim of public nuisance and arguing that there have yet to be appropriate reparations for the harm caused by the 1921 Race Riot and its aftermath.

Notes

Preface

[1] The 'Windrush Scandal' refers to the treatment of commonwealth citizens (primarily Black Caribbean citizens) who came to the UK between 1948 and 1973. These citizens are known as the 'Windrush Generation' after the name of the HMT Empire Windrush ship which brought one of the first large group of Black citizens to the UK to address labour shortages after World War II. Those of the Windrush Generation who settled in the UK were automatically British subjects and in principle were free to live and work in the UK. However, in 2018, the UK government adopted a 'Hostile Environment' policy constructed to strictly enforce immigration rules intended to make the UK unliveable for undocumented immigrants. Because many of the Windrush Generation had arrived in the UK on their parents' passports and because the UK Home Office had destroyed landing cards and other documents relating to their arrival, many of the Windrush Generation were unable to prove their immigration status and became subject to the threat of deportation. Media reporting of the 'criminalization' of mostly Black citizens who had lived in the UK for many years but were now being threatened with removal provoked a public outcry and a review of the government's policy (The Joint Council for the Welfare of Immigrants, 2020). In March 2019, the UK government set up a compensation scheme to financially compensate those affected (and their families) for losses linked to being classified as immigration offenders. Yet in 2021 a National Audit Office (NAO) inspection found that the compensation scheme had only paid out to 633 people out of an original estimate of 15,000 claimants. In addition, it was estimated that 21 people had died while waiting for compensation (Gentleman, 2021).

Chapter 1

[1] In its report the EJI notes that this figure is at least 800 more lynchings in these states than had been previously reported.
[2] The 2011 murder of James Craig Anderson in Mississippi is considered the last recorded fatal lynching in the United States.
[3] See, for example, Article 7 of the Universal Declaration on Human Rights which provides for a ban on discrimination and notes that everyone is equal before the law and should not be subject to discrimination of any kind particularly on grounds such as race, colour, sex, language, religion, political or other opinion, national or social origin, property, birth or other status. Similar provisions are included in other human rights instruments such as the ECHR and the Inter-American Convention on Human Rights.
[4] This book assesses litigation as at September 2020 with a primary focus on US and UK cases and litigation attempts.

Chapter 2

1. Black citizens in the Antebellum South were denied certain rights including exclusion from the right to marry, follow trade, travel, own land or property, enter into contracts, testify in court and seek judicial remedy.
2. Paragraph 3 of Article 7 clarifies that for the purpose of the Statute, the term 'gender' should be taken to refer to the legal classification of two sexes, male and female, within the context of society.
3. See also Chapter 8's case study on systematic racism in policing in the US as an alleged crime against humanity, according to the 2021 Commission of Inquiry into the matter.
4. It should, however, be noted that there are still some proponents of modified eugenics theories as well as the existence of White supremacists who continue to believe that Black races are inferior.
5. For detailed discussion of the Abolitionist movements see, for example, Stewart (2008).
6. The Legacies of British Slave-Ownership project at UCL (UK) created a database that contains the identity of all slave-owners in the British colonies at the time slavery ended and details of all the estates in the British Caribbean colonies. The project provided details of the slave-owning histories of estates and tracked details of compensation paid. Details of the project are available at: Legacies of British Slave-ownership (ucl.ac.uk).

Chapter 3

1. This book assesses litigation as at September 2020 with a focus on US and UK cases and litigation attempts.
2. See the discussion of the Chicago police brutality reparations claims later in this chapter.
3. The 18 corporations were identified as FleetBoston Financial Corporation, CSX Corporation, Aetna Inc., Brown Brothers Harriman, New York Life Insurance Company, Norfolk Southern Corporation, Lehman Brothers, Lloyd's of London, Union Paciac Railroad, J.P. Morgan Chase Manhattan Bank, Westpoint Stevens Inc., RJ Reynolds Tobacco Company, Brown and Williamson, Liggett Group Inc., Loews Corporation, Canadian National Railway, Southern Mutual Insurance Company, and American International Group (AIG).
4. §502 of the statute defines a public nuisance as: 'A public nuisance is one which affects at the same time an entire community or neighbourhood, or any considerable number of persons, although the extent of the annoyance or damage inflicted upon the individuals may be unequal.'

Chapter 5

1. While it is beyond the scope of this chapter to fully explore the nature of Holocaust denial it is worth mentioning that some commentators have expressed the view that the Holocaust was either greatly exaggerated or that the evidence for the existence of gas chambers and mass killing of Jews is lacking. The matter has been partly litigated in the case of *Irving v Penguin Books Limited*, Deborah E. Lipstat [2000] EWHC QB 115. David Irving (a historian) initiated libel proceedings against Professor Deborah Lipstat. He claimed that her book '*Denying the Holocaust: The Growing Assault on Truth and Memory*' contained passages that accused him of being a Nazi apologist and an admirer of Hitler, and that in his work he had distorted facts and manipulated documents in support of his contention that the Holocaust did not take place. Lipstat's defence was one of justification, essentially that she and the publishers could prove the truth of what they published. Irving accepted at trial that perhaps as many as 1.5 million Jews were killed on the authority of Heydrich (a state official) and on a systematic basis and at paragraphs 13.155 to 13.159 of

the judgement the trial judge commented that Irving had appeared to shift his position on the number of Jews killed and also on the existence of, for example, gas chambers at Auschwitz. While the case was not about proving the existence of the Holocaust, the trial judge concluded that Lipstat and Penguin Books had substantially justified what they had published and so the defence of justification had been established and judgement went in their favour.
2   A further complication was that the Yugoslavian law was in conflict with California law where the claims were issued (Bazyler, 2000: 22–3).

Chapter 8
1   It is beyond the scope of this book's discussion to do justice to the complexity of South Africa's political and racial system during the apartheid era, or the political and international factors that either created the apartheid regime or led to its downfall. For further reading on the subject the following books provide some additional context: Pauw, J. (2017) *Into the Heart of Darkness: Confessions of Apartheid's Assassins*; Clark, N. and Worger, W. (2016) *South Africa: The Rise and Fall of Apartheid*, Routledge; Welsh, D. (2010) *The Rise and Fall of Apartheid: From Racial Domination to Majority Rule*, Jonathan Ball Publishers; Guethke, A. (2004) *Rethinking the Rise and Fall of Apartheid: South Africa and World Politics*, Palgrave. At time of writing, the website of South Africa's Truth and Recommission, containing documents and evidence from the Commission's hearings, is also available online at: Truth and Reconciliation Commission (www.justice.gov.za/trc/).
2   'Ubuntu' is derived from the Nguni languages of Zulu and Xhosa to broadly mean values of compassion and humanity. In a political sense, ubuntu could be considered as incorporating working towards the country's shared moral ideals, spirit of togetherness and ability to work together towards a common goal.

Chapter 9
1   As noted earlier in this book, slaveholders in both the US and UK were ultimately compensated by governments for the loss of their 'legal' property rights when emancipation deprived them of their property.
2   Darity (2008) suggested that the present-day value of 40 acres and a mule could provide the basis for a calculation on reparations owed to African Americans.
3   Govtrack notes that these factors are based on correlations which may not indicate causation.
4   Miller's specific argument in relation to unfair and unlawful practices is linked to suits pursued under the California private attorney general doctrine. But the principle behind his argument is extended in this chapter's discussion.

References

Agence France-Presse (2017) 'Burundi becomes first nation to leave International Criminal Court', *The Guardian*. Available at: www.theguardian.com/law/2017/oct/28/burundi-becomes-first-nation-to-leave-international-criminal-court [Accessed 14 February 2021].

Aiyetoro, A. (2003) 'Formulating Reparations Litigation through the Eyes of the Movement', *NYU Annual Survey of American Law*, 58: 457–74.

Ajdukovic, D. (2004) 'Social Contexts of Trauma and Healing', *Medicine, Conflict and Survival*, 20(2): 120–35, doi: 10.1080/1362369042000234717

Alexander, M. (2019) *The New Jim Crow: Mass Incarceration in the Age of Colourblindness*, London: Penguin.

America, R.F. (1988) 'Unjust Enrichment and Restitution: Defining and Measuring Current Benefits from Past Wrongs Estimation and Policy Implications', *NYLS Journal of Human Rights*, 5(2): 413–23. Available at: https://digitalcommons.nyls.edu/journal_of_human_rights/vol5/iss2/7 [Accessed 30 January 2021].

Anderson, K. (2017) '"Who Was I to Stop the Killing?" Moral Neutralization among Rwandan Genocide Perpetrators', *Journal of Perpetrator Research*, 1(1): 39–63, doi: 10.21039/jpr.v1i1.49

Apel, D. (2004) *Imagery of Lynching: Black Men, White Women, and the Mob*, New Brunswick, NJ: Rutgers University Press.

Arat, Z.F.K. (2006) 'Forging a Global Culture of Human Rights: Origins and Prospects of the International Bill of Rights', *Human Rights Quarterly*, 28(2), 416–37.

Armstrong, M. (2002) 'Reparations Litigation: What about Unjust Enrichment?', *Oregon Law Review*, 81 (3): 771–82.

Ashworth, A. (2004) 'Criminal Justice Act 2003: (2) Criminal Justice Reform: Principles, Human Rights and Public Protection', *Criminal Law Review*, (July): 516–32.

Associated Press (2007) 'Chicago to Pay $20M to Settle Lawsuits Filed by Former Death Row Inmates'. Available at: www.foxnews.com/story/chicago-to-pay-20m-to-settle-lawsuits-filed-by-former-death-row-inmates [Accessed 20 February 2021].

Baer, A. (2018) 'Dignity Restoration and the Chicago Police Torture Reparations Ordinance', 92 *Chicago-Kent Law Review*, 769. Available at: https://scholarship.kentlaw.iit.edu/cklawreview/vol92/iss3/6 [Accessed 4 February 2021].

Banner, S. (2006) 'Traces of Slavery: Race and the Death Penalty in Historical Perspective', in C.J. Ogletree, Jr. and A. Sarat (eds) *From Lynch Mobs to the Killing State: Race and the Death Penalty in America*, New York: New York University Press.

Barlow, J.N. (2018) 'Restoring Optimal Black Mental Health and Reversing Intergenerational Trauma in an Era of Black Lives Matter', *Biography*, 41(4): 895–908. *Project MUSE*, doi:10.1353/bio.2018.0084

Bassiouni, M. (1979) 'International Law and the Holocaust', *California Western International Law Journal*.

Baumgartner, S.P. (2005) 'Human Rights and Civil Litigation in United States Courts: The Holocaust-Era Cases'. Available at: https://ssrn.com/abstract=720224 [Accessed 19 September 2020].

Bazyler, M.J. (2000) 'Nuremberg in America: Litigating the Holocaust in United States Courts', *University of Richmond Law Review*, 34.

Bazyler, M.J. (2002) 'The Holocaust Restitution Movement in Comparative Perspective', *Berkeley Journal of International Law*, 20(1): 11–34. Available at: http://scholarship.law.berkeley.edu/bjil/vol20/iss1/2 [Accessed 12 September 2020].

Bazyler, M.J. (2017) *Holocaust, Genocide, and the Law: A Quest for Justice in a Post-Holocaust World*, Oxford: Oxford University Press.

Berg, M. (2011) *Popular Justice: A History of Lynching in America*, Lanham, MD: Rowman and Littlefield.

Bilenker, S. (1997) 'In Re Holocaust Victims' Assets Litigation: Do the US Courts Have Jurisdiction over the Lawsuits Filed by Holocaust Survivors Against the Swiss Banks?', *Maryland Journal of International Law*, 251. Available at: http://digitalcommons.law.umaryland.edu/mjil/vol21/iss2/5 [Accessed 19 September 2020].

Bilsky, L. (2012) 'Transnational Holocaust Litigation', *European Journal of International Law*, 23(2): 349–75, doi: 10.1093/ejil/chs021

Biondi, M. (2003) 'The Rise of the Reparations Movement', *Radical History Review*, 87: 5–18. Available at: www.muse.jhu.edu/article/47386 [Accessed 20 February 2021].

Birks, P. (2005) *Unjust Enrichment*, Oxford: Oxford University Press.

Bittker, B. (1973) *The Case for Black Reparations* (2003 edition), Boston, MA: Beacon Press.

Blum, L. (2020) '"Black Lives Matter": Moral Frames for Understanding the Police Killings of Black Males', in A. Amaya and M. Del Mar (eds) *Imaginations, Virtues, and Emotion and Imagination in Law and Legal Reasoning*, London: Bloomsbury.

Bond, P. and Sharife, K. (2009) 'Apartheid Reparations and the Contestation of Corporate Power in Africa', *Review of African Political Economy*, 36(119): 115–25, doi: 10.1080/03056240902910156

Bonilla-Silva, E. (2015) 'The Structure of Racism in Colour-Blind, "Post-Racial" America', *American Behavioral Scientist*, 59(11): 1358–76, doi: 10.1177/0002764215586826

Boukli, A., Yanacopulos, H. and Papanicolaou, G. (2020) 'Genealogies of Slavery', in J. Winterdyk and J. Jones (eds) *The Palgrave International Handbook of Human Trafficking*, Cham: Palgrave Macmillan, pp 207–25, doi: 10.1007/978-3-319-63058-8_11

Bowling, B. and Philips, C. (2002) *Racism, Crime and Justice*, Harlow: Pearson Education Limited.

Bowling, B. and Phillips, C. (2007) 'Disproportionate and Discriminatory: Reviewing the Evidence on Police Stop and Search', *The Modern Law Review*, 70: 936–61, doi:10.1111/j.1468-2230.2007.00671.x

Boxill, B. (2016) 'Black Reparations', *The Stanford Encyclopedia of Philosophy* (Summer 2016 edition), Edward N. Zalta (ed). Available at: https://plato.stanford.edu/archives/sum2016/entries/black-reparations/ [Accessed 20 September 2021].

Braithwaite, J. (2002) *Restorative Justice and Responsive Regulation*, Oxford: Oxford University Press.

Braithwaite, J. (2004) 'Restorative Justice: Theories and Worries, Visiting Experts Papers', 123rd International Senior Seminar, Resource Material Series No. 63, pp 47–56. Tokyo: United Nations Asia and Far East Institute for the Prevention of Crime and the Treatment of Offenders.

Brandler, S. (2000) 'Practice Issues: Understanding Aged Holocaust Survivors', *Families in Society*, 81(1): 66–75, doi: 10.1606/1044-3894.1094

Bravo, K. (2007) 'Exploring the Analogy Between Modern Trafficking in Humans and the Transatlantic Slave Trade', *Boston University International Law Journal*, 25: 207–95.

Breen, C. (2007) 'When Is a Child Not a Child? Child Soldiers in International Law', *Human Rights Review*, 8:71–103, doi: 10.1007/BF02881667

Brophy, A. (2001) 'The Tulsa Race Riot of 1921 in the Oklahoma Supreme Court', *Oklahoma Law Review*, 54(1): 67–148.

Brophy, A. (2003) 'Some Conceptual and Legal Problems in Reparations for Slavery', *New York University Annual Survey of American Law*, 58(4): 497–555.

Brophy, A. (2004) 'The Cultural War over Reparations for Slavery'. Available at: https://ssrn.com/abstract=561441 [Accessed 16 February 2021].

Brown, M., Carnoy, M., Curriee, E., Duster, T., Oppenheiner, D., Shultz, M. and Wellman, D. (2007) 'Race Preferences and Race Privileges', in M.T. Martin and M. Yaquinto (eds) *Redress for Historical Injustices in the United States*, Durham and London: Duke University Press, pp 55–90.

Brown, W. (1993) 'Wounded Attachments', *Political Theory*, 21(3): 390–410. Available at: www.jstor.org/stable/191795 [Accessed 20 February 2021].

Bryant, E., Schimke, E.B., Brehm, H.N. and Uggen, C. (2018) 'Techniques of Neutralization and Identity Work Among Accused Genocide Perpetrators', *Social Problems*, 65(4): 584–602, doi: 10.1093/socpro/spx026

Buchanan, S. (2009) 'Questioning the Political Question Doctrine: Inconsistent Applications in Reparations and Alien Tort Claims Act Litigation', *Cardozo Journal of International Law*.

Buckner Inniss, L. (2010) 'A Critical Legal Rhetoric Approach to In Re African-American Slave Descendants Litigation', *St John's Journal of Legal Commentary*, 24(4): 649–96.

Buergenthal, T. (2003) *International Law and the Holocaust*, United States Holocaust Memorial Museum. Available at: Buergenthal3.doc (ushmm.org)

Bunce, L., King, N., Saran, S. and Talib, N. (2019) 'Experiences of Black and Minority Ethnic (BME) Students in Higher Education: Applying Self-determination Theory to Understand the BME Attainment Gap', *Studies in Higher Education*, doi: 10.1080/03075079.2019.1643305

Burch, T. (2015) 'Skin Colour and the Criminal Justice System: Beyond Black-White Disparities in Sentencing', *Journal of Empirical Legal Studies*, 12: 395–420.

Bush, J. (2009) 'The Prehistory of Corporations and Conspiracy in International Criminal Law: What Nuremberg Really Said', *Columbia Law Review*, 109(5): 1094–262. Available at: www.jstor.org/stable/40380399 [Accessed 19 September 2020].

Buttaro, A., Battle, J. and Pastrana, Jr., A. (Jay) (2010) 'The Aspiration–Attainment Gap: Black Students and Education', *The Journal of Negro Education*, 79(4): 488–502. Available at: www.jstor.org/stable/41341091 [Accessed 15 February 2021].

Cabraser, E.J. (2004) 'Human Rights Violations as Mass Torts: Compensation as a Proxy for Justice in the United States Civil Litigation System', *Vanderbilt Law Review*, 57(6): 2211–38.

Calomiris, C.W. and Pritchett. J. (2016) 'Betting on Secession: Quantifying Political Events Surrounding Slavery and the Civil War', *American Economic Review*, 106(1): 1–23.

Cambridge Dictionary (2020) Modern Slavery. Available at: https://dictionary.cambridge.org/dictionary/english/modern-slavery [Accessed 27 September 2020].

Campbell, R.B. (ed) (2010) *The Laws of Slavery in Texas: Historical Documents and Essays*, Austin: University of Texas Press.

Capers, B. (2014) 'Critical Race Theory' in M.D. Dubber and T. Hörnle (eds) *The Oxford Handbook of Criminal Law*, Oxford: Oxford University Press, pp 25–37.

CARICOM Reparations Commission (CRC) (2021) 10-Point Reparation Plan, Guyana: Caricom Reparations Commission. Available at: 10-Point Reparation Plan – Caribbean Reparations Commission (caricomreparations.org) [Accessed 14 February 2021].

Carrell, S. (2019) 'Glasgow University to pay £20m in slave trade reparations', *The Guardian*. Available at: www.theguardian.com/uk-news/2019/aug/23/glasgow-university-slave-trade-reparations [Accessed 18 February 2021].

Cassese, A. (1999) 'The Statute of the International Criminal Court: Some Preliminary Reflections', *European Journal of International Law*, 10(1): 144–71, doi: 10.1093/ejil/10.1.144

Casteel, C. and Marks, J. (2005) 'Race-riot recourse blocked Supreme Court refuses appeal after decisions', *The Oklahoman*, 17 May. Available at: www.oklahoman.com/article/2896719/race-riot-recourse-blocked-br-supreme-court-refuses-appeal-after-decisions [Accessed 13 February 2021].

Christensen, K. (2021) 'The Tulsa Race Massacre at 100: An Imperative for International Accountability and Justice', Stanford Law School. Available at: https://law.stanford.edu/2021/02/11/the-tulsa-race-massacre-at-100-an-imperative-for-international-accountability-and-justice/ [Accessed 13 February 2021].

Christopher, A.J. (1990) 'Apartheid and Urban Segregation Levels in South Africa', *Urban Studies*, 27(3): 421–40, doi: 10.1080/00420989020080361

Claims Conference (2019) 'Negotiations with the German Government Result in Increased Social Welfare Services for Holocaust Survivors and First Ever Payment for Surviving Spouse', New York: Conference on Jewish Material Claims Against Germany, Inc. Available at: www.claimscon.org/2019/07/negotiations-with-the-german-government-result-in-increased-social-welfare-services-for-holocaust-survivors-and-first-ever-payment-for-surviving-spouse/ [Accessed 12 September 2020].

Clarke, K.M., Knottnerus, A.S. and de Volder, E. (eds) (2016) *Africa and the ICC*, Cambridge: Cambridge University Press.

Clegg, P. (2014) 'The Caribbean Reparations Claim: What Chance of Success?', The Round Table, 103(4): 435–7, doi: 10.1080/00358533.2014.941207

Coates, T. (2014) 'The Case for Reparations', *The Atlantic*.

Cohen, S. (2006) *States of Denial: Knowing about Atrocities and Suffering*, Cambridge: Polity Press.

Colvin, C. (2006) 'Overview of the Reparations Program in South Africa', in P. de Greiff (ed) *The Handbook of Reparations*, Oxford: Oxford University Press.

Commission of Inquiry on Systemic Racist Police Violence Against People of African Descent in the United States (2021) Report of the Commission, International Commission of Inquiry. Available at: https://inquirycommission.org/ [Accessed 27 April 2021].

Committee Against Torture (2006) *Consideration of Reports Submitted by States Parties Under Article 19 of the Convention, Conclusions and Recommendations of the Committee Against Torture*, 7, U.N. Doc. CAT/C/USA/CO/2

Concepcion, N.P. (2001) 'Legislative Focus: Reparations for African-Americans', *Human Rights Brief*, 8(2): 16.

Corlett, J.A. (2007) 'Reparations to African Americans?', in M.T. Martin and M. Yaquinto (eds) *Redress for Historical Injustices in the United States*, Durham, NC: Duke University Press.

Corlett, J.A. (2011) 'Reparations', in W. Edelglass and J.L. Garfield (eds) *The Oxford Handbook of World Philosophy*, Oxford: Oxford University Press.

Craemer, T. (2015) 'Estimating Slavery Reparations: Present Value Comparisons of Historical Multigenerational Reparations Policies', *Social Science Quarterly*, 96: 639–55, doi: 10.1111/ssqu.12151

Craemer T. (2019) 'Comparative Analysis of Reparations for the Holocaust and for the Transatlantic Slave Trade', *The Review of Black Political Economy*, 2018, 45(4): 299–324, doi:10.1177/0034644619836263

Croall, H. (2013) 'Food Crime: A Green Criminology Perspective', in N. South and A. Brisman (eds) *Routledge International Handbook of Green Criminology*, pp 167–83.

Cuccia, A. (2019) 'Doing What Has Never Been Done': GUSA Senate Passes Reconciliation Referendum for GU272, *The Georgetown Voice*. Available at: https://georgetownvoice.com/2019/02/15/doing-what-has-never-been-done-gusa-senate-passes-reconciliation-referendum-for-gu/ [Accessed 18 February 2021].

Cuthbertson, A. (2020) 'Eleven charts that show extent of racial inequality in the UK', *The Independent*. Available at: www.independent.co.uk/news/uk/home-news/racism-uk-inequality-black-lives-matter-wealth-economic-health-a9567461.html [Accessed 19 February 2021].

Dagan, H., Hylton, K.N. and Sebok, A.J. (2004) 'Symposium: The Jurisprudence of Slavery Reparations', *Boston University Law Review*, 1135. Available at: https://larc.cardozo.yu.edu/faculty-articles/293 [Accessed 20 February 2021].

Daly, E. (2003) 'Reparations in South Africa: A Cautionary Tale', *University of Memphis Law Review*, 33: 367–407. Available at: https://ssrn.com/abstract=1562009 [Accessed 20 February 2021].

Dardick, H. (2015) 'Burge torture accusers seek reparations', *The Chicago Tribune*. Available at: www.chicagotribune.com/news/breaking/ct-burge-torture-reparations-met-0116-20150115-story.html [Accessed 12 June 2021].

Darity, Jr., W. (1990) 'Forty Acres and a Mule: Placing the Price Tag on Oppression', in R.F. America (ed) *The Wealth of Races: The Present Value of Benefits From Past Injustices*, Westport, CT: Preager.

Darity, Jr., W. (2008) 'Forty Acres and a Mule in the 21st Century', *Social Science Quarterly*, 89(3): 656–64, doi: 10.1111/j.1540-6237.2008.00555.x

Davies, P., Francis, P. and Greer, C. (2017) *Victims, Crime and Society: An Introduction*, London: Sage Publications Ltd.

De Greiff, P. (2006) 'Justice and Reparations', in P. De Greiff (ed) *The Handbook of Reparations*, Oxford: Oxford University Press.

Department of Justice (2011) 'Former Chicago Police Officer Jon Burge Sentenced for Lying about Police Torture'. Available at: www.justice.gov/opa/pr/former-chicago-police-officer-jon-burge-sentenced-lying-about-police-torture [Accessed 14 February 2021].

Department of Justice and Constitutional Development (2021) *Truth and Reconciliation Commission*. Available at: www.justice.gov.za/trc/ [Accessed 10 January 2021].

Dervin, F. (2015). 'Discourses of Othering', in K. Tracy, T. Sandel and C. Ilie (eds) *The International Encyclopedia of Language and Social Interaction*, doi: 10.1002/9781118611463.wbielsi027

Dickerson, M. (2019) 'Designing Slavery Reparations: Lessons from Complex Litigation', *Texas Law Review*, 98: 1255–82.

Dixon, T.L. and Williams, C.L. (2015) 'The Changing Misrepresentation of Race and Crime on Network and Cable News', *Journal of Communication*, 65(1): 24–39.

Dodd, V. (2021) '"Eye watering": top police officer laments rate of stop and search on young black men', *The Guardian*. Available at: www.theguardian.com/uk-news/2021/jan/19/eye-watering-top-police-officer-laments-rate-of-stop-and-search-on-young-black-men [Accessed 14 February 2021].

Dreyfus, H.L. and Rabinow, P. (1982) *Michel Foucault: Beyond Structuralism and Hermeneutics*, Chicago: University of Chicago Press.

Du Plessis, M. (2007) 'Reparations and International Law. How are Reparations to be Determined (Past Wrong or Current Effects), Against Whom, and What Form Should They take?', in M. du Plessis and S. Pete (eds) *Repairing the Past? International Perspectives on Reparations for Gross Human Rights Abuses*, Oxford, UK: Intersentia, pp 147–77.

Dubinsky, P.R. (2004) 'Justice for the Collective: The limits of the Human Rights Class Action', *Michigan Law Review*, 102(6): 1152–90.

Eades, C., Grimshaw, R., Silvestri, A. and Solomon, E. (2007) *'Knife Crime': A Review of Evidence and Policy*, London: Centre for Crime and Justice Studies. Available at: Layout 1 (crimeandjustice.org.uk)

Ellis, M. and Hutton, E. (2002) 'Policy Implications of World War II Reparations and Restitution as Applied to the Former Yugoslavia', *Berkeley Journal of International Law*.

Emmanuel, A. (2015) 'Chicago to create fund to compensate victims of Burge police torture', *The Chicago Reporter*. Available at: www.chicagoreporter.com/chicago-to-create-fund-to-compensate-victims-of-burge-police-torture/ [Accessed 12 June 2021].

Epps, G. (2006) *Democracy Reborn: The Fourteenth Amendment and the Fight for Equal Rights in Post-Civil War America*, New York: Henry Holt.

Epstein, R. (2014) *The Case Against Reparations for Slavery*, Stanford, CA: Hoover Institution. Available at: www.hoover.org/research/case-against-reparations-slavery [Accessed 24 January 2021].

Equal Justice Initiative (EJI) (2017) *Lynching in America: Confronting the Legacy of Racial Terror* (Third edition). Available at: https://lynchinginamerica.eji.org/report/ [Accessed 30 December 2020].

European Court of Human Rights (2020) *Guide on Article 4 of the European Convention on Human Rights: Prohibition of slavery and forced labour*, Strasbourg: Council of Europe/European Court of Human Rights.

Fagan, N. and Thompson, L. (2009) 'Corporate Responsibility and Group Redress Mechanisms', *Business Law International*, 10(1): 51–60.

Feagin, J. (2000) 'Documenting the Costs of Slavery, Segregation, and Contemporary Discrimination: Are Reparations in Order for African Americans?' (CSD Working Paper No. 00–10). St. Louis, MO: Washington University, Centre for Social Development.

Feagin J. (2004) 'Documenting the Costs of Slavery, Segregation, and Contemporary Racism: Why Reparations Are in Order for African Americans', *Harvard BlackLetter Law Journal*, 20: 49–81.

Feagin, J. and Elias, S. (2013) 'Rethinking Racial Formation Theory: A Systemic Racism Critique', *Ethnic and Racial Studies*, 36(6): 931–60, doi: 10.1080/01419870.2012.669839

Feinberg, J. (1970) *Doing and Deserving*, Princeton, NJ: Princeton University Press.

Fernandez. L. (1999) 'Reparation for Human Rights Violations Committed by the Apartheid Regime in South Africa', in A. Randelzhofer and C. Tomuschat (eds) *State Responsibility and the Individual: Reparation in Instances of Grave Violations of Human Rights*, Leiden: Brill.

Ferrell, C. (2005) *The Abolitionist Movement*, Westport, CT: Greenwood Press.

Finkelman, P. (ed) (2001) *Slavery and the Law*, Wisconsin: Madison House.

Flaherty, P. and Carlisle, J. (2004) *The Case Against Slave Reparations*, Virginia: National Legal and Policy Centre.

Flint Taylor, G. (2015) 'How Activists Won Reparations for the Survivors of Chicago Police Torture', *In These Times*. Available at: https://inthesetimes.com/article/jon-burge-torture-reparations [Accessed 14 February 2021].

Flint Taylor, G. (2016) 'The Long Path to Reparations for the Survivors of Chicago Police Torture', *Northwestern Journal of Law and Social Policy*, 11(3): 330–53. Available at: http://scholarlycommons.law.northwestern.edu/njlsp/vol11/iss3/1 [Accessed 14 February 2021].

Foster, D., Haupt, P. and De Beer, M. (2005) *The Theatre of Violence: Narratives of Protagonists in the South African Conflict*, Cape Town: University of Cape Town.

Fox, M.J. (2005) 'Child Soldiers and International Law: Patchwork Gains and Conceptual Debates', *Human Rights Review*, 7: 27–48, doi: 10.1007/s12142-005-1001-4

Franklin, V.P. (2013) 'Commentary: Reparations as a Development Strategy: The CARICOM Reparations Commission', *The Journal of African American History*, 98(3): 363–6.

Freeland, S. (2008) 'Mere Children or Weapons or War – Child Soldiers and International Law', *La Verne Law Review*.

Gates, E.F. (2004) 'The Oklahoma Commission to Study the Tulsa Race Riot of 1921', *Harvard Blackletter Law Review*, 20: 83–9.

Gentleman, A. (2021) 'Windrush victims not compensated quickly enough, report finds', *The Guardian*. Available at: www.theguardian.com/uk-news/2021/may/21/windrush-victims-not-compensated-quickly-enough-report-finds [Accessed 30 May 2021].

Georgetown Working Group on Slavery, Memory and Reconciliation (2016) Report of the Working Group, Washington, DC: Georgetown University. Available at: www.elon.edu/u/commemoration-project/wp-content/uploads/sites/922/2019/10/Georgetown-2016.pdf [Accessed 14 February 2021].

González-Pérez, J., Remond-Roa, R., Rullan-Salamanca, O. and Vives-Miró, S. (2016) 'Urban Growth and Dual Tourist City in the Caribbean. Urbanization in the Hinterlands of the Tourist Destinations of Varadero (Cuba) and Bávaro-Punta Cana (Dominican Republic)', *Habitat International*, 58: 59–74.

Goodin, R. (2013) 'Disgorging the Fruits of Historical Wrongdoing', *American Political Science Review*, Cambridge University Press, 107(3): 478–91, doi: 10.1017/S0003055413000233

Gordon, P. (1990) *Racial Violence and Harassment*, London: Runnymede Trust.

Gottschalk, K. (2002) 'The Rise and Fall of Apartheid's Death Squads', in B. Campbell and A. Brenner (eds) *Death Squads in Global Perspective: Murder with Deniability*, Basingstoke: Palgrave Macmillan, pp 229–60.

Govtrack (2021) *H.R. 40: Commission to Study and Develop Reparation Proposals for African Americans Act*. Available at: www.govtrack.us/congress/bills/117/hr40 [Accessed 19 February 2021].

Graf, G. (2014) 'The Intergenerational Trauma of Slavery and Its Aftermath', *The Journal of Psychohistory*, 41(3): 181–97.

Green, P. and Ward, T. (2004) *State Crime: Governments, Violence and Corruption*, London: Pluto.

Green, S. (2019) 'The Case Against Reparations', Merion West. Available at: https://merionwest.com/2019/09/15/the-case-against-reparations/ [Accessed 20 February 2021].

Groark, V. (2002) 'Slave policies', *The New York Times*, 2 May.

Hall, C. (2016) 'Writing History, Making "Race": Slave-Owners and Their Stories', *Australian Historical Studies*, 47(3): 365–80, doi: 10.1080/1031461X.2016.1202291

Hall, C. (2020) 'The Slavery Business and the Making of "Race" in Britain and the Caribbean', *Current Anthropology*, 61, supplement 22: S172–82.

Hall, C., Draper, N., McCleland, K., Donington, K. and Lang, R. (2014) *Legacies of British Slave-Ownership: Colonial Slavery and the Formation of Victorian Britain*, Cambridge: Cambridge University Press.

Halloran, M.J. (2019) 'African American Health and Posttraumatic Slave Syndrome: A Terror Management Theory Account', *Journal of Black Studies*, 50(1): 45–65, doi: 10.1177/0021934718803737

Hamilton, C. (2020) 'Georgetown Explained: The GU272', *The Georgetown Voice*. Available at: https://georgetownvoice.com/2020/08/28/georgetown-explained-the-gu272/ [Accessed 20 January 2021].

Hamilton, D. and Darity, Jr., W. (2010) 'Can "Baby Bonds" Eliminate the Racial Wealth Gap in Putative Post-Racial America?', *The Review of Black Political Economy*, 37(3–4): 207–16, doi: 10.1007/s12114-010-9063-1

Hardaway, A.B. (2015) 'A Substantive Right to Reparations', *NYU Review of Law and Social Change*, 39: 525–65.

Harding, W. (2017) 'Spectacle Lynching and Textual Responses, *Miranda*, 15. Available at: https://journals.openedition.org/miranda/10493 [Accessed 10 February 2021].

Harold, C. and DeLuca. K.M. (2005) 'Behold the Corpse: Violent Images and the Case of Emmett Till', *Rhetoric & Public Affairs*, 8(2): 263–86, doi:10.1353/rap.2005.0075

Harris, F. (2011) 'Brands Corporate Social Responsibility and Reputation Management', in A. Voiculescu and H. Yanacopulos (eds), *The Business of Human Rights: An Evolving Agenda for Corporate Responsibility*, London: Zed Books/The Open University.

Hatamiya, L.T. (1993) *Righting a Wrong: Japanese Americans and the Passage of the Civil Liberties Act of 1988*, Stanford: Stanford University Press.

Heath, D. (2020) 'The Case for Reparations in Tulsa, Oklahoma, Human Rights Watch'. Available at: www.hrw.org/news/2020/05/29/case-reparations-tulsa-oklahoma [Accessed 13 February 2021].

Henry, C. P. (2007) 'The Politics of Reparations', in M.T. Martin and M. Yaquinto (eds) *Redress for Historical Injustices in the United States*, Durham: Duke University Press, pp 353–70.

Hodges, C. (2008) *The Reform of Class and Representative Actions in European Legal Systems: A New Framework for Collective Redress in Europe*, Oxford: Hart Publishing.

Howard-Hassmann, R. (2004) 'Getting to Reparations: Japanese Americans and African Americans', *Social Forces*, 83(2): 823–40, doi: 10.1353/sof.2005.0012

Howard-Hassmann, R. and Lombardo, A. (2007) 'Framing Reparations Claims: Differences between the African and Jewish Social Movements for Reparations' *African Studies Review*, 50(1): 27–48, doi:10.2307/20065339

Humphrey, J.P. (1976) 'The International Bill of Rights: Scope and Implementation', *William and Mary Law Review*, 17(3): 527–41.

Hylton, K. (2004) 'A Framework for Reparations Claims', *Boston College Third World Law Journal*, 31. Available at: https://scholarship.law.bu.edu/faculty_scholarship/660 [Accessed 6 February 2021].

Ince, J., Rojas, F. and Davis, C. (2017) 'The Social Media Response to Black Lives Matter: How Twitter Users Interact with Black Lives Matter through Hashtag Use', *Ethnic and Racial Studies*, 40(11): 1814830, doi: 10.1080/01419870.2017.1334931

International Centre for Transitional Justice (ICTJ) (2021) *Reparations*, New York: International Centre for Transitional Justice. Available at: www.ictj.org/our-work/transitional-justice-issues/reparations [Accessed 17 January 2021].

International Court of Justice (2005) Case concerning armed activities on the territory of the Congo (Democratic Republic of the Congo v Uganda (2005). Available at: 116-20051219-JUD-01-00-EN.pdf (icj-cij.org) [Accessed 09 August 2021].

Jackson, J. and Brunger, Y. (2015) 'Witness Preparation in the ICC: An Opportunity for Principled Pragmatism', *Journal of International Criminal Justice*, 13(3): 601–24, doi: 10.1093/jicj/mqv024

Jackson, J. and Weidman, N. (2005) 'The Origins of Scientific Racism', *The Journal of Blacks in Higher Education*, 50: 66–79.

Jolly, J. (2020) 'Barclays, HSBC and Lloyds among UK banks that had links to slavery', *The Guardian*. Available at: www.theguardian.com/business/2020/jun/18/barclays-hsbc-and-lloyds-among-uk-banks-that-had-links-to-slavery [Accessed 17 February 2021].

Jordan, E.C. (2003) 'A History Lesson: Reparations for What?', *Annual Survey of American Law*, 58: 557–613.

Kahn, J. (2020) 'George Floyd protests force Britain to reckon with its role in slavery, leading some companies to pay reparations', *Fortune*, 18 June. Available at: https://fortune.com/2020/06/18/george-floyd-protests-uk-slavery-reparations/ [Accessed 16 February 2021].

Kahn, R. (2004) *Holocaust Denial and the Law: A Comparative Study*, Basingstoke: Palgrave Macmillan.

Keim, R. (2003) 'Filling the Gap Between Morality and Jurisprudence: The Use of Binding Arbitration to Resolve Claims of Restitution Regarding Nazi-Stolen Art,' *Pepperdine Dispute Resolution Law Journal*, 3(2): 295–315.

Kelley, R.D.G. (2007) 'A Day of Reckoning: Dreams of Reparation', in M.T. Martin and M. Yaquinto (eds) *Redress for Historical Injustices in the United States*, Durham and London: Duke University Press, pp 203–31.

King, M. (2021) 'Reparations bill approved out of committee in historic vote, Politico'. Available at: www.politico.com/news/2021/04/15/reparations-bill-committee-historic-vote-481811 [Accessed 12 June 2021].

Klein, H., Engerman, S., Haines, R. and Shlomowitz, R. (2001) 'Transoceanic Mortality: The Slave Trade in Comparative Perspective', *The William and Mary Quarterly*, 58(1): 93–118, doi:10.2307/2674420

Kleintop, A.L. (2018) 'Life, Liberty, and Property in Slaves: White Mississippians Seek "Just Compensation" for Their Freed Slaves in 1865', *Slavery & Abolition*, 39(2): 383–404, doi: 10.1080/0144039X.2017.1397334

Kramer, R.C., Michalowski, R.J. and Kauzlarich, D. (2002) 'The Origins and Development of the Concept and Theory of State-Corporate Crime', *Crime & Delinquency*, 48(2): 263–82, doi: 10.1177/0011128702048002005

Kreder, J.A. (2017) 'Analysis of the Holocaust Expropriated Art Recovery Act of 2016', *Chapman Law Review*, 2017. Available at: https://ssrn.com/abstract=2859132 [Accessed 14 September 2020].

Kull, A. (2004) 'Restitution in Favour of Former Slaves', *Boston University Law Review*, 84: 1278–80.

Lammy, D. (2017) 'Lammy Review: Final Report'. Available at: www.gov.uk/government/publications/lammy-review-final-report [Accessed 12 September 2020].

Lartey, J. and Morris, S. (2018) 'How White Americans used lynchings to terrorize and control black people', *The Guardian*. Available at: www.theguardian.com/us-news/2018/apr/26/lynchings-memorial-us-south-montgomery-alabama [Accessed 31 December 2020].

Leary, J.D. (2005) *Post Traumatic Slave Syndrome: America's legacy of enduring injury and healing*, Milwaukie, OR: Uptone Press.

Levine, M. and Levine, A.G. (2014) 'Coming from Behind: A Historical Perspective on Black Education and Attainment', *American Journal of Orthopsychiatry*, 84(5): 447–54, doi: 10.1037/h0099861

Llewellyn, J. (2002) 'Dealing with the Legacy of Native Residential School Abuse in Canada: Litigation, ADR, and Restorative Justice', *The University of Toronto Law Journal*, 52(3): 253–300.

Lockhart, P.R. (2019) 'America Is Having an Unprecedented Debate about Reparations: What Comes Next?', *Vox*. Available at: www.vox.com/identities/2019/6/20/18692949/congress-reparations-slavery-discrimination-hr-40-coates-glover [Accessed 18 February 2021].

Longman-Mills, S., Mitchell, C. and Abel, W. (2019) 'The Psychological Trauma of Slavery: The Jamaican Case Study', *Social and Economic Studies*, 68 (3 and 4).

Lu, C. (2017) *Justice and Reconciliation in World Politics*, Cambridge: Cambridge University Press.

Lutz, C.E. (2008) 'The Death Knell Tolls for Reparations in *In re African-American Slave Descendants Litigation*', *Seventh Circuit Review*, 3(2): 532–56. Available at: http://scholarship.kentlaw.iit.edu/seventhcircuitreview/vol3/iss2/4 [Accessed 13 February 2021].

Lynch, M. (2010) 'Critical Criminology, Oxford Bibliographies'. Available at: www.oxfordbibliographies.com/view/document/obo-9780195396607/obo-9780195396607-0064.xml [Accessed 11 June 2021].

Lyons, D. (2007) 'Racial Injustices in US History and Their Legacy', in M.T. Martin and M. Yaquinto (eds) *Redress for Historical Injustices in the United States*, Durham and London: Duke University Press, pp 33–54.

Magarrell, L. (2003) 'Reparations for Massive or Widespread Human Rights Violations: Sorting out Claims for Reparations and the Struggle for Social Justice', *Windsor Yearbook of Access to Justice*.

Magill, K. (2005) 'From J.P. Morgan Chase, an Apology And $5 Million in Slavery Reparations', *The New York Sun*. Available at: www.nysun.com/business/from-jp-morgan-chase-an-apology-and-5-million/8580/ [Accessed 15 February 2021].

Marketti, J. (1990) 'Estimated Present Value of Income Diverted During Slavery', in R.F. America (ed) *The Wealth of Races: The Present Value of Benefits from Past Injustices*, Westport, CT: Prager, pp 107–12.

Marshall, T.F. (1999) *Restorative Justice: An Overview*, London, Home Office.

Martin, M.T. and Yaquinto, M. (2007a) 'On Redress for Racial Injustice', in M.T. Martin and M. Yaquinto (eds) *On Reparations for Slavery, Jim Crow and Their Legacies*, Durham, NC: Duke University Press.

Martin, M.T. and Yaquinto, M. (eds) (2007b) *Redress for Historical Injustices in the United States*, Durham and London: Duke University Press.

Martinez, J. (2012) *The Slave Trade and the Origins of International Human Rights Law*, Oxford: Oxford University Press.

Massey, C. (2004) 'Some Thoughts on the Law and Politics of Reparations for Slavery', *Boston College Third World Law Journal*, 24(1):157–76. Available at: http://lawdigitalcommons.bc.edu/twlj/vol24/iss1/9 [Accessed 1 February 2021].

Mawby, R. and Walklate, S. (1994) *Critical Victimology*, London: Sage.

Mazurkiewicz, P. (2004) 'Corporate Environmental Responsibility: Is a Common CSR Framework Possible?', World Bank. Available at: https://documents.worldbank.org/en/publication/documents-reports/documentdetail/577051468339093024/corporate-environmental-responsibility-is-a-common-csr-framework-possible [Accessed 17 February 2021].

Mazzocco, P., Brock, T., Brock, G., Olson, K. and Banaji, M.R. (2006) 'The Cost of Being Black: White Americans' Perceptions and the Question of Reparations', *Du Bois Review*, 3(2): 261–97. Available at: https://ssrn.com/abstract=1838491 [Accessed 19 February 2021].

Mbengue, M.M. and McClellan, K. (2018) 'The ICC and Africa: Should the Latter Remain Engaged?', in Z. Yihdego, M. Desta, M. Hailu and F. Merso (eds) *Ethiopian Yearbook of International Law*, Cham: Springer, doi: 10.1007/978-3-319-90887-8_8

McCarthy, C. (2009) 'Reparations under the Rome Statute of the International Criminal Court and Reparative Justice Theory', *International Journal of Transitional Justice*, 3(2): 250–71, doi: 10.1093/ijtj/ijp001

McDuff, N., Tatam, J., Beacock, O. and Ross, F. (2018) 'Closing the Attainment Gap For Students From Black and Minority Ethnic Backgrounds through Institutional Change', *Widening Participation and Lifelong Learning*, 20(1): 79–101.

McIntosh, K., Moss, E., Nunn, R. and Shambaugh, J. (2020) 'Examining the Black-White Wealth Gap', Brookings Institute. Available at: www.brookings.edu/blog/up-front/2020/02/27/examining-the-black-white-wealth-gap/ [Accessed 19 February 2021].

McShane, M.D. and Williams, F.P. (1992) 'Radical Victimology: A Critique of the Concept of Victim in Traditional Victimology', *Crime & Delinquency*, 38(2): 258–71, doi: 10.1177/0011128792038002009

Meron, T. (2006) 'Reflections on the Prosecution of War Crimes by International Tribunals', *American Journal of International Law*, 100(3): 551–79.

Mesic, A., Franklin, L., Cansever, A., Potter, F., Sharma, A., Knopov, A. and Siegel, M. (2018) 'The Relationship Between Structural Racism and Black-White Disparities in Fatal Police Shootings at the State Level', *Journal of the National Medical Association*, 110(2): 106–16.

Messer, C.M. (2011) 'The Tulsa Race Riot of 1921: Toward an Integrative Theory of Collective Violence', *Journal of Social History*, 44(4): 1217–32. Available at: www.muse.jhu.edu/article/439314 [Accessed 13 February 2021].

Messer, C.M. and Bell, P. (2010) 'Mass Media and Governmental Framing of Riots: The Case of Tulsa, 1921', *Journal of Black Studies*, 40(5): 851–70. Available at: www.jstor.org/stable/40648610 [Accessed 13 February 2021].

Messer, C.M., Shriver, T.E. and Beamon, K.K. (2018) 'Official Frames and the Tulsa Race Riot of 1921: The Struggle for Reparations', *Sociology of Race and Ethnicity*, 4(3): 386–99, doi: 10.1177/2332649217742414

Michalowski, R.J. and Kramer, R. (eds) (2006) *State-Corporate Crime: Wrongdoing at the Intersection of Business and Government*, New Brunswick, NJ: Rutgers University Press.

Michalowski, R.J. and Kramer, R. (2007) 'State-Corporate Crime and Criminological Inquiry', in H.N. Pontell and G. Geis (eds) *International Handbook of White-Collar and Corporate Crime*, Boston, MA: Springer, doi: 10.1007/978-0-387-34111-8_10

Miksch, K.L. and Ghere, D. (2004) 'Teaching Japanese-American Incarceration', *The History Teacher*, 37(2): 211–27, doi:10.2307/1555653

Miles, J. (2000) 'Standing under the Human Rights Act 1998: Theories of Rights Enforcement and the Nature of Public Law Adjudication', *The Cambridge Law Journal*, 59(1): 133–67.

Miller, E.J. (2004) 'Representing the Race: Standing to Sue in Reparations Lawsuits', *Harvard BlackLetter Law Journal*, 20: 91–114. Available at: https://ssrn.com/abstract=692641 [Accessed 13 February 2021].

Miller, J. (1981) 'Mortality in the Atlantic Slave Trade: Statistical Evidence on Causality', *The Journal of Interdisciplinary History*, 11(3): 385–423, doi:10.2307/203625

Miller, J. (2016) *An African Volk: The Apartheid Regime and Its Search for Survival*, Oxford: Oxford University Press.

Miller, J. and Kumar, R. (eds) (2007) *Reparations: Interdisciplinary Inquiries*, Oxford: Oxford University Press.

Miller, M.C. (2018) 'Destroyed by Slavery? Slavery and African American Family Formation Following Emancipation', *Demography*, 55: 1587–609, doi: 10.1007/s13524-018-0711-6

Ministry of Justice (2013) Victim Personal Statement. Available at: www.gov.uk [Accessed 20 October 2020].

Moffett, L. and Schwarz, K. (2018) 'Reparations for the Transatlantic Slave Trade and Historical Enslavement: Linking Past Atrocities with Contemporary Victim Populations', *Netherlands Quarterly of Human Rights*, doi: 10.1177/0924051918801612

Mosley, A. (2003) 'Affirmative Action as a form of Reparations', *University of Memphis Law Review*, 33: 353–66.

Muhammad, P.M. (2003) 'The Trans-Atlantic Slave Trade: A Forgotten Crime Against Humanity as Defined by International Law', *American University International Law Review*, 19(4): 883–947.

Muhammad, P.M. (2020) 'The US Reparations Debate: Where Do We Go From Here?' (5 February). *N.Y.U. Review of Law and Social Change: The Harbinger, 2020*. Available at: https://ssrn.com/abstract=3532158

Mullins, C. (2020) 'State Crime', *Oxford Bibliographies*. Available at: www.oxfordbibliographies.com/view/document/obo-9780195396607/obo-9780195396607-0014.xml [Accessed 9 January 2021].

Mutua, M. (2016) 'Closing the "Impunity Gap" and the Role of State Support for ICC', *Contemporary Issues Facing the International Criminal Court*, pp 99–111. Available at: https://ssrn.com/abstract=3026289 [Accessed 20 September 2020].

Nadya Sadat, L.D. (2013) 'Crimes Against Humanity in the Modern Age', *The American Journal of International Law*, 107(2): 334–77, doi:10.5305/amerjintelaw.107.2.0334

Nagata, D.K., Kim, J.H.J. and Nguyen, T.U. (2015) 'Processing Cultural Trauma: Intergenerational Effects of the Japanese American Incarceration', *Journal of Social Issues*, 71: 356–70, doi: 10.1111/josi.12115

Nathan, C. (2016) 'Rehabilitation for the Jewish Victims of the Holocaust Sixty Years of the Claims Conference, the Scope of Reparations, and the Changing Nature of Rehabilitation', *International Human Rights Law Review*, 5: 217–40.

Nattrass, N. (1999) 'The Truth and Reconciliation Commission on Business and Apartheid: A Critical Evaluation', *African Affairs*, 98(392): 373–91, doi: 10.1093/oxfordjournals.afraf.a008045

Neuborne, B. (2003) 'Holocaust Reparations Litigation: Lessons for the Slavery Reparations Movement', *NYU Annual Survey of American Law*, 58(4): 615–20.

Nurse, A. (2015) 'Creative Compliance, Constructive Compliance: Corporate Environmental Crime and the Criminal Entrepreneur', in G. McElwee and R. Smith (eds) *Exploring Criminal and Illegal Enterprise: New Perspectives on Research Policy and Practice: 5 (Contemporary Issues in Entrepreneur Research)*, Bingley: Emerald Publishing.

Nurse, A. (2016) *An Introduction to Green Criminology and Environmental Justice*, London: Sage.

Nurse, A. (2020a) *The Citizen and the State: Criminal Justice and Civil Liberties in Conflict*, London: Emerald Publishing.

Nurse, A. (2020b) 'Law, the Environment and Narrative Storytelling', in N. Creutzfeldt, M. Mason and K. McConachie (eds) *Routledge Handbook of Socio-Legal Theory and Methods*, Abingdon: Routledge, pp 301–14.

OHCHR (2019) Universal Declaration of Human Rights, Office of the High Commissioner for Human Rights. Available at: eng.pdf (ohchr.org)

Ogletree, Jr., C. (2007) 'Tulsa Reparations', in M.T. Martin and M. Yaquinto (eds) (2007) *Redress for Historical Injustices in the United States*, Durham, NC: Duke University Press.

Oklahoma Commission to Study the Tulsa Race Riot of 1921 (2001) 'The Tulsa Race Riot, Oklahoma City', UK: 1921 Tulsa Race Riot Commission. Available at: www.okhistory.org/research/forms/freport.pdf [Accessed 10 February 2021].

Oliver, M. and Shapiro, T. (2007) 'A Sociology of Wealth and Racial Inequality', in M.T. Martin and M. Yaquinto (eds) *Redress for Historical Injustices in the United States*, Durham and London: Duke University Press, pp 91–116.

Olson, W. (2008) 'So long, slavery reparations', *Los Angeles Times*. Available at: www.latimes.com/archives/la-xpm-2008-oct-31-oe-olson31-story.html [Accessed 30 January 2021].

REFERENCES

Orentlicher, D. (1994) 'Addressing Gross Human Rights Abuses: Punishment and Victim Compensation', *Studies in Transnational Legal Policy*, 26: 425–75.

Pemberton, A., Mulder, E. and Aarten, P.G.M. (2019) 'Stories of Injustice: Towards a Narrative Victimology', *European Journal of Criminology*, 16(4): 391–412, doi: 10.1177/1477370818770843

Personal Justice Denied: Report of the Commission on Wartime Relocation and Internment of Civilians (1997 [1982/83]). Seattle; London: University of Washington Press. Available at: www.jstor.org/stable/j.ctvcwnm2s [Accessed 18 February 2021].

Pettit, B. (2012) *Invisible Men: Mass Incarceration and the Myth of Black Progress*, New York: Russel Sage Foundation.

Posner, E. and Vermeule, A. (2003) 'Reparations for Slavery and Other Historical Injustices', *Columbia Law Review*, 103: 689.

Pradier, A., Rubin, M. and van der Merwe, H. (2018) 'Between Transitional Justice and Politics: Reparations in South Africa, South African', *Journal of International Affairs*, 25(3): 301–21, doi: 10.1080/10220461.2018.1514528

Priel, D. (2014) 'The Justice in Unjust Enrichment' *Osgoode Hall Law Journal*, 51(3): 813–58. Available at: https://digitalcommons.osgoode.yorku.ca/cgi/viewcontent.cgi?referer=&httpsredir=1&article=2757&context=ohlj [Accessed 30 January 2021].

Quinney, R. (1963) 'Occupational Structure and Criminal Behavior: Prescription Violation by Retail Pharmacists', *Social Problems*, 11(2): 179–185.

Quinney, R. (1964) 'The Study of White Collar Crime: Toward a Reorientation in Theory and Research', *Journal of Criminal Law, Criminology and Police Science*, 55(2): 208–14.

Ramchandani, T.K. (2007) 'Judicial Recognition of the Harms of Slavery: Consumer Fraud as an Alternative to Reparations Litigation', *Harvard Civil Rights-Civil Liberties Law Review*, 42(2): 541–56.

Ray, R., Brown, M., Fraistat, N. and Summers, E. (2017) 'Ferguson and the Death of Michael Brown on Twitter: #BlackLivesMatter, #TCOT, and the Evolution of Collective Identities', *Ethnic and Racial Studies*, 40(11): 1797–813, doi: 10.1080/01419870.2017.1335422

Reid, O., Mims, S. and Higginbottom, L. (2005) *Post Traumatic Slavery Disorder: Definition, Diagnosis, and Treatment*, Charlotte, NC: Conquering Books.

Richardson, J.T. (2015) 'The Under-attainment of Ethnic Minority Students in UK Higher Education: What We Know and What We Don't Know', *Journal of Further and Higher Education*, 39(2): 278–91, doi: 10.1080/0309877X.2013.858680

Rickford, R. (2016) 'Black Lives Matter: Toward a Modern Practice of Mass Struggle', *New Labour Forum*, 25(1), 34–42.

Rising, D. (2012) 'Germany increases reparations for Holocaust survivors', *The Times of Israel*, 16 November.

Rojas, D. (2020) 'Chicago Passed Torture Reparations 5 Years Ago. Were they Implemented?' CARICOM. Available at: https://caricomreparations.org/chicago-passed-police-torture-reparations-5-years-ago-were-they-implemented/ [Accessed 12 June 2021].

Rosenne, S. (1989) *World Court: What It Is and How It Works* (Legal Aspects of International Organizations), Cham: Springer.

Rosensaft, M. and Rosensaft, J. (2002) 'The Early History of German-Jewish Reparations', *Fordham International Law Journal*, 25(6): S-1–45.

Rothe, D.L. (2020) 'Moving Beyond Abstract Typologies? Overview of State and State-Corporate Crime', *Journal of White Collar and Corporate Crime*, 1(1): 7–15, doi: 10.1177/2631309X19872438

Ruggiero, V. (2015) *Power and Crime*, Abingdon: Routledge.

Sacerdote, B. (2006) 'Slavery and the Intergenerational Transmission of Human Capital', *The Review of Economics and Statistics*, 87(2): 217–34.

Saito, N.T. (2001) 'Symbolism Under Siege: Japanese American Redress and the "Racing" of Arab Americans as "Terrorists"', *Asian Law Journal*, 8(1):1–30.

Sarkin, J. (1996) 'The Trials and Tribulations of South Africa's Truth and Reconciliation Commission', *South African Journal on Human Rights*, 12:4, 617–40, doi: 10.1080/02587203.1996.11834930

Sarkin, J. (1997) 'The Truth and Reconciliation Commission in South Africa', *Commonwealth Law Bulletin*, 23:1–2, 528–542, doi: 10.1080/03050718.1997.9986472

Sarkin, J. (1998) 'The Development of a Human Rights Culture in South Africa', *Human Rights Quarterly*, 20(3): 628–65.

Schabas, W. (2012) *Unimaginable Atrocities: Justice, Politics, and Rights at the War Crimes Tribunals*, Oxford: Oxford University Press.

Schlesinger, P. and Tumber, H. (1994) *Reporting Crime: The Media Politics of Criminal Justice*, Oxford: Oxford University Press.

Scruggs, G. (2013) 'CARICOM Nations Intensify Push for Slavery Reparations', *Latin American Digital Beat (LADB)*. Available at: https://digitalrepository.unm.edu/noticen/10120 [Accessed 14 February 2021].

Seebok, A.J. (2003) 'Reparations, Unjust Enrichment, and the Importance of Knowing the Difference Between the Two', *NYU Annual Survey of American Law*, 58: 651–8.

Sherwin, E. (2001) 'Restitution and Equity: An Analysis of the Principle of Unjust Enrichment', *Texas Law Review*, 79(7): 2083–113.

Sherwin, E. (2004) 'Reparations and Unjust Enrichment', *Boston University Law Review*, 84(4): 1443–65. Available at: http://scholarship.law.cornell.edu/lsrp_papers/6 [Accessed 30 January 2021].

Simmons, B. (2009) 'Civil Rights in International Law: Compliance with Aspects of the "International Bill of Rights"', *Indiana Journal of Global Legal Studies*, 16(2): 437–81. Available at: www.repository.law.indiana.edu/ijgls/vol16/iss2/4 [Accessed 1 August 2020].

Simmons, B. and Danner, A. (2010) 'Credible Commitments and the International Criminal Court', *International Organization*, 64(2): 225–56. Available at: www.jstor.org/stable/40608014 [Accessed 18 February 2021].

Smith, D. (2006) 'Blair: Britain's "sorrow" for shame of slave trade', *The Observer*. Available at: www.theguardian.com/politics/2006/nov/26/race.immigrationpolicy [Accessed 15 February 2021].

Smith Lee, J.R. and Robinson, M.A. (2019) '"That's My Number One Fear in Life. It's the Police": Examining Young Black Men's Exposures to Trauma and Loss Resulting From Police Violence and Police Killings', *Journal of Black Psychology*, 45(3): 143–84, doi: 10.1177/0095798419865152

Spiga, V. (2010) 'Indirect Victims' Participation in the *Lubanga* Trial', *Journal of International Criminal Justice*, 8(1): 183–98, doi: 10.1093/jicj/mqq009

Stenson, A.F., Rooij, S., Sierra E., Carter, S., Powers, A. and Tanja Jovanovic, T. (2021) 'A Legacy of Fear: Physiological Evidence for Intergenerational Effects of Trauma Exposure on Fear and Safety Signal Learning among African Americans', *Behavioural Brain Research*, 402, doi: 10.1016/j.bbr.2020.113017

Stewart, J.B. (2008) *Abolitionist Politics and the Coming of the Civil War*, Amherst, MA: University of Massachusetts Press.

Swarns, R.L (2019) 'Is Georgetown's $400,000-a-year plan to aid slave descendants enough?', *The New York Times*. Available at: www.nytimes.com/2019/10/30/us/georgetown-slavery-reparations.html [Accessed 14 February 2021].

Swinton, D.H. (1990) 'Racial Inequality and Reparations', in R.F. America (ed) *The Wealth of Races: The Present Value of Benefits From Past Injustices*, Westport, CT: Prager.

Sykes, G. M. and Matza, D. (1957) 'Techniques of Neutralization: A Theory of Delinquency', *American Sociological Review*, 22: 664–73.

Tapley, J. and Davies, P. (eds) (2020) *Victimology: Research, Policy and Activism*, Basingstoke: Palgrave Macmillan.

The Joint Council for the Welfare of Immigrants (2020) 'Windrush Lessons Learned Review: Briefing', London: JCWI. Available at: www.jcwi.org.uk/windrush-lessons-learned-review [Accessed 30 May 2021].

Thomas, H. (1999) *The Slave Trade: The Story of the Atlantic Slave Trade: 1440–1870*, New York, NY: Touchstone/Simon and Schuster.

Thorne, S. (2012) 'Capitalism and Slavery Compensation', *Small Axe*, 16(1(37)): 154–67, doi: 10.1215/07990537-1548155

Tibbles, A. (2008) 'Facing Slavery's Past: The Bicentenary of the Abolition of the British Slave Trade', *Slavery & Abolition*, 29(2): 293–303, doi: 10.1080/01440390802028200

Topalli, V. (2005) 'When Being Good Is Bad: An Expansion of Neutralization Theory', *Criminology*, 43: 797–836, doi: 10.1111/j.0011-1348.2005.00024.x

Torpey, J. (2004) 'Paying for the Past?: The Movement for Reparations for African-Americans', *Journal of Human Rights*, 3(2): 171–87, doi: 10.1080/1475483042000210702

Torpey, J. and Burkett, M. (2010) 'The Debate over African American Reparations', *Annual Review of Law and Social Science*, 6: 449–67.

Torres, J. (2015) 'Race/Ethnicity and Stop-and-Frisk: Past, Present, Future', *Sociology Compass*, 9: 931–9, doi: 10.1111/soc4.12322

Tourse, R.W., Hamilton-Mason, J. and Wewiorski, N. (2018) *Systemic Racism in the United States: Scaffolding as Social Construction*, Cham: Springer.

Treviño, A.J., Harris, M.A. and Wallace, D. (2008) 'What's so Critical about Critical Race Theory?', *Contemporary Justice Review*, 11(1): 7–10, doi: 10.1080/10282580701850330

Truth and Reconciliation Commission (1998) *Truth and Reconciliation Commission of South Africa, Volume Five*. Available at: www.justice.gov.za/trc/report/finallreport/Volume5.pdf [Accessed 20 February 2021].

Turvey, B. (2014) 'Victimity: Entering the Criminal Justice System', in B. Turvey, *Forensic Victimology* (Second edition), Oxford: Academic Press/Elsevier, pp 31–65.

UN Human Rights Council (2016) *Report of the Working Group of Experts on People of African Descent on its mission to the United States of America, United Nations*. Available at: https://digitallibrary.un.org/record/848570 [Accessed 10 February 2021].

United Nations (1948) 260 B (III) *Study by the International Law Commission of the Question of an International Criminal Tribunal*. Available at: A/RES/3/260 B - Study by the International Law Commission of the Question of an International Criminal Tribunal - UN Documents: Gathering a body of global agreements (un-documents.net) [Accessed 10 September 2020].

US Congress (2019) H.R.40 – 116th Congress (2019–2020). Available at: www.congress.gov/bill/116th-congress/house-bill/40 [Accessed 14 February 2021].

Vilmer, J-B. (2016) 'The African Union and the International Criminal Court: Counteracting the Crisis', *International Affairs*, 92(6): 1319–42, doi: 10.1111/1468-2346.12747

Wacquant, L. (2002) 'From Slavery to Mass Incarceration: Rethinking the "Race Question" in the US', *New Left Review*, 13: 41–60.

Walker, M. (2006) 'Restorative Justice and Reparations', *Journal of Social Philosophy*, 37(3): 377–95.

Walkerdine, V., Olsvold, A. and Rudberg, M. (2013) 'Researching Embodiment and Intergenerational Trauma Using the Work of Davoine and Gaudilliere: History Walked in the Door', *Subjectivity*, 6: 272–97, doi: 10.1057/sub.2013.8

Walklate, S. and McGarry, R. (eds) (2015) *Criminology and War: Transgressing the Borders*, Abingdon: Routledge.

Walklate, S., Maher, J.M., McCulloch, J., Fitz-Gibbon, K. and Beavis, K. (2019) 'Victim Stories and Victim Policy: Is There a Case for a Narrative Victimology?', *Crime, Media, Culture*, 15(2): 199–215, doi: 10.1177/1741659018760105

Walling, C.B. (2000) 'The History and Politics of Ethnic Cleansing', *The International Journal of Human Rights*, 4(3–4): 47–66, doi: 10.1080/13642980008406892

Walvin, J. (2007) *A Short History of Slavery*, London: Penguin Books.

Walvin, J. (2013) *Crossings: Africa, the Americas and the Atlantic Slave Trade*, London: Reaktion Books.

Waterhouse, C.M. (2011) 'Total Recall: Restoring the Public Memory of Enslaved African-Americans and the American System of Slavery through Rectificatory Justice and Reparations', *Journal of Gender, Race and Justice*, 14. Available at: https://ssrn.com/abstract=1916416

Webb, C. (2009) 'What Is Unjust Enrichment?', *Oxford Journal of Legal Studies*, 29(2): 215–43, doi: 10.1093/ojls/gqp008

Weinrib, E.J. (2000) 'Restitutionary Damages as Corrective Justice', *Theoretical Inquiries in Law*, 1(1): 1–37.

Weitz, Y. (2009) 'Rwandan Genocide: Taking Notes from the Holocaust Reparations Movement' *Cardozo Journal of Law and Gender*, 15(2): 357–81.

Wenar, L. (2006) 'Reparations for the Future', *Journal of Social Philosophy*, 37(3): 396–405.

Wenger, K.D. (2006) 'Causation and Attenuation in the Slavery Reparations Debate', *University of San Francisco Law Review*, TJSL Public Law Research Paper No. 05–16, Available at: https://ssrn.com/abstract=600021 or http://dx.doi.org/10.2139/ssrn.600021 [Accessed 14 February 2021].

Wenger, K.D. (2009) 'Apology Lite: Truths, Doubts, and Reconciliations in the Senate's Guarded Apology for Slavery', *Connecticut Law Review*, 42(1): 1–11.

Wenger, K.D. (2018) 'The Unconscionable Impossibility of Reparations for Slavery; Or, Why the Master's Mules Will Never Dismantle the Master's House', in A. Bloom et al (eds) *Injury and Injustice*, Cambridge: Cambridge University Press.

Wilkins, D. (2020) 'Understanding Historical Slavery, Its Legacies, and Its Lessons for Combating Modern-Day Slavery and Human Trafficking', in J. Winterdyk and J. Jones (eds) *The Palgrave International Handbook of Human Trafficking*, Cham: Palgrave Macmillan, doi: 10.1007/978-3-319-63058-8_1

Williams, J. (1985) 'Redefining Institutional Racism', *Ethnic and Racial Studies*, 8(3): 323–48, doi: 10.1080/01419870.1985.9993490

Williams, Y. (2008) *Black Politics White Power, Civil Rights, Black Power, and the Black Panthers in New Haven*, New Haven, CT: Blackwell Press.

Williams-Washington, K.N. and Mills, C.P. (2018) 'African American Historical Trauma: Creating an Inclusive Measure', *Journal of Multicultural Counselling and Development*, 46: 246–63, doi: 10.1002/jmcd.12113

Williamson, K. (2014) 'The Case Against Reparations', *National Review*. Available at: www.nationalreview.com/2014/05/case-against-reparations-kevin-d-williamson/ [Accessed 20 January 2021].

Wolff, L. (2014) 'Let's Talk about Lex: Narrative Analysis as Both Research Method and Teaching Technique in Law', *Adelaide Law Review*, 35(1): 3–21.

Womack, S. (2016) 'I Know I Can't: The Negative Effects of Post Traumatic Slave Syndrome's on the Well-Being of African American College Students', *The Vermont Connection,* 37(1). Available at: https://scholarworks.uvm.edu/tvc/vol37/iss1/15 [Accessed 30 September 2020].

Wood, A.L. (2011) *Lynching and Spectacle: Witnessing Racial Violence in America, 1890–1940*, Chapel Hill, NC: University of North Carolina Press.

Woolford, A. and Wolejszo, S. (2006) 'Collecting on Moral Debts: Reparations for the Holocaust and Porajmos', *Law & Society Review*, 40: 871–902, doi: 10.1111/j.1540-5893.2006.00284.x

Xie, M. and McDowall, D. (2008) 'Escaping Crime: The Effects of Direct and Indirect Victimization on Moving', *Criminology*, 46: 809–40, doi: 10.1111/j.1745-9125.2008.00133.x

Yamamoto, E.K. (1998) 'Racial Reparations: Japanese American Redress and African American Claims', *Boston College Third World Law Journal*, 19(1), 477–523. Available at: http://lawdigitalcommons.bc.edu/twlj/vol19/iss1/13 [Accessed 30 January 2021].

Index

A
abolition 4, 27
accountability 10–11, 62–3, 87–8, 108–10, 121, 128
accounting 36, 79
Adenauer, Konrad 63
affirmative action 94
African nations
  redress for impoverishment 2
  reparations from European governments 113
  social harms 94
African-American Reconciliation Study Commission Act of 2003 5
African-American Slave Descendants Litigation 30, 35–8, 46, 50, 77, 78–9, 82, 117, 121, 122
Aiyetoro, A. 74, 76
Ajdukovic, D. 52
Alexander, M. 10
Alien Tort Claims Act 36
America, R.F. 79, 81
American Civil War 4, 27, 28, 31, 35
American Convention on Human Rights 105
Anderson, K. 22
Angiolini Report (UK, 2017) 9
anti-discrimination legislation 125
anti-racism laws 7–9
anti-racism protests (2020) 8
apartheid 20, 91, 107, 113
Apel, D. 25
apologies
  Chicago police brutality cases 40
  contemporary reparations narratives 111, 113, 115–16, 123, 124, 128
  as type of reparation 21
  unjust enrichment 81
  value of reparations 88, 90
appeals courts 42
appropriation of funds 44, 80
Armed Activities on the Territory of the Congo 104
Armenian genocide 71

Armstrong, M. 75
Artuković, Andrija 66
artworks, stolen 66–7
Ashworth, A. 125
Atonement, Reparation and Justice Act 106

B
Baer, A. 38
Bank of England 123
banks 67, 68–9, 109, 120–1
Baumgartner, S.P. 69
Bazyler, M.J. 48, 65, 66, 67, 69, 70–1
Bell, P. 41
Berg, M. 26
Bilenker, S. 67
Bilsky, L. 67
Birks, P. 74, 75–9
Bittker, B. 118
Black Codes 5
black crime 26
Black Lives Matter 2, 9–11, 121, 128–9
Black Panthers 2
#BlackLivesMatter 10
Black-on-Black crime 26
blame 23–4, 25–6
  see also victim blaming
Block, Robert 82–3
bodily integrity 69
Bond, P. 109
Bonilla-Silva, E. 51
Boukli, A. 78
Bowling, B. 1, 54, 125
Boxill, B. 80
Braithwaite, J. 87, 89
Brixton Riots (1981) 10
Brookings Institute 91
Brophy, A. 21, 117, 127
Brown, M. 8, 26, 54
Brown, Michael 9, 10, 105
Brown, W. 119–20
Bryant, E. 22
Buchanan, S. 32
Buckner Inniss, L. 35, 37, 38
Burge (Chicago police brutality) reparations cases 38–41, 46, 105, 127, 131

burials and exhumations 109
Burkett, M. 112
Bush, J. 67–8

C

Cabraser, E.J. 68
Cameron, David 94
Capers, B. 124–5
Caribbean nations
  CARICOM reparations commission 94, 112–15, 128
  psychological effects 52
  redress for impoverishment 2
  social harms 94
Carlisle, J. 46, 51, 83, 120
Cassese, A. 18
Castile, Philando 105
Cato v United States (1995) 30, 33–5, 37–8, 50, 78, 81, 84, 95
causal links, difficulty in establishing 33, 60
charity donations 122
chattel slavery 4, 9, 16, 21, 50, 113
Chicago police brutality cases 38–41, 46, 105, 127
child soldiers 51
civic trust 89
Civil Liberties Act (1988,US) 58
civil litigation 18, 31, 40, 65–7, 71
  see also class actions; tort law
Civil Rights Act (1964, US) 7
civil rights legislation 59
civil rights movement 2, 7–9, 31, 51, 120
civil rights violations 42
class actions 31, 32, 66, 67, 69–70, 72, 117, 124
Clegg, P. 115
closure 88
C.N. v the United Kingdom, 103
Coates, Ta-Nehisi 117, 119
coerced labour 6
Cohen, S. 21, 22, 23, 24, 26, 27, 49, 56
collective memory 116–17
collective perpetrators 31–2
collective psyche 52
collective victims 50, 55, 81
college scholarships 122, 131
colonialism 2, 4, 19, 21, 23, 28, 52, 90, 99
colour-blindness 8, 10
Colvin, C. 109
Commission of Inquiry on Systemic Racist Police Violence (the Commission) 105–7, 110
Commission to Study Reparations for African Americans 115
Commonwealth subjects 7
community empowerment programmes 124
community-level victimhood 50, 55, 81
compensation
  calculating 33, 86

Cato v United States (1995) 81, 95
form of reparations 128
Holocaust reparations 61–72
H.R.40 116
ICC (International Criminal Court) 20
Japanese American reparations 59
making good the consequences of illegal acts 104
In re African-American Slave Descendants Litigation 35–8
refusal of 113
Reparations for Burge Torture Victims Ordinance (Chicago City Council, 2015) 40
reparations law 21, 27–8
versus restitution 76, 77–8
slave compensation payments 121
South Africa 109
condemn the condemners 27, 47
Conference on Jewish Material Claims against Germany (Claims Conference) 63–4, 65
Congress members 115
contemporary reparations narratives 111–29
convict leasing 5
Conyers Jr., John 115, 116
Corlett, J.A. 59, 70, 86
Corporate Social Responsibility (CSR) policies 121–2
corporations
  corporate involvement in slavery 35–8
  Holocaust 65–8
  knowledge of slavery as human rights violation 77
  litigation against 30
  predecessor corporations 121, 122
  profits and compensation 33
  reparations 120–2
  responsibility for historical actions 79
  South Africa 109–10
  state-corporate crime 16, 17–18, 30
  unjust enrichment 75, 82
corrective justice 71, 80, 84, 86, 90, 111, 126
'cost' of slavery 85–96
counsellling 40
cover-ups 42
co-victims 51
Covid-19 92
Craemer, T. 69, 70, 92, 93
CRC (CARICOM Reparations Commission) 15, 94, 112–15, 128
crime of apartheid 20
crimes against humanity (CAH)
  corporations' knowledge 77
  genocide 62
  Holocaust 67
  international law 98, 99
  legality of 128
  museums and cultural institutions 114
  nature of harm 49

INDEX

In re African-American Slave Descendants Litigation 35
  reparations litigation 36
  reparations mechanisms 104
  slavery as 112
  state crime 17, 18–20
crimes of the powerful 16, 30
criminal justice agencies 1, 10, 18, 23, 26, 102, 125
  see also police
criminal justice reparations discourse 86
criminal liability 67
criminal record expunges 109
criminological conceptions of value 86–90
criminological focus of book 15, 16–29
critical race theory (CRT) 124–5
critical victimology 64
cruel and unusual punishment 67
Cuccia, A. 123
cultural appropriation 80
cultural heritage, theft of 66
culture of victimization 54
Cuthbertson, A. 92
cycles of victimhood 29

D
Dagan, h. 75
Danner, A. 99
Darity Jr., W. 31, 92, 94, 115
Davies, P. 29, 50
De Grieff, P. 21, 89
dead offenders 49, 127
dead victims 32, 33, 38, 45, 48, 49, 70
death certificates 109
debt wiping 128
defences 46, 74, 78–9
  see also neutralization techniques
deflection techniques 27
dehumanization 21, 24, 26
Democratic Republic of the Congo v Uganda 104
denial 21, 22–5, 33, 45–6, 49, 56
derivative harm 33
Dervin, F. 24
descendants
  African-American Slave Descendants Litigation 46, 50, 77, 78–9, 82, 117, 121, 122
  anonymity problem 82
  apologies to` 115–16
  continuing discrimination 9, 12, 34
  Holocaust 70, 71
  indirect harm 33
  Jim Crow era 32, 47
  nature of harm 49, 50, 83
  reparations 60
  reparations to 2–3, 13–14, 15, 35–8, 42–3, 81–4, 90
  unjust enrichment claims 76
  value of reparations 85–96

'deserving' victims 46, 54, 55
dignity 65, 75, 109
discriminatory employment 75
disgorgement 82
distribution of wealth 72, 76–7
distributional justice 90
'doing justice' model of reparations claims 72
domestic servitude 103
Du Pleiss, M. 97

E
economic reasons for slavery 16, 23, 27–8
education 92, 114
effective remedy, right to 104–5, 106
elder care funding 64, 65
Ellis, M. 62
emancipation 4, 5, 14, 27, 51, 70, 85, 93, 113
emotional effects 44, 55
  see also psychological effects
employment discrimination 94
enslavement, definition of 19–20
Epstein, R. 28
Equal Justice Initiative (EJI) 6–7
equal rights legislation 2, 120, 125
Equality Act (2010, UK) 8
equity, principle of 74, 90, 126
ethnic cleansing 20, 26
ethnic discrimination 32, 64
European Convention on Human Rights (ECHR) 4, 99, 102, 104, 127
European Court of Human Rights (ECtHR) 4, 102–3
evidence-gathering 41–2, 49–50, 66, 82–3
exploited labour, slavery as 17–18, 75

F
Fagan, N. 124
failed reparations cases 32–3, 34–5
false confessions 40
Far East trials 62, 70
Farmer-Paellmann, Deadria 35
Farmer-Paellmann v FleetBoston Fin. Corp. (2002) 35, 45, 46, 81, 121
Feagin, J.R. 1, 75, 76, 77, 84, 93, 94
federal commission 115
federal court 30, 32, 35, 42, 67
Feinberg, J. 90
Ferguson protests (2014) 9, 10
'few bad apples' 10, 23–4, 49
financial institutions' links to slavery 120–1, 122–3
financial reparations *see* compensation
Flaherty, P. 46, 51, 83, 120
Flint Taylor, G. 39, 40
Floyd, George 54, 105
'following orders' 23
forced labour 67, 103
forced migration 113
forgiveness 89, 111, 126

159

Foucault, M. 89
Franklin, V.P. 112
Fraser, Simon 123
fraud 36
freed slaves, land given to 6
Freedmen's Bureau Bill 6
freedom, denial of 102
Friedman, Jacob 67

G

Garner, Eric 9, 54
Geneva Convention 66
genocide
  dehumanization 26
  denial 21–2, 24, 49
  genocide reparations in principle 62–3
  Holocaust 64
  and the ICC 99
  international law 14, 16, 18
  of native Caribbean population 114
  reparations mechanisms 104
  slavery 113
Georgetown University 123
Glasgow University 123
global anti-racist advocacy 112
González-Pérez, J. 95
Goodin, R. 82
Gordon, P. 9
government officials, culpability of 62
Graf, G. 52, 53
Green, S. 17, 18, 119

H

Hague Convention 66
Hall, C. 28, 121
Halloran, M.J. 53
Hamilton, C. 123
Hamilton, D. 92
Hardaway, A. 31
harm
  admissions of 90
  case against reparations 117–20
  and the concept of reparations 31, 32
  in concepts of victimization 29, 55, 86
  contemporary reparations narratives 56–7
  contextualizing unjust enrichment 79–80
  criminological perspectives on reparations 124–5
  denial of injury 24–5, 45–6
  denial of responsibility 46
  derivative harm 33
  indirect harm 50–1, 55, 64, 82, 83
  legal recognition of 87
  making good the consequences of illegal acts 104
  nature of 49–51
  offender understandings of 88
  proving personal injury 37–8
  recognition via monetary compensation 64
  repeated 'minor' incidents 53
  restitution 81
  restorative justice 87
  and trauma 52
  who suffers? 48–60
  wider criminological context 50
Harris, F. 121
Hatamiya, L.T. 59
healing and rehabilitation 109, 113
health inequalities 52, 64, 65
Heath, D. 44
Henry, C.P. 59, 60, 115
higher loyalty, appealing to 27–8
Hirabayashi v U.S .3 58
historical injustices
  calculating financial reparations 91–3
  versus correcting current 79
  correction of 90
  nature of harm 49–50
  reparations 76, 82
  responsibility for 24, 71, 78–9
  see also descendants
historical wisdom, challenging 57
Hobley, Madison 40
Hodges, C. 124
Holocaust 23, 48, 60, 61–72, 75, 81, 116, 118, 119
Holocaust Victim Assets Litigation (2000) 68
House Judiciary Subcommittee on the Constitution, Civil Rights, and Civil Liberties 120
housing 92, 94
Howard, Stanley 40
Howard-Hassmann, R.E. 60, 69, 70
H.R.40 89, 106, 115–17, 118, 128
human rights
  anti-discrimination 8–9
  civil redress 62–3
  Corporate Social Responsibility (CSR) policies 121
  international human rights mechanisms 99–102
  and international law 62–3
  Japanese American reparations 59
  and modern slavery 3–4
  nature of reparations 97–110
  notions of unfairness 77
  police brutality 39, 106
  reparations 89
  restorative justice 87
  South Africa 108
  Swiss banks 69
  Tulsa riots 44
  and victimology 54
  violations 32
Human Rights Act (1998,UK) 8, 104
human trafficking 3
'Hurdle' plaintiffs 35
Hutton, E. 62
Hylton, K. 35, 72, 90

INDEX

I
ICC (International Criminal Court) 18–19, 20, 21, 51, 63, 98, 99, 106, 107
ICJ (International Court of Justice) 98, 104
identity negotiation 22
identity politics 119–20
ideological conflict 26
illiteracy 114
indentured servitude, value of 85, 93
Independent Anti-slavery Commissioner 3
indigenous peoples 75, 81
indirect harm 50–1, 55, 64, 82, 83
inheritance 37, 92
injury, denial of 24–5, 45–6
injury personal 33, 34, 37, 45, 48, 75
injury-in-fact 38
inquiries 9, 41, 105–7
institutionalized racism 9, 24, 53, 55
intangible interests 74
Inter-American Commission on Human Rights (IACHR) 39
interest convergence principle 125
intergenerational justice 70
intergenerational trauma 29, 51, 52–3, 89, 114
International Bill of Rights (UN) 102
International Centre for Transitional Justice (ICTJ) 21
International Convention on the Elimination of All Forms of Racial Discrimination 105
International Covenant on Civil and Political Rights (ICCPR) 101–2, 104–5
International Covenant on Economic, Social and Cultural Rights (ICESCR) 102
International Criminal Tribunal for the Former Yugoslavia 63, 89
international law
  contemporary reparations narratives 112
  crimes against humanity 36
  Holocaust 48, 54–5, 59, 62, 66, 67–8
  international criminal law 21
  international human rights law 39, 99–102
  international humanitarian law 103, 119
  and reparations 97–9, 103–5
  state compliance with international law 98–9
  unjust enrichment 75
Isaac Hawkins Legacy Group 123

J
Jackson Lee, Sheila 115
Japanese American reparations 57–60, 61, 90, 118, 119
Jewish Agency 63
Jewish people, reparations to 63–70, 119
Jim Crow laws/era
  institutionalized racism 5
  and international law 99

lynching 5, 6, 6–7, 25, 25–6, 41, 117
present-day descendants 83
reparations 2, 32, 41–4, 50
segregation 9, 28
and trauma 52
Johnson, President 6
Jolly, J. 120–1
Jordan, E.C. 70, 116, 117
JP Morgan Chase 122
jury trials 66
just satisfaction 21, 98

K
Kahn, J. 123
Kahn, R. 64
Kelley, R.D.G. 6
King, M. 116
King, Rodney 9
Kitchen and Reeves v Chicago (2012) 40, 131
Korematsu v U.S .4 58
Kramer, R.C. 17, 18
Kreder, J.A. 66

L
lack of standing 32, 37–8, 65, 127
Lammy, D. 1, 125
Lartey, J. 6
Lawrence, Stephen 10
left-wing identity politics 119
legal precedent 59
legal title to interests 74
legality of slavery 17, 69, 71, 73, 90, 99, 128
liability 60, 67, 127–8
libel 67
life expectancy 91
litigation attempts 30–47, 81–3, 130–1
living victims 32, 33, 42, 43, 44, 48, 60, 70, 71
Llewellyn, J. 87
Lloyd's of London 121, 122
Lockhart, P.R. 120
Lombardo, A. 69, 70
Longman-Mills, S. 52
looted property 66, 67, 68, 104
Los Angeles 1991 riots 9
lost wages reparations 33, 92–4
Lu, C. 29
Lutz, C.E. 5, 32, 33
Lynch, M. 31
lynching 5, 6–7, 25–6, 41, 117
Lyons, D. 6

M
Marketti, J. 93
Martin, M.T. 2, 33, 45, 115, 116
mass harm 18, 21, 62, 104, 105
mass tort claims 72
see also class actions
Massey, C. 83

master-slave relationship, lasting impact of 53
Matza, D. 21–3, 45, 88
Mawby, R. 53
Mazurkiewicz, P. 121
Mazzocco, P. 91
McCarthy, C. 20
McIntosh, K. 91, 92
mediation 87–8, 89
memorials 40, 109, 123, 128
memory preservation 116–17
Messer, C.M. 41
Metropolitan Police 10
Michalowski, R.J. 17, 18
Miles, J. 127
Miller, E.J. 32, 33, 126
Miller, J. 23, 86, 108
Miller, M.C. 50
misappropriation 37, 44, 65, 68
mobs 26, 43, 57
modern slavery 3–4, 103
Modern Slavery Act (2015, UK) 3
Moffett, L. 97
morality 3–4, 77, 79, 119, 121
Morris, S. 6
motives, criticism of plaintiffs' 27, 47
Muhammad, P.M. 17, 116
Mullins, C. 17
Multidistrict Litigation Panel 35

N
Nadya Sadat, L.D. 62
Nagata, D.K. 58
naming of institutions 123, 128
narrative victimology 56–7, 65
Nathan, C. 65
National Legal and Policy Centre 82–3
Native American reparations 118
Nattrass, N. 110
Neal, Larry 93
neutralization techniques 21–8, 45–7, 49, 88, 119
Nicaragua v United States of America 98
Norgle, Judge 46, 117
nuisance laws 43–4, 83
Nuremburg trials 62, 67, 69–70
Nurse, A. 31, 49, 56, 57, 72, 87, 121

O
obedience to authority 22–3
Ogletree Jr., C. 34, 42, 44
Oklahoma Commission to Study the Tulsa Race Riot of 1921 42
Oliver, M. 1
Olson, W. 83
omission, acts of 55
one-parent families 53
oral history projects 123
Orange, Leroy 40
Orentlicher, D. 62

'othering' 21, 24, 26, 55

P
Pan-African Congress on Reparations 112
parenting, effects on 53
Patterson, Aaron 40
Pearl Harbor 58, 61
Pemberton, A. 56
pensions 64
personal injury 33, 34, 37, 45, 48, 75
Phillips, C. 1, 54, 125
physical health 52, 114
pillaging 66
piracy 36
police
 arrest rates by race 92
 Black citizens as service users 54
 Chicago police brutality cases 38–41, 46, 105, 127
 Commission of Inquiry on Systemic Racist Police Violence 105–7
 cultural issues 55
 deaths in police custody 9–10
 denial 23
 'few bad apples' 10, 23–4, 49
 and international law 102
 police brutality 105–7, 110
 police killings 106, 110
 police reform 9, 10
 racial discrimination 54, 92, 106, 125
 responses to racial violence 9
 stop and search 1, 54, 92, 106
 and trauma 52
 Tulsa race riot reparations litigation (2003 and 2020) 43
 use of force 9, 10, 26, 54
 victim blaming 26
Police and Criminal Evidence Act (1984, UK) 125
political case against reparations 118–19
political office 1, 115
political reparations movement 115–17
Posner, E. 49, 126
post-traumatic slave syndrome/post-traumatic slavery disorder (PTSlaveryD) 53
power 54, 55, 89
predecessor corporations 121, 122
present-day victims *see* living victims
prevention of future harm 74, 89
Priel, D. 77, 80
prisons 1, 9, 10
private attorney general doctrine 32
profiting from Holocaust 67
profiting from slavery 17, 33, 35–8, 74, 76, 79
 see also unjust enrichment
progressive politics 120
property, slaves as 23, 50, 69, 71, 92
 see also chattel slavery

INDEX

property rights 71, 104
property theft 66–7, 68
Prosecutor v Thomas Lubanga Dyilo 51
psychological effects 52, 53, 55, 64, 86, 126
Public Nuisance Law 43–4, 83
public resources, redirection of 44
punishment 25–6, 31, 71, 74, 86
punitive damages 66

Q
Quinney, R. 17

R
Race Relations Act (1976,UK) 7–8
racial castes 6, 10
racial discrimination
  case against reparations 120
  civil rights movement 7–9
  links to slavery 32, 36, 37, 116
  police 106
  redesign of 10
  and trauma 52
  as victimization 51
racial inequality 91–2
racial realism 54
'racism as a thing of the past' 54
radical victimology 53–5
Raines v Byrd (1997) 37
Ramchandani, T.K. 32, 36
Randle, Lessie Benningfield 43, 44, 57
Randle and Others v City of Tulsa and Others, 2020 43, 44, 57
rationalization 21–2, 23
Ray, R. 10, 54
recognition 89
reconciliation 108–9
Reconstruction Era 5–6, 7
redistributive taxation 82
reframing 22, 24
rehabilitation 20, 21
reintegrative shaming 89
repairing uncorrected harms 72
reparations
  case against 117–20
  contemporary debates 111–29
  crimes against humanity discourse 18–20
  definition 21
  Holocaust 48, 61–72
  Japanese American reparations 57–60
  nature of 97–110
  overview of litigation 30–47
  police brutality 40
  political, legal and social mechanisms 20–2
  post-slavery period 5
  precedents 59
  state crime 18
  value of 85–96
  and victimology 53–5
  see also apologies; compensation

Reparations Assessment group 83
Reparations for Burge Torture Victims Ordinance (Chicago City Council, 2015) 40
reparative justice 20, 21, 107, 113, 124
repatriations 113–14
Report of the Working Group of Experts on People of African Descent on Its Mission to the United States of America 110
resettlement 6, 113–14
Resolution 40 *see* H.R.40
responsibility, denial of 22–4
restitution versus compensation 76, 77–8
restorative justice 31, 80, 87–9, 97–110, 113, 123, 124–5, 128
Restorative Justice Council 87
retaliation 79, 81
retrospective application of laws 71
Revici v Jewish Material Claims (1958) 65
Richardson, J.T. 1
right to compensation 77
right to fair and equal treatment 78
right to restitution 74, 77
riots 9, 10, 41–4, 57, 80
Rising, D. 63, 64, 65
Rome Statute of the ICC 18, 19–20, 21, 51, 62–3, 99, 106
Ruggiero, V. 11

S
Saito, N.T. 58
San Francisco 5
savages, slaves seen as 24, 28
Scarman Report 10
Schabas, W. 19
scholarships 42
Schwarz, K. 97
Scruggs, G. 112, 115
secondary victims 51, 125
Seebok, A.J. 80
sentencing 1, 21, 86
service users versus victims 54
servitude, definition 102–3
settlement calculations 87
settlement waivers 69
Shapiro, T. 1
Sharett, Moshe 63
Sharife, K. 109
Sherman, William T. 6
Sherwin, E. 74, 79, 81
Simmons, B. 99, 102
Slave Compensation Commission (UK) 28
slave insurance policies 35, 82
slavery
  continuing effects of 16–29, 32–47, 48–60, 116, 127
  criminological view of 16–29
  definition 3–4
  legacy of contemporary anti-Black racism 2

163

as legal wrong 3–4
as moral wrong 3–4
as 'natural' state 24
and police brutality 39–40
see also descendants
Slavery Abolition Act (1833, UK) 4
Slavery Convention 1926 4
social harms 18, 57, 73, 78, 85, 94–5, 119, 126
social justice 86, 90, 91, 117, 124
social media 10
social solidarity 89
social welfare funding 64, 65
social welfare suits 72
socio-economic disadvantage 1, 52, 53, 91, 94
South Africa 89, 91, 107–10
sovereign immunity 32, 34
Spiga, V. 51, 83
standing 32, 37–8, 65, 127
state apparatus 60, 64, 72
state crime 16, 17–18, 30, 42, 50, 60, 72, 118–19
state-corporate crime 16, 17–18, 30
statue of limitations 32, 33, 44, 49, 119–20
Stephen Lawrence Inquiry 10
still-living plaintiffs *see* living victims
stop and search 1, 54, 92, 106
structural/systematic racism 2, 3, 9, 53–5, 77–8, 101, 120
structural/systemic inequality 2, 52, 91–2
successor corporation laws 82
Supreme Court (US) 42, 59
survivors, use of terminology of 51
Swarns, R.L. 123
Swinton, D.H. 93
Sykes, G.M. 21–3, 45, 88

T
Tapley, J. 29
Taylor, Breonna 54, 105
terrorism 5, 6–7, 43, 83
theft 66–7, 68
third party liability 36–7
third party mediation 89
Thirteenth Amendment 34
Thomas, H. 4
Thompson, L. 124
Till, Emmett 7
Topalli, V. 22
Torpey, J. 35, 112
tort law 18, 32, 36, 72, 116, 117
tourism 44, 94
traditional class claims 32–3, 95, 118, 126
traditional news media 10
traffic stops 106
transgenerational haunting 53
transitional justice 21
trauma 52–3, 56–7, 64, 65

trials, value of 62, 66
Truth and Reconciliation Commission (TRC) 89, 108–9
truth-seeking 109, 128
Tucker Act 34
Tulsa race riot reparations litigation (2003 and 2020) 40, 41–4, 46, 47, 50, 57, 80, 83, 90, 118, 120
Tulsa Reconciliation Education and Scholarship Program 42
Turvey, B. 54

U
ubuntu 108
UCL slave ownership project 121, 122–3
Uganda 104
unemployment 92
Unfair Deceptive Acts and Practices (UDAP) in 36
United Nations (UN)
  Committee Against Torture (UNCAT) 39
  Declaration on Basic Principles of Justice for Victims of Crime and Abuse of Power 55
  General Assembly 99
  Human Rights Council (UNHRC) 105, 110
  inquiries 105
  International Bill of Rights (UN) 102
  Working Group of Experts on People of African Descent 105, 110
  World Conference Against Racism, Racial Discrimination, Xenophobia and Related Intolerance 112
United States Constitution 37
Universal Declaration of Human Rights (UDHR) 99–101, 102, 104
universities 120, 121, 123–4
unjust enrichment 31, 32, 36, 37, 44, 72, 73–84
unjust impoverishment 75
unpaid labour costs 2, 37, 72, 75–6, 83, 92–3

V
value of reparations, calculating 83, 85–96
Van der Mussele v Belgium, 1983 103
vengeance 108
Vermeule, A. 49, 126
victim blaming 25–6, 46, 54, 55
victim movements 65
Victim Personal Statement scheme (VPS) 86
victim-centred identities 120
victimhood, social construction of 53–5
victim-offender mediation 87–8
victimology 28–9, 50, 53–5
Victims' Code and Witness Charter 86
violence
  against abolitionists 27
  disproportionate use of force 10

lynching 5, 6–7, 25–6, 41, 117
post facto rationalization 22
post-slavery period 6
reframing 24
and reparations 117
responses to racial violence 46
South Africa 107
supposed propensity of Black citizens to 24
third party liability 36–7
UK racial violence 9
victim blaming 25

W
Wacquant, L. 4, 6, 9
Walkerdine, V. 52
Walklate, S. 18, 53, 56
Walvin, J. 4, 23
war crimes 51, 67, 99
Waterhouse, C.M. 116, 117
wealth distribution 72, 76–7
Webb, C. 80

Weinrib, E.J. 71
Weitz, Y. 62, 65
Wenar, L. 29
Wenger, K.D. 50, 82, 128
White labourers during slavery 75
White superiority 28, 107
White supremacy 2, 4, 7, 20, 24, 119
white-dominated power structures 25
Williamson, K. 119
Wilson, Darren 10
Wolejszo, S. 64
Wolff, L. 56
Womack, S. 53
Woolford, A. 64

Y
Yamamoto, E.K. 59, 60
Yaquinto, M. 2, 33, 45, 115, 116

Z
zemiological perspectives 73, 78, 85, 94–5

www.ingramcontent.com/pod-product-compliance
Lightning Source LLC
Chambersburg PA
CBHW071205070526
44584CB00019B/2918